Presented to:

Julia Perona

Presented by:

Grandma & Grandpa E.

Date:

12/20/09

Love is the fairest bloom in God's garden.

The Greatest Love Stories of All Time

Published by Standard Publishing, Cincinnati, Ohio
www.standardpub.com

Printed in China.

Product developed by Bordon Books, Tulsa, Oklahoma.
Manuscript compiled by Patricia Lutherbeck and Rebecca Currington in association with SnapdragonGroupSM Editorial Services, Tulsa, Oklahoma.
Bible stories retold by Vicki J. Kuyper. Used by permission of the writer.
Minor vocabulary and punctuation changes have been made to public domain works in this manuscript to improve clarity and readability.
Cover Design by Greg Jackson, Thinkpen Design.

All Scripture quotations, unless otherwise indicated, are taken from the *Holy Bible, New International Version*®. (North American Edition)®. Copyright © 1973, 1978, 1984 by International Bible Society. Used by permission of Zondervan. All rights reserved.

Just As I Am: The Autobiography of Billy Graham by Billy Graham. Excerpt used by permission of HarperSanFrancisco.

A Man Called Peter by Catherine Marshall. Excerpt used by permission of Baker Books, Grand Rapids, Michigan.

C. S. Lewis: Through the Shadowlands by Brian Sibley. Excerpt used by permission of Fleming H. Revell, a division of Baker Publishing Group, copyright 1985, 1994.

Romeo and Juliet by William Shakespeare, adapted narrative by Charles and Mary Lamb, 1892, reworked by SnapdragonGroupSM Editorial Services, Tulsa, Oklahoma. Used by permission.

The compiler has sought to locate and secure permission for the inclusion of all copyrighted material in this book. If any such acknowledgments have been inadvertently omitted, the compiler and publisher would appreciate receiving the information so that proper credit may be given in future editions.

ISBN: 0-7847-1954-3

13 12 11 10 09 08 07   9 8 7 6 5 4 3 2 1

THE
GREATEST
LOVE
STORIES
OF ALL TIME

Celebrate Love with

Timeless Writings from Classic Authors

Standard
PUBLISHING
Bringing The Word to Life™

Cincinnati, Ohio

Love alone is capable of uniting living beings
in such a way as to complete and fulfill them,
for it alone takes them and joins them
by what is deepest in themselves.

PIERRE TEILHARD DE CHARDIN

Introduction

Love makes the world go 'round—even the Bible says so in 1 Corinthians 13:13: "Now these three remain: faith, hope and love. But the greatest of these is love." It's a big job for such a little word, but somehow it manages to hold its own—and has done so throughout the millennia of human history.

Though there are many varieties of love, romantic love is one of the earliest entries in love's exhaustive résumé. It began the moment Adam laid eyes on Eve—the perfect partner created exclusively for him by God himself. It is God's own great idea and His own splendid gift.

The Greatest Love Stories of All Time was compiled to celebrate God's gift of romantic love. It contains stories of love won and love lost, love cherished and love scorned, love that brings new life and love that gives its life for the object of its affection.

We hope that you will revel in this book right down to the very last word, that you will enjoy both the laughter and the tears, the hope and the sorrow, the triumph and the defeat—and that you will see God's hand in it all.

If I speak in the tongues of men and of angels, but have not love,
I am only a resounding gong or a clanging cymbal. If I have the gift of
prophecy and can fathom all mysteries and all knowledge, and if I have a
faith that can move mountains, but have not love, I am nothing.
If I give all I possess to the poor and surrender my body to the flames,
but have not love, I gain nothing.

Love is patient, love is kind. It does not envy, it does not boast,
it is not proud. It is not rude, it is not self-seeking, it is not easily
angered, it keeps no record of wrongs. Love does not delight in evil but
rejoices with the truth. It always protects, always trusts, always hopes,
always perseveres. Love never fails.

1 Corinthians 13:1-8

Contents

JANE EYRE

CHARLOTTE BRONTË

AN EXCERPT

Jane Eyre was published in 1847 and is probably a partially fictionalized autobiography of its author. The heroine, Jane, begins her life as a girl orphaned without a penny to her name.

Left in the care of her aunt, Mrs. Reed, she is treated cruelly. At the age of ten, she is sent to live at a charitable institution for orphans, where she is trained as a teacher. She teaches there at the school for several years, but when her mentor marries, Jane decided to leave as well and seek a position as a governess, and her inquiry is soon answered by a Mr. Rochester who is seeking her services as a tutor for his young daughter.

The unconventional hero figure finds himself drawn to Jane not for her plain features but for her intellect and indomitable spirit. As she attends her duties, Jane soon realizes that she has fallen in love with Mr. Rochester, and he with her. They plan to marry, but on their wedding day, she learns that her beloved already has a wife. When confronted, he confesses the truth. Rochester explained that his first marriage was a travesty arranged by his unscrupulous father out of greed. His wife, Bertha, is insane and must be kept in an isolated attic room where she will not harm herself or others.

Devastated by the news, Jane leaves Thornfield, and after some days, is taken in by two kind sisters and their brother, St. John Rivers, and offered a teaching job at a local country school. In time, St. John falls in love with Jane. He plans to leave for India as a missionary and wants to marry Jane and take her with him. But she refuses, realizing that her heart still belongs to Mr. Rochester. Soon after, Jane learns two things. She has been left a fortune by a kind aunt, and the Rivers' siblings are her cousins. She splits her newfound wealth four ways and plans to return to Thornfield to check on Mr. Rochester.

When she arrives, she finds that Rochester's tormented wife has burned Thornfield to the ground. She is told that Mr. Rochester saved the servants from the fire and tried to save his wife, but could not reach her before she jumped from the roof. The fire has left him blind and scarred. His arm is a useless stump and he is emotionally devastated.

The parlor looked gloomy; a neglected handful of fire burnt low in the grate; and, leaning over it, with his head supported against the high, old-fashioned mantel-piece, appeared the blind tenant of the room. His old dog, Pilot, lay on one side, removed out of the way, and coiled up as if afraid of being inadvertently trodden upon. Pilot pricked up his ears when I came in: then he jumped up with a yelp and a whine, and bounded toward me— almost knocking the tray from my hands. I set it on the table; then patted him, and said softly, "Lie down!" Mr. Rochester turned mechanically to see what the commotion was: but as he saw nothing, he returned and sighed.

"Give me the water, Mary," he said.

I approached him with the now only half-filled glass. Pilot followed me, still excited.

"What is the matter?" he inquired.

"Down, Pilot!" I again said. He checked the water on its way to his lips, and seemed to listen: he drank, and put the glass down. "This is you, Mary, is it not?"

"Mary is in the kitchen," I answered.

He put out his hand with a quick gesture, but not seeing where I stood, he did not touch me. "Who is this? Who is this?" he demanded, trying, as it seemed, to see with those sightless eyes—unavailing and distressing attempt! "Answer me—speak again!" he ordered, imperiously and aloud.

"Will you have a little more water, sir? I spilt half of what was in the glass," I said.

"Who is it? What is it? Who speaks?"

"Pilot knows me, and John and Mary know I am here. I came only this evening," I answered.

"Great God!—what delusion has come over me? What sweet madness has seized me?"

"No delusion—no madness. Your mind, sir, is too strong for delusion, your health too sound for frenzy."

"And where is the speaker? Is it only a voice? Oh! I cannot see, but I must feel, or my heart will stop and my brain burst. Whatever—whoever you are—be perceptible to the touch or I cannot live!"

He groped; I arrested his wandering hand, and imprisoned it in both of mine.

"Her very fingers!" he cried; "her small, slight fingers! If so, there must be more of her!"

The muscular hand broke from my custody; my arm was seized, my shoulder—neck—waist—I was entwined and gathered to him.

"Is it Jane? What is it? This is her shape—this is her size—"

"And this is her voice," I added. "She is all here—her heart as well. God bless you, sir! I am glad to be so near you again."

"Jane Eyre—Jane Eyre," was all he said.

"My dear master," I answered, "I am Jane Eyre: I have found you out—I am come back to you."

"In truth—in the flesh? My living Jane?"

"You touch me, sir,—you hold me, and fast enough: I am not like a corpse, nor vacant like air, am I?"

"My living darling? These are certainly her limbs, and these her features; but I cannot be so blest, after all my misery. It is a dream—such dreams as I have had at night when I have clasped her once more to my heart, as I do now, and kissed her, as thus—and felt that she loved me, and trusted that she would not leave me."

"Which I never will, sir, from this day."

"Never will, says the vision? But I always woke and found it an empty mockery, and I was desolate and abandoned—my life dark, lonely, hopeless— my soul athirst and forbidden to drink—my heart famished and never to be fed. Gentle, soft dream, nestling in my arms now, you will fly, too, as your sisters have all fled before you. But kiss me before you go—embrace me, Jane."

"There, sir—and there!"

I pressed my lips to his once brilliant and now rayless eyes. I swept his hair from his brow and kissed that too. He suddenly seemed to arouse himself, the reality of all this seizing him.

"It is you—is it, Jane? You are come back to me, then?"

"I am."

"And you do not lie dead in some ditch under some stream? And you are not a pining outcast amongst strangers?"

"No, sir; I am an independent woman now."

"Independent! What do you mean, Jane?"

"My uncle in Madeira is dead, and he left me five thousand pounds."

"Ah, this is practical—this is real!" he cried: "I should never dream that. Besides, there is that peculiar voice of hers, so animating and piquant, as well as soft. It cheers my withered heart; it puts life into it. What, Janet! Are you an independent woman? A rich woman?"

"Quite rich, sir. If you won't let me live with you, I can build a house of my own close up to your door, and you may come and sit in my parlor when you want company of an evening."

"But as you are rich, Jane, you have now, no doubt, friends who will look after you and not suffer you to devote yourself to a blind lamenter like me."

"I told you I am independent, sir, as well as rich. I am my own mistress."

"And you will stay with me?"

"Certainly—unless you object. I will be your neighbor, your nurse, your housekeeper. I find you lonely so I will be your companion—to read to you, to walk with you, to sit with you, to wait on you, to be eyes and hands to you. Cease to look so melancholy, my dear master; you shall not be left desolate, so long as I live."

He replied not. Instead he seemed serious—abstracted. He sighed, half-opened his lips as if to speak. Then closed them again. I felt a little embarrassed. Perhaps I had too rashly overleaped conventionalities, and he, like St. John, saw impropriety in my inconsiderateness. I had indeed made my proposal from the idea that he wished and would ask me to be his wife. An expectation that he would claim me at once as his own—not the less certain because unexpressed—had buoyed me up. But no hint to that effect escaped him, and his countenance became more overcast. I suddenly remembered that I might have been all wrong and was perhaps playing the fool unwittingly. I began gently to withdraw myself from his arms—but he eagerly snatched me closer.

"No—no—Jane; you must not go. No—I have touched you, heard you, felt the comfort of your presence—the sweetness of your consolation: I cannot give up these joys. I have little left in myself—I must have you. The world may laugh—may call me absurd, selfish—but it does not matter. My very soul demands you. It will be satisfied or it will take deadly vengeance on its frame."

"Well, sir, I will stay with you—I have said so."

"Yes—but you understand one thing by staying with me, and I understand another. You, perhaps, could make up your mind to be about my hand and chair, to wait on me as a kind little nurse (for you have an affectionate heart and a generous spirit, which prompt you to make sacrifices for those you pity), and that ought to suffice for me, no doubt. I suppose I should now entertain none but fatherly feelings for you: do you think so? Come—tell me."

"I will think what you like, sir. I am content to be only your nurse, if you think it better."

"But you cannot always be my nurse, Janet. You are young—you must marry one day."

"I don't care about being married."

"You should care, Janet. If I were what I once was, I would try to make you care—but—a sightless block!"

He relapsed again into gloom. I, on the contrary, became more cheerful and took fresh courage. These last words gave me an insight as to where the difficulty lay—and as it was no difficulty for me, I felt quite relieved from my previous embarrassment. I resumed a livelier vein of conversation.

"It is time some one undertook to rehumanize you," said I, parting his thick and long uncut locks, "for I see you are being metamorphosed into a lion or something of that sort. You have a 'faux air' of Nebuchadnezzar in the fields about you, that is certain. Your hair reminds me of eagles' feathers— whether your nails are grown like birds' claws or not, I have not yet noticed."

"On this arm, I have neither hand nor nails," he said, drawing the mutilated limb from his breast, and showing it to me. "It is a mere stump—a ghastly sight! Don't you think so, Jane?"

"It is a pity to see it; and a pity to see your eyes—and the scar of fire on your forehead. And the worst of it is, one is in danger of loving you too well for all this and making too much of you."

"I thought you would be revolted, Jane, when you saw my arm, and my scarred visage."

"Did you? Don't tell me so—lest I should say something disparaging to your judgment. Now, let me leave you an instant to make a better fire and have the hearth swept up. Can you tell when there is a good fire?"

"Yes; with the right eye I see a glow—a ruddy haze."

"And you see the candles?"

"Very dimly—each is a luminous cloud."

"Can you see me?"

"No, my fairy—but I am only too thankful to hear and feel you."

"When do you take supper?"

"I never take supper."

"But you shall have some tonight. I am hungry. So are you, I daresay, only you forget."

Summoning Mary, I soon had the room in more cheerful order: I prepared him, likewise, a comfortable repast. My spirits were excited, and with pleasure and ease I talked to him during supper and for a long time after. There was no harassing restraint, no repression of glee and vivacity with him—for with him I was at perfect ease, because I knew I suited him. All I said or did seemed either to console or revive him. Delightful consciousness! It brought to life and light my whole nature. In his presence I thoroughly lived. And he lived in mine. Blind as he was, smiles played over his face, joy dawned on his forehead, his lineaments softened and warmed.

After supper, he began to ask me many questions—where I had been, what I had been doing, how I had found him out—but I gave him only very partial replies. It was too late to enter into particulars that night. Besides, I wished to touch no deep-thrilling chord—to open no fresh well of emotion in his heart. My sole present aim was to cheer him. Cheered, as I have said, he was, and yet but by fits. If a moment's silence broke the conversation, he would turn restless, touch me, then say, "Jane."

"You are altogether a human being, Jane? You are certain of that?"

"I conscientiously believe so, Mr. Rochester."

"Yet how, on this dark and doleful evening, could you so suddenly rise on my lone hearth? I stretched my hand to take a glass of water from a hireling, and it was given me by you. I asked a question, expecting John's wife to answer me, and your voice spoke at my ear."

"Because I had come in Mary's stead with the tray."

"And there is enchantment in the very hour I am now spending with you. Who can tell what a dark, dreary, hopeless life I have dragged on for months past? Doing nothing, expecting nothing. I merged night into day, feeling but the sensation of cold when I let the fire go out, of hunger when I forgot to eat, and then a ceaseless sorrow, and, at times, a very delirium of desire to behold my Jane again. Yes: for her restoration I longed, far more than for that of my lost sight. How can it be that Jane is with me, and says she loves me? Will she not depart as suddenly as she came? To-morrow, I fear I shall find her no more."

A common-place, practical reply—out of the train of his own disturbed ideas—was, I was sure, the best and most reassuring for him in this frame of mind. I passed my finger over his eyebrows and remarked that they were scorched. I would apply something that should make them grow as broad and black as ever.

"What is the use of doing me good in any way, beneficent spirit, when, at some fatal moment, you will again desert me—passing like a shadow, whither and how to me unknown and for me remaining afterward undiscoverable?"

"Have you a pocket-comb about you, sir?"

"What for, Jane?"

"Just to comb out this shaggy black mane. I find you rather alarming when I examine you close at hand. You talk of my being a fairy, but I am sure, you are more like a brownie."

"Am I hideous, Jane?"

"Very, sir—you always were, you know."

"Humph! The wickedness has not been taken out of you wherever you have sojourned."

"Yet I have been with good people far better than you—a hundred times better people, possessed of ideas and views you never entertained in your life, quite more refined and exalted."

"Who the deuce have you been with?"

"If you twist in that way you will make me pull the hair out of your head; and then I think you will cease to entertain doubts of my substantiality."

"Who have you been with, Jane?"

"You shall not get it out of me tonight, sir. You must wait till tomorrow. To leave my tale half-told, will, you know, be a sort of security that I shall appear at your breakfast table to finish it. By-the-by, I must mind not to appear on your hearth with only a glass of water: I must bring an egg at the least, to say nothing of fried ham."

"You mocking changeling—fairy-born and human-bred! You make me feel as I have not felt these twelve months. If Saul could have had you for his David, the evil spirit would have been exorcised without the aid of the harp."

"There, sir, you are made decent. Now I'll leave you. I have been traveling these last three days, and I believe I am tired. Good-night."

"Just one word, Jane. Were there only ladies in the house where you have been?"

I laughed and made my escape, still laughing as I ran upstairs. "A good idea!" I thought, with glee. "I see I have the means of fretting him out of his melancholy for some time to come."

Very early the next morning, I heard him up and astir, wandering from one room to another. As soon as Mary came down, I heard the question: "Is Miss Eyre here?" Then: "Which room did you put her into? Was it dry? Is she up? Go and ask if she wants anything and when she will come down."

I came down as soon as I thought there was a prospect of breakfast. Entering the room very softly, I had a view of him before he discovered my presence. It was mournful indeed to witness the subjugation of that vigorous spirit to a corporeal infirmity. He sat in his chair,—still, but not at rest—expectant evidently; the lines of now habitual sadness marking his strong features. His countenance reminded one of a lamp quenched, waiting to be relit—and alas! it was not himself that could now kindle the luster of animated expression. He was dependent on another for that office! I had meant to be gay and careless, but the powerlessness of the strong man touched my heart to the quick: still I accosted him with what vivacity I could.

"It is a bright, sunny morning, sir," I said. "The rain is over and gone, and there is a tender shining after it. You shall have a walk soon."

I had wakened the glow—his features beamed.

"Oh, you are indeed there, my skylark! Come to me. You are not gone, not vanished? I heard one of your kind an hour ago, singing high over the wood. But its song had no music for me, any more than the rising sun had rays. All the melody on earth is concentrated in my Jane's tongue to my ear (I am glad it is not naturally a silent one). All the sunshine I can feel is in her presence."

The water stood in my eyes to hear this avowal of his dependence—just as if a royal eagle chained to a perch should be forced to entreat a sparrow to become its purveyor. But I would not be tearful. I dashed off the salt drops, and busied myself with preparing breakfast.

Most of the morning was spent in the open air. I led him out of the wet and wild wood into some cheerful fields. I described to him how brilliantly green they were, how the flowers and hedges looked refreshed, how sparklingly blue was the sky. I sought a seat for him in a hidden and lovely spot—a dry stump of a tree—and I did not refuse to let him, when seated, place me on his knee. Why should I, when both he and I were happier near than apart? Pilot lay beside us—all was quiet. He broke out suddenly while clasping me in his arms.

"Cruel, cruel deserter! Oh, Jane, what did I feel when I discovered you had fled from Thornfield, and when I could nowhere find you, and, after examining your apartment, ascertained that you had taken no money, nor anything that could serve as an equivalent! A pearl necklace I had given you lay untouched in its little casket, your trunks were left corded and locked as they had been prepared for the bridal tour. What could my darling do, I asked, left destitute and penniless? And what did she do? Let me hear now."

Thus urged, I began the narrative of my experience for the last year. I softened considerably what related to the three days of wandering and starvation, because to have told him all would have been to inflict unnecessary pain. The little I did say lacerated his faithful heart deeper than I wished.

I should not have left him thus, he said, without any means of making my way. I should have told him my intention. I should have confided in him. He would never have forced me to be his mistress. Violent as he had seemed in his despair, he, in truth, loved me far too well and too tenderly to constitute himself my tyrant. He would have given me half his fortune without demanding so much as a kiss in return rather than seeing me fling myself friendless on the wide world. I had endured, he was certain, more than I had confessed to him.

"Well, whatever my sufferings had been, they were very short," I answered. Then I proceeded to tell him how I had been received at Moor House, how I had obtained the office of schoolmistress, etc. The accession of fortune and the discovery of my relations followed in due order. Of course, St. John Rivers' name came in frequently in the progress of my tale. When I was done, that name was immediately taken up.

"This St. John, then, is your cousin?"

"Yes."

"You have spoken of him often. Did you like him?"

"He was a very good man, sir; I could not help liking him."

"A good man? Does that mean a respectable, well-conducted man of fifty? What does it mean?"

"St. John was only twenty-nine, sir."

"Jeune encore, as the French say. Is he a person of low stature, phlegmatic, and plain? A person whose goodness consists rather in his guiltlessness of vice, than in his prowess in virtue?"

"He is untiringly active. Great and exalted deeds are what he lives to perform."

"But his brain? That is probably rather soft? He means well, but you shrug your shoulders to hear him talk?"

"He talks little, sir. What he does is ever to the point. His brain is first-rate. I should think not impressive, but vigorous."

"Is he an able man, then?"

"Truly able."

"A thoroughly educated man?"

"St. John is an accomplished and profound scholar."

"His manners, I think you said, are not to your taste?—priggish and parsonic?"

"I never mentioned his manners; but, unless I have very bad taste, they must suit it. They are polished, calm, and gentlemanlike."

"His appearance—I forget what description you gave of his appearance. A sort of raw curate, half strangled with his white neck cloth, and stilted up on his thick-soled high-lows, was it?"

"St. John dresses well. He is a handsome man—tall, fair with blue eyes and a Grecian profile."

"Did you like him, Jane?"

"Yes, Mr. Rochester, I liked him—but you asked me that before."

I perceived, of course, the drift of my interlocutor. Jealousy had gotten hold of him. She had stung him, but the sting was salutary—It gave him respite from the gnawing fang of melancholy. I would not, therefore, immediately charm the snake.

"Perhaps you would rather not sit any longer on my knee, Miss Eyre?" was the next somewhat unexpected observation.

"Why not, Mr. Rochester?"

"The picture you have just drawn is suggestive of a rather too overwhelming contrast. Your words have delineated very prettily a graceful Apollo. He is present to your imagination—tall, fair, blue-eyed, and with a Grecian profile. Your eyes dwell on a Vulcan—a real blacksmith, brown, broad-shouldered—blind and lame into the bargain."

"I never thought of it, before, but you certainly are rather like a Vulcan, sir."

"Well—you can leave me, ma'am: but before you go" (and he retained me by a firmer grasp than ever), "you will be pleased just to answer me a question or two." He paused.

"What questions, Mr. Rochester?"

He then followed this cross-examination.

"St. John made you schoolmistress of Morton before he knew you were his cousin?"

"Yes."

"You would often see him? He would visit the school sometimes?"

"Daily."

"He would approve of your plans, Jane? I know they would be clever, for you are a talented creature."

"He approved of them—yes."

"He would discover many things in you he could not have expected to find? Some of your accomplishments are not ordinary."

"I don't know about that."

"You had a little cottage near the school, you say. Did he ever come there to see you?"

"Now and then."

"Of an evening?"

"Once or twice."

A pause.

"How long did you reside with him and his sisters after the cousinship was discovered?"

"Five months."

"Did Rivers spend much time with the ladies of his family?"

"Yes—the back parlor was both his study and ours. He sat near the window, and we by the table."

"Did he study much?"

"A good deal."

"What?"

"Hindostanee."

"And what did you do meantime?"

"I learned German, at first."

"Did he teach you?"

"He did not understand German."

"Did he teach you nothing?"

"A little Hindostanee."

"Rivers taught you Hindostanee?"

"Yes, sir."

"And his sister also?"

"No."

"Only you?"

"Only me."

"Did you ask to learn?"

"No."

"He wished to teach you?"

"Yes."

A second pause.

"Why did he wish it? Of what use could Hindostanee be to you?"

"He intended me to go with him to India."

"Ah! Here I reach the root of the matter. He wanted you to marry him?"

"He asked me to marry him."

"That is a fiction—an impudent invention to vex me."

"I beg your pardon, it is the literal truth. He asked me more than once and was as stiff about urging his point as ever you could be."

"Miss Eyre, I repeat it—you can leave me. How often am I to say the same thing? Why do you remain impertinently perched on my knee when I have given you notice to quit?"

"Because I am comfortable there."

"No, Jane, you are not comfortable there, because your heart is not with me. It is with this cousin—this St. John. Oh, till this moment, I thought my little Jane was all mine! I had a belief she loved me even when she left me—that was an atom of sweet in much bitter. Long as we have been parted, hot tears as I have wept over our separation, I never thought that while I was mourning her, she was loving another! But it is useless grieving. Jane, leave me—go and marry Rivers."

"Shake me off, then, sir—push me away, for I'll not leave you of my own accord."

"Jane, I ever like your tone of voice—it still renews hope, it sounds so truthful. When I hear it, it carries me back a year. I forget that you have formed a new tie. But I am not a fool—go—"

"Where must I go, sir?"

"Your own way—with the husband you have chosen."

"Who is that?"

"You know—this St. John Rivers."

"He is not my husband nor ever will he be. He does not love me: I do not love him. He loves (as he can love, and that is not as you love) a beautiful young lady called Rosamond. He wanted to marry me only because he thought I should make a suitable missionary's wife, which she would not have done. He is good and great, but severe; and, for me, cold as an iceberg. He is not like you, sir. I am not happy at his side, nor near him, nor with him. He has no indulgence for me—no fondness. He sees nothing attractive in me; not even youth—only a few useful mental points, Must I then leave you, sir, to go to him?"

I shuddered involuntarily, and clung instinctively closer to my blind but beloved master. He smiled.

"What, Jane! Is this true? Is such really the state of matters between you and Rivers?"

"Absolutely, sir. Oh, you need not be jealous! I wanted to tease you a little to make you less sad. I thought anger would be better than grief. But if you wish me to love you, could you but see how much I do love you, you would be proud and content. All my heart is yours, sir. It belongs to you; and with you it would remain, were fate to exile the rest of me from your presence for ever."

Again, as he kissed me, painful thoughts darkened his aspect.

"My seared vision! My crippled strength!" he murmured regretfully.

I caressed, in order to soothe him. I knew of what he was thinking. I wanted to speak for him—but dared not. As he turned aside his face a minute, I saw a tear slide from under the sealed eyelid and trickle down his manly cheek. My heart swelled.

"I am no better than the old lightning-struck chestnut-tree in Thornfield orchard," he remarked. "And what right would that ruin have to bid a budding woodbine cover its decay with freshness?"

"You are no ruin, sir—you are no lightning-struck tree. I see a man who is green and vigorous. Plants will grow about your roots, whether you ask them to or not, because they take delight in your bountiful shadow. And as they grow they will lean toward you, and wind round you, because your strength offers them so safe a prop."

Again he smiled: I gave him comfort.

"You speak of friends, Jane?" he asked.

"Yes; of friends," I answered, rather hesitatingly—for I knew I meant more than friends, but could not tell what other word to employ. He helped me!

"Ah! Jane. But I want a wife."

"Do you, sir?"

"Yes—is it news to you?"

"Of course. You said nothing about it before."

"Is it unwelcome news?"

"That depends on circumstances, sir—on your choice."

"Which you shall make for me, Jane. I will abide by your decision."

"Choose then, sir—her who loves you best."

"I will at least choose—her I love best. Jane, will you marry me?"

"Yes, sir."

"A poor blind man whom you will have to lead about by the hand?"

"Yes, sir."

"A crippled man, twenty years older than you, whom you will have to wait on?"

"Yes, sir."

"Truly, Jane?"

"Most truly, sir."

"Oh! my darling! God bless and reward you!"

"Mr. Rochester, if ever I did a good deed in my life—if ever I thought a good thought—if ever I prayed a sincere and blameless prayer—if ever I wished a righteous wish—I am rewarded now. To be your wife is, for me, to be as happy as I can be on earth."

"Because you delight in sacrifice."

"Sacrifice! What do I sacrifice? Famine for food, expectation for content. To be privileged to put my arms round what I value—to press my lips to what I love—to repose on what I trust. Is that to make a sacrifice? If so, then certainly I delight in sacrifice."

"And to bear with my infirmities, Jane—to overlook my deficiencies."

"Which are none, sir, to me. I love you better now—when I can really be useful to you—than I did in your state of proud independence, when you disdained every part but that of the giver and the protector."

"Hitherto I have hated to be helped—to be led. Henceforth, I feel, I shall hate it no more. I did not like to put my hand into a hireling's, but it is pleasant to feel it circled by Jane's little fingers. I preferred utter loneliness to the constant attendance of servants; but Jane's soft ministry will be a perpetual joy. Jane suits me. Do I suite her?"

"To the finest fiber of my nature, sir."

"The case being so, we have nothing in the world to wait for. We must be married instantly."

He looked and spoke with eagerness, his old impetuosity rising.

"We must become one flesh without any delay, Jane. There is but the license to get—then we marry."

"Mr. Rochester, I have just discovered the sun is far declined from its meridian, and Pilot is actually gone home to his dinner. Let me look at your watch."

"Fasten it into your girdle, Janet, and keep it henceforward. I have no use for it."

"It is nearly four o'clock in the afternoon, sir. Don't you feel hungry?"

"The third day from this must be our wedding-day, Jane. Never mind fine clothes and jewels, now—all that is not worth a fillip."

"The sun has dried up all the raindrops, sir. The breeze is still. It is quite hot."

"Do you know, Jane, I have your little pearl necklace at this moment fastened round my bronze scrag under my cravat? I have worn it since the day I lost my only treasure. I kept it as a memento of her."

"We will go home through the wood. That will be the shadiest way."

He pursued his own thoughts without heeding me.

"Jane! You think me, I daresay, an irreligious dog, but my heart swells with gratitude to the beneficent God of this earth just now. He sees not as man sees, but far clearer, judges not as man judges, but far more wisely. I did wrong. I would have sullied my innocent flower—breathed guilt on its purity, therefore, the Omnipotent snatched it from me. I, in my stiff-necked rebellion, almost cursed the dispensation. Instead of bending to the decree, I defied it. Divine justice pursued its course; disasters came thick on me: I was forced to pass through the valley of the shadow of death. His chastisements are mighty; and one smote me that has humbled me for ever. You know I was proud of my strength. But what is it now, when I must give it over to foreign guidance as a child does its weakness? Of late, Jane—only—only of late—I began to see and acknowledge the hand of God in my doom. I began to experience remorse, repentance; the wish for reconcilement to my Maker. I began sometimes to pray—very brief prayers they were, but very sincere.

"Some days since, nay, I can number them—four. It was last Monday night, a singular mood came over me—one in which grief replaced frenzy, sorrow, sullenness. I had long had the impression that since I could nowhere find you, you must be dead. Late that night—perhaps it might have been between eleven and twelve o'clock—before I retired to my dreary rest, I supplicated God. I asked that, if it seemed good to Him, I might soon be taken from this life, and admitted to that world to come—a world where there was still hope of rejoining Jane.

"I was in my own room sitting by an open window. It soothed me to feel the balmy night-air, though I could see no stars and only by a vague, luminous haze, knew the presence of a moon. I longed for thee, Janet! Oh, I longed for thee both with soul and flesh! I asked of God, at once in anguish and humility, if I had not been long enough desolate, afflicted, tormented; and might not soon taste bliss and peace once more. I acknowledged that I merited all I endured. I pleaded that I could scarcely endure more, and the alpha and omega of my heart's wishes broke involuntarily from my lips in the words—'Jane! Jane! Jane!'"

"Did you speak these words aloud?"

"I did, Jane. If any listener had heard me, he would have thought me mad: I pronounced them with such frantic energy."

"And it was last Monday night—somewhere near midnight?"

"Yes; but the time is of no consequence; what followed is the strange point. You will think me superstitious—some superstition I have in my blood, and always had. Nevertheless, this is true—true at least that I heard what I now relate.

"As I exclaimed 'Jane! Jane! Jane!' a voice—I cannot tell from whence the voice came, but I know whose voice it was—replied, 'I am coming: wait for me.' A moment after the words—'where are you?' went whispering on the wind.

"I'll tell you, if I can, the idea, the picture these words opened to my mind—yet it is difficult to express what I want to express. Ferndean is buried, as you see, in a heavy wood, where sound falls dull and dies unreverberating. 'Where are you?' seemed spoken amongst mountains; for I heard a hill-sent echo repeat the words. Cooler and fresher at the moment, the gale seemed to visit my brow, I could have deemed that in some wild, lone scene, Jane and I were meeting. In spirit, I believe we must have met. You no doubt were, at that hour, in unconscious sleep, Jane. Perhaps your soul wandered from its cell to comfort mine, for those were your accents—as certain as I live—they were yours!"

Reader, it was on Monday night—near midnight—that I too had received the mysterious summons—those being the very words by which I replied to it. I listened to Mr. Rochester's narrative; but made no disclosure in return. The coincidence struck me as too awful and inexplicable to be communicated or discussed. If I told anything, my tale would be such as must necessarily make a profound impression on the mind of my hearer. And that mind, yet from its sufferings too prone to gloom, needed not the deeper shade of the supernatural. I kept things then, and pondered them in my heart.

"You cannot now wonder," continued my master, "that when you rose upon me so unexpectedly last night, I had difficulty in believing you any other than a mere voice and vision—something that would melt to silence and annihilation, as the midnight whisper and mountain echo had melted before. Now I thank God! I knew it to be otherwise. Yes, I thank God!"

"I thank my Maker that in the midst of judgment he has remembered mercy. I humbly entreat my Redeemer to give me strength to lead henceforth a purer life than I have done hitherto!"

Then he stretched his hand out to be led. I took that dear hand, held it a moment to my lips, then let it pass round my shoulder—being so much lower of stature than he, I served both for his prop and guide. We entered the wood and wended homeward.

Reader, I married him. We had a quiet wedding—he and I, the parson and the clerk, were alone present. When we got back from church, I went into the kitchen of the manor house where Mary was cooking the dinner and John cleaning the knives, and I said:

"Mary, I have been married to Mr. Rochester this morning." The housekeeper and her husband both are of that decent phlegmatic order of people to whom one may at any time safely communicate a remarkable piece of news without incurring the danger of having one's ears pierced by some shrill shout and subsequently stunned by a torrent of wordy wonderment. Mary did look up, and she did stare at me. The ladle with which she was basting a pair of chickens roasting at the fire, did for some three minutes hang suspended in the air. And for the same space of time John's knives also had a rest from the polishing process. But Mary, bending again over the roast, said only—

"Have you, Miss? Well, for sure!"

I have now been married ten years. I know what it is to live entirely for and with what I love best on earth. I hold myself supremely blest—blest beyond what language can express, because I am my husband's life as fully as he is mine. No woman was ever nearer to her mate than I am. No woman ever more absolutely bone of his bone and flesh of his flesh. I know no weariness of my Edward's company, and he knows none of mine, any more than we each do of the pulsation of the heart that beats in our separate bosoms. Consequently, we are ever together. To be together is for us to be at once as free as in solitude, as gay as in the presence of others. We talk, I believe, all day long. To talk to each other is but a more animated and audible thinking. All my confidence is bestowed on him; all his confidence is devoted to me. We are precisely suited in character and perfect concord is the result.

Mr. Rochester continued blind the first two years of our union. Perhaps it was that circumstance that drew us so very near—that knit us so very close! For I was then his vision, as I am still his right hand. Literally, I was (what he often called me) the apple of his eye. He saw nature—he saw books through me, and never did I weary of conducting him where he wished to go, or doing for him what he wished to be done. And there was a pleasure in my services, most full, most exquisite, even though sad—because he claimed these services without painful shame or damping humiliation. He loved me so truly, that he knew no reluctance in profiting by my attendance. He felt that I loved him so fondly that to yield that attendance was to indulge my sweetest wishes.

One morning at the end of the two years, as I was writing a letter to his dictation, he came and bent over me, and said—

"Jane, have you a glittering ornament round your neck?"

I had a gold watch-chain. I answered "Yes."

"And have you a pale blue dress on?"

I had. He informed me then that for some time he had fancied the obscurity clouding one eye was becoming less dense; and that now he was sure of it.

He and I went up to London. He had the advice of an eminent oculist, and eventually recovered the sight of that one eye. He cannot now see very distinctly. He cannot read or write much. But he can find his way without being led by the hand—the sky is no longer blank to him, the earth no longer a void. When his first-born was put into his arms, he could see that the boy had inherited his own eyes as they once were—large, brilliant, and black. On that occasion, he again, with a full heart, acknowledged that God had tempered judgment with mercy.

ADAM BEDE

GEORGE ELIOT

AN EXCERPT

Adam Bede is a young English workman and foreman of a carpentry shop.
He has two brothers, Seth and Arthur, and a sister, Lisbeth. Dinah Morris is
a young Methodist preacher, who sometimes comes to their town to preach and
minister to the sick. When the boy's father dies unexpectedly, she comes by the
house to comfort Lisbeth.

When Adam's fiancée is found guilty of murder, Dinah goes to see her in
prison, summons Adam, and succeeds in helping Hetty to reach out to God and
Adam for forgiveness. Afterward, her death sentence is commuted from death
to exile, and Dinah returns to her home in Snowfield.

Eighteen months later, Adam contacts Dinah while she is visiting relatives
at the nearby Hall Farm, asking that she pay a visit to his ailing mother. In
time, he learns from his sister that Dinah loves him, and realizes that he loves
her as well.

※

ADAM AND DINAH

It was about three o'clock when Adam entered the farmyard
and roused Alick and the dogs from their Sunday dozing. Alick said
everybody was gone to church "but th' young missis"—so he called
Dinah; but this did not disappoint Adam, although the "everybody" was
so liberal as to include Nancy the dairymaid, whose works of necessity
were frequently incompatible with church-going.

There was perfect stillness about the house. The doors were all closed,
and the very stones and tubs seemed quieter than usual. Adam heard

the water gently dripping from the pump—that was the only sound, and he knocked at the house door rather softly, as was suitable in that stillness.

The door opened, and Dinah stood before him, coloring deeply with the great surprise of seeing Adam at this hour, when she knew it was his regular practice to be at church. Yesterday he would have said to her without any difficulty, "I came to see you, Dinah. I knew the rest were not at home." But today something prevented him from saying that, and he put out his hand to hers in silence. Neither of them spoke, and yet both wished they could speak, as Adam entered, and they sat down. Dinah took the chair she had just left at the corner of the table near the window. There was a book laying on the table, but it was not open. She had been sitting perfectly still, looking at the small bit of clear fire in the bright grate. Adam sat down opposite her in Mr. Poyser's three-cornered chair.

"Your mother is not ill again, I hope, Adam?" Dinah said, recovering herself. "Seth said she was well this morning."

"No, she's very hearty today," said Adam, happy in the signs of Dinah's feeling at the sight of him, but shy.

"There's nobody at home, you see," Dinah said; "but you'll wait. You've been hindered from going to church today, doubtless."

"Yes," Adam said, and then paused, before he added, "I was thinking about you—that was the reason."

This confession was very awkward and sudden, Adam felt, for he thought Dinah must understand all he meant. But the frankness of the words caused her immediately to interpret them into a renewal of his brotherly regrets that she was going away, and she answered calmly—

"Do not be careful and troubled for me, Adam. I have all things and abound at Snowfield. And my mind is at rest, for I am not seeking my own will in going."

"But if things were different, Dinah," said Adam, hesitatingly—"if you knew things that perhaps you don't know now—"

Dinah looked at him inquiringly. But instead of going on, he reached a chair and brought it near the corner of the table where she was sitting. She wondered and was afraid—and the next moment her thoughts flew to the past. *Was it something about those distant unhappy ones that she didn't know?*

Adam looked at her. It was so sweet to look at her eyes, which had now a self-forgetful questioning in them—for a moment he forgot that he wanted to say anything or that it was necessary to tell her what he meant.

"Dinah," he said suddenly, taking both her hands between his, "I love you with my whole heart and soul. I love you next to God who made me."

Dinah's lips became pale—like her cheeks—and she trembled violently under the shock of painful joy. Her hands were cold as death between Adam's. She could not draw them away, because he held them fast.

"Don't tell me you can't love me, Dinah. Don't tell me we must part and pass our lives away from one another."

The tears were trembling in Dinah's eyes, and they fell before she could answer. But she spoke in a quiet low voice.

"Yes, dear Adam, we must submit to another will. We must part."

"Not if you love me, Dinah—not if you love me," Adam said, passionately. "Tell me—tell me if you can love me better than a brother."

Dinah was too entirely reliant on the Supreme guidance to attempt to achieve any end by a deceptive concealment. She was recovering now from the first shock of emotion, and she looked at Adam with simple sincere eyes as she said—

"Yes, Adam, my heart is drawn strongly toward you; and of my own will, if I had no clear showing to the contrary, I could find my happiness in being near you and ministering to you continually. I fear I should forget to rejoice and weep with others—nay, I fear I should forget the Divine presence and seek no love but yours."

Adam did not speak immediately. They sat looking at each other in delicious silence—for the first sense of mutual love excludes other feelings; it will have the soul all to itself.

"Then, Dinah," Adam said at last, "how can there be anything contrary to what's right in our belonging to one another and spending our lives together? Who put this great love into our hearts? Can anything be holier than that? For we can help one another in everything as is good. I'd never think o' putting myself between you and God, and saying you oughtn't to do this and you oughtn't to do that. You'd follow your conscience as much as you do now."

"Yes, Adam," Dinah said, "I know marriage is a holy state for those who are truly called to it, and have no other drawing; but from my childhood upward I have been led toward another path. All my peace and my joy have come from having no life of my own, no wants, no wishes for myself, and living only in God and those of his creatures whose sorrows and joys he has given me to know. Those have been very blessed years to me. I feel that if I were to listen to any voice that would draw me aside from that path, I should be turning my back on the light that has shone upon me, and darkness and doubt would take hold of me. We could not bless each other, Adam, if there were doubts in my soul. If I yearned, when it was too late, after that better part which had once been given me and I had put away from me."

"But if a new feeling has come into your mind, Dinah, and if you love me so as to be willing to be nearer to me than to other people, isn't that a sign that it's right for you to change your life? Doesn't the love make it right when nothing else would?"

"Adam, my mind is full of questionings about that—for now. Since you tell me of your strong love for me, what was clear to me has become dark again. I felt before that my heart was too strongly drawn toward you, and that your heart was not as mine. The thought of you had taken hold of me, so that my soul had lost its freedom, and was becoming enslaved to an earthly affection that made me anxious and careful about what should befall me.

For in all other affection, I had been content with any small return or with none; but my heart was beginning to hunger after an equal love from you. I had no doubt that I must wrestle against that as a great temptation, and the command was clear that I must go away."

"But now, dear, dear Dinah—now you know I love you better than you love me. It's all different now. You won't think of going. You'll stay, and be my dear wife, and I shall thank God for giving me my life as I never thanked him before."

"Adam, it's hard for me to turn a deaf ear. You know it's hard. But a great fear is upon me. It seems to me as if you are stretching out your arms to me and beckoning me to come and take my ease and live for my own delight. And Jesus, the Man of Sorrows, is standing looking toward me, and pointing to the sinful, and suffering, and afflicted. I have seen that again and again when I have been sitting in stillness and darkness—and a great terror has come upon me lest I should become hard, and a lover of self, and no more bear willingly the Redeemer's cross."

Dinah had closed her eyes, and a faint shudder went through her. "Adam," she went on, "you wouldn't desire that we should seek a good through any unfaithfulness to the light that is in us—you wouldn't believe that could be a good. We are of one mind in that."

"Yes, Dinah," said Adam sadly, "I'll never be the man to urge you against your conscience. But I can't give up the hope that you may come to see differently. I don't believe your loving me could shut up your heart. It's only adding to what you've been before—not taking away from it—for it seems to me it's the same with love and happiness as with sorrow. The more we know of it the better we can feel what other people's lives are or might be, and so we shall only be more tender to 'em, and wishful to help 'em. The more knowledge a man has, the better he'll do's work; and feeling's a sort o' knowledge."

Dinah was silent, her eyes fixed in contemplation of something visible only to herself. Adam went on presently with his pleading, "And you can do almost as much as you do now. I won't ask you to go to church with me of a Sunday. You shall go where you like among the people and teach 'em. For though I like church best, I don't put my soul above yours, as if my words was better for you to follow than your own conscience. And you can help the sick just as much, and you'll have more means of making 'em a bit comfortable. You'll be among all your own friends as love you, and you can help 'em and be a blessing to 'em till their dying day. Surely, Dinah, you'd be as near to God as if you were living lonely and away from me."

Dinah made no answer for some time. Adam was still holding her hands and looking at her with almost trembling anxiety when she turned her grave loving eyes on his and said, in rather a sad voice—

"Adam there is truth in what you say. There's many of the brethren and sisters who have greater strength than I have and find their hearts enlarged by the cares of husband and kindred. But I have not faith that it would be so with me. Since my affections have been set above measure on you, I have had less peace and joy in God. I have felt as it were a division in my heart. And think how it is with me, Adam. That life I have led is like a land I have trodden in blessedness since my childhood. If I long for a moment to follow the voice that calls me to another land that I know not, I cannot but fear that my soul might hereafter yearn for that early blessedness which I had forsaken. And where doubt enters there is not perfect love. I must wait for clearer guidance. I must go from you, and we must submit ourselves entirely to the Divine Will. We are sometimes required to lay our natural lawful affections on the altar."

Adam dared not plead again, for Dinah's was not the voice of caprice or insincerity. But it was very hard for him. His eyes grew dim as he looked at her.

"But you may come to feel satisfied, to feel that you may come to me again, and we may never part, Dinah?"

"We must submit ourselves, Adam. With time, our duty will be made clear. It may be when I have entered on my former life, I shall find all these new thoughts and wishes vanish, and become as things that were not. Then I shall know that my calling is not toward marriage. But we must wait."

"Dinah," said Adam, mournfully, "you can't love me so well as I love you, else you'd have no doubts. But it's natural you shouldn't—for I'm not so good as you. I can't doubt it's right for me to love the best thing God's ever given me to know."

"Nay, Adam. It seems to me that my love for you is not weak. My heart waits on your words and looks almost as a little child waits on the help and tenderness of the strong on whom it depends. If the thought of you took slight hold of me, I should not fear that it would be an idol in the temple. But you will strengthen me. You will not hinder me in seeking to obey to the uttermost."

"Let us go out into the sunshine, Dinah, and walk together. I'll speak no word to disturb you."

They went out and walked toward the fields where they would meet the family coming from church. Adam said, "Take my arm, Dinah," and she took it. That was the only change in their manner to each other since they were last walking together. But no sadness in the prospect of her going away—in the uncertainty of the issue—could rob the sweetness from Adam's sense that Dinah loved him. He thought he would stay at the Hall Farm all that evening. He would be near her as long as he could.

"Heyday! There's Adam along wi' Dinah," said Mr. Poyser, as he opened the far gate into the Home Close. "I couldna think how he happened away from church. Why," added good Martin, after a moment's pause, "what dost think has just jumped into my head?"

"Summat as hadna far to jump, for it's just under our nose. You mean as Adam's fond o' Dinah."

"Ay! Hast ever had any notion of it before?"

"To be sure I have," said Mrs. Poyser, who always declined, if possible, to be taken by surprise. "I'm not one o' those as can see the cat i' the dairy an' wonder what she's come after."

"Thee never saidst a word to me about it."

"Well, I aren't like a bird-clapper, forced to make a rattle when the wind blows on me. I can keep my own counsel when there's no good i' speaking."

"But Dinah'll ha' none o' him; dost think she will?"

"Nay," said Mrs. Poyser, not sufficiently on her guard against a possible surprise. "She'll never marry anybody if he isn't a Methodist and a cripple."

"It 'ud ha' been a pretty thing though for 'em t' marry," said Martin, turning his head on one side, as if in pleased contemplation of his new idea. "Thee'dst ha' liked it too, wouldstna?"

"Ah! I should. I should ha' been sure of her then, as she wouldn't go away from me to Snowfield, well thirty mile off, and me not got a creature to look to, only neighbors, as are no kin to me, an' most of 'em women as I'd be ashamed to show my face, if my dairy things war like their'n. There may well be streaky butter i' the market. An' I should be glad to see the poor thing settled like a Christian woman, with a house of her own over her head. We'd stock her well wi' linen and feathers, for I love her next to my own children. An' she makes one feel safer when she's i' the house, for she's like the driven snow—anybody might sin for two as had her at their elbow."

THE MEETING ON THE HILL

Adam understood Dinah's haste to go away and drew hope rather than discouragement from it. She was fearful lest the strength of her feeling toward him should hinder her from waiting and listening faithfully for the ultimate guiding voice from within.

I wish I'd asked her to write to me, though, he thought. *And yet even that might disturb her a bit, perhaps. She wants to be quite quiet in her old way for a while. And I've no right to be impatient and interrupting her with my wishes. She's told me what her mind is, and she's not a woman to say one thing and mean another. I'll wait patiently.*

That was Adam's wise resolution, and it throve excellently for the first two or three weeks on the nourishment it got from the remembrance of

Dinah's confession that Sunday afternoon. There is a wonderful amount of sustenance in the first few words of love. But toward the middle of October the resolution began to dwindle perceptibly and showed dangerous symptoms of exhaustion. The weeks were unusually long: Dinah must surely have had more than enough time to make up her mind. Let a woman say what she will after she has once told a man that she loves him—he is a little too flushed and exalted with that first draught she offers him to care much about the taste of the second. He treads the earth with a very elastic step as he walks away from her and makes light of all difficulties. But that sort of glow dies out. Memory gets sadly diluted with time and is not strong enough to revive us. Adam was no longer so confident as he had been. He began to fear that perhaps Dinah's old life would have too strong a grasp upon her for any new feeling to triumph. If she had not felt this, she would surely have written to him to give him some comfort, but it appeared that she held it right to discourage him. As Adam's confidence waned, his patience waned with it, and he thought he must write her. He must ask Dinah not to leave him in painful doubt longer than was needful. He sat up late one night to write her a letter, but the next morning he burnt it, afraid of its effect. It would be worse to have a discouraging answer by letter than from her own lips, for her presence reconciled him to her will.

You perceive how it was. Adam was hungering for the sight of Dinah; and when that sort of hunger reaches a certain stage, a lover is likely to still it though he may have to put his future in pawn.

But what harm could he do by going to Snowfield? Dinah could not be displeased with him for it. She had not forbidden him to go—she must surely expect that he would go before long. By the second Sunday in October, this view of the case had become so clear to Adam that he was already on his way to Snowfield—on horseback this time—for his hours were precious now. He had borrowed Jonathan Burge's good nag for the journey.

What keen memories went along the road with him! He had often been to Oakbourne and back since that first journey to Snowfield. But beyond Oakbourne the gray stone walls, the broken country, the meager trees seemed to be telling him afresh the story of that painful past he knew so well by heart. But no story is the same to us after a lapse of time; or rather, we who read it are no longer the same interpreters. Adam this morning brought with him new thoughts through that gray country—thoughts that gave an altered significance to its story of the past.

It is a base and selfish, even a blasphemous, spirit, that rejoices and is thankful over the past evil that has blighted or crushed another, because it has been made a source of unforeseen good to ourselves: Adam could never cease to mourn over that mystery of human sorrow that had been brought so close to him. He could never thank God for another's misery. And if I were capable of that narrow-sighted joy in Adam's behalf, I should still know he was not the kind of man to feel it for himself. He would have shaken his head at such a sentiment and said, "Evil's evil, and sorrow's sorrow, and you can't alter it's natur' by wrapping it up in other words. Other folks were not created for my sake that I should think all square when things turn out well for me."

But it is not ignoble to feel that the fuller life a sad experience has brought us is worth our own personal share of pain. Surely it is not possible to feel otherwise any more than it would be possible for a man with cataracts to regret the painful process by which his dim blurred sight of men as trees walking had been exchanged for clear outline and effulgent day. The growth of higher feeling within us is like the growth of faculty, bringing with it a sense of added strength. We can no more wish to return to a narrower sympathy than a painter or a musician can wish to return to his cruder manner or a philosopher to his less complete formula.

Something like this sense of enlarged being was in Adam's mind this Sunday morning as he rode along in vivid recollection of the past. His feeling toward Dinah, the hope of passing his life with her, had been the distant unseen point toward which that hard journey from Snowfield eighteen months ago had been leading him. Tender and deep as his love for Hetty had been—so deep that the roots of it would never be torn away—his love for Dinah was better and more precious to him, for it was the outgrowth of that fuller life that had come to him from his acquaintance with deep sorrow. "It's like as if it were a new strength to me," he said to himself, "to love her and know as she loves me. I shall look t' her to help me to see things right. For she's better than I am—there's less o' self in her, and pride. And it's a feeling as gives you a sort o' liberty, as if you could walk more fearless, when you've more trust in another than y' have in yourself. I've always been thinking I knew better than them as belonged to me, and that's a poor sort o' life when you can't look to them nearest to you t' help you with a bit better thought than what you've got inside you a'ready."

It was more than two o'clock in the afternoon when Adam came in sight of the gray town on the hillside and looked searchingly toward the green valley below for the first glimpse of the old thatched roof near the ugly red mill. The scene looked less harsh in the soft October sunshine than it had in the eager time of early spring. And there was one grand charm it possessed in common with all wide-stretching woodless regions—that it filled you with a new consciousness of the overarching sky and had a milder, more soothing influence than usual on this almost cloudless day. Adam's doubts and fears melted under this influence as the delicate web-like clouds had gradually melted away into the clear blue above him. He seemed to see Dinah's gentle face assuring him, with its looks alone, of all he longed to know.

He did not expect Dinah to be at home at this hour, but he got down from his horse and tied it at the little gate so he might ask where she was gone today. He had set his mind on following her and bringing her home. She was gone to Sloman's End, a hamlet about three miles off over the hill, the old woman told him—had set off directly after morning chapel to preach in a cottage there, as was her habit. Anybody at the town would tell him the way to Sloman's End.

So Adam got on his horse again and rode to the town, putting up at the old inn and taking a hasty dinner there in the company of the too-chatty landlord—from whose friendly questions and reminiscences he was glad to escape as soon as possible—and set out toward Sloman's End.

With all his haste it was nearly four o'clock before he could set off, and he thought that as Dinah had gone so early, she would perhaps already be near returning. The little, gray, desolate-looking hamlet, unscreened by sheltering trees, lay in sight long before he reached it. As he came near he could hear the sound of voices singing a hymn. *Perhaps that's the last hymn before they come away,* Adam thought. *I'll walk back a bit, and turn again to meet her farther from the village.* He walked back till he got nearly to the top of the hill again and seated himself on a loose stone, against the low wall to watch till he should see the little black figure leaving the hamlet and winding up the hill. He chose this spot, almost at the top of the hill, because it was away from all eyes—no house, no cattle, not even a nibbling sheep near—no presence but the still lights and shadows and the great embracing sky.

She was much longer coming than he expected. He waited an hour at least, watching for her and thinking of her while the afternoon shadows lengthened and the light grew softer. At last he saw the little black figure coming from between the gray houses and gradually approaching the foot of the hill. Slowly, Adam thought, but Dinah was really walking at her usual pace, with a light quiet step. Now she was beginning to wind along the path up the hill, but Adam would not move yet, not wanting to meet her too soon. He had set his heart on meeting her in this assured loneliness. And now he began to fear lest he should startle her too much. *Yet,* he thought, *she's not one to be over-startled. She's always so calm and quiet, as if she were prepared for anything.*

What was she thinking of as she wound up the hill? Perhaps she had found complete repose without him and ceased to feel any need of his love. On the verge of a decision we all tremble—hope pauses with fluttering wings.

But now at last she was very near, and Adam rose from the stone wall. It happened that just as he walked forward, Dinah had paused and turned round to look back at the village. Who does not pause and look back in mounting a hill? Adam was glad, for with the fine instinct of a lover, he felt it would be best for her to hear his voice before she saw him. He came within three paces of her and then said, "Dinah!" She started without looking round, as if she connected the sound with no place. "Dinah!" Adam said again. He knew quite well what was in her mind. She was so accustomed to thinking of impressions as purely spiritual monitions that she looked for no material visible accompaniment of the voice.

But this second time she looked round. What a look of yearning love it was that the mild gray eyes turned on the strong dark-eyed man! She did not start again at the sight of him. She said nothing but moved toward him so that his arm could clasp her round.

And they walked on so in silence while the warm tears fell. Adam was content, and said nothing. It was Dinah who spoke first.

"Adam," she said, "it is the Divine Will. My soul is so knit to yours that it is but a divided life I live without you. And this moment, now you are with me, and I feel that our hearts are filled with the same love. I have a fullness of strength to bear and do our heavenly Father's Will that I had lost before."

Adam paused and looked into her sincere eyes.

"Then we'll never part any more, Dinah, till death parts us."

And they kissed each other with a deep joy.

What greater thing is there for two human souls than to feel that they are joined for life—to strengthen each other in all labor, to rest on each other in all sorrow, to minister to each other in all pain, to be one with each other in silent unspeakable memories at the moment of the last parting?

In little more than a month after that meeting on the hill—on a rimy morning in departing November—Adam and Dinah were married.

THE GIFT OF THE MAGI

O. HENRY

One dollar and eighty-seven cents. That was all. And sixty cents of it was in pennies. Pennies saved one and two at a time by bulldozing the grocer and the vegetable man and the butcher until one's cheeks burned with the silent imputation of parsimony that such close dealing implied. Three times Della counted it. One dollar and eighty-seven cents. And the next day would be Christmas.

There was clearly nothing to do but flop down on the shabby little couch and howl. So Della did it, which instigates the moral reflection that life is made up of sobs, sniffles, and smiles—with sniffles predominating.

While the mistress of the home is gradually subsiding from the first stage to the second, take a look at the home. A furnished flat at $8 per week. It did not exactly beggar description, but it certainly had that word on the lookout for the mendicancy squad.

In the vestibule below was a letter box into which no letter would go and an electric button from which no mortal finger could coax a ring. Also appertaining thereunto was a card bearing the name "Mr. James Dillingham Young."

The "Dillingham" had been flung to the breeze during a former period of prosperity when its possessor was being paid $30 per week. Now, when the income was shrunk to $20, though, they were thinking seriously of contracting to a modest and unassuming D. But whenever Mr. James Dillingham Young came home and reached his flat above, he was called "Jim" and greatly hugged by Mrs. James Dillingham Young, already introduced to you as Della—which is all very good.

Della finished her cry and attended to her cheeks with the powder rag. She stood by the window and looked out dully at a gray cat walking a gray fence in a gray backyard. Tomorrow would be Christmas Day, and she had only $1.87 with which to buy Jim a present. She had been saving every penny she could for months, with this result. Twenty dollars a week doesn't go far. Expenses had been greater than she had calculated. They always are. Only $1.87 to buy a present for Jim. Her Jim. Many a happy hour she had spent planning for something nice for him. Something fine and rare and sterling— something just a little bit near to being worthy of the honor of being owned by Jim.

There was a pier glass between the windows of the room. Perhaps you have seen a pier glass in an $8 flat. A very thin and very agile person may, by observing his reflection in a rapid sequence of longitudinal strips, obtain a fairly accurate conception of his looks. Della, being slender, had mastered the art.

Suddenly she whirled from the window and stood before the glass. Her eyes were shining brilliantly, but her face had lost its color within twenty seconds. Rapidly she pulled down her hair and let it fall to its full length.

Now, there were two possessions of the James Dillingham Youngs in which they both took a mighty pride. One was Jim's gold watch that had been his father's and his grandfather's. The other was Della's hair. Had the queen of Sheba lived in the flat across the airshaft, Della would have let her hair hang out the window some day to dry just to depreciate Her Majesty's jewels and gifts. Had King Solomon been the janitor, with all his treasures piled up in the basement, Jim would have pulled out his watch every time he passed, just to see him pluck at his beard from envy.

So now Della's beautiful hair fell about her rippling and shining like a cascade of brown waters. It reached below her knee and made itself almost a garment for her. And then she did it up again nervously and quickly. Once she faltered for a minute and stood still while a tear or two splashed on the worn red carpet.

On went her old brown jacket; on went her old brown hat. With a whirl of skirts and with the brilliant sparkle still in her eyes, she fluttered out the door and down the stairs to the street.

Where she stopped the sign read: "Mme. Sofronie. Hair Goods of All Kinds." One flight up Della ran and collected herself, panting. Madame, large, too white, chilly, hardly looked the "Sofronie."

"Will you buy my hair?" asked Della.

"I buy hair," said Madame. "Take yer hat off and let's have a sight at the looks of it."

Down rippled the brown cascade.

"Twenty dollars," said Madame, lifting the mass with a practiced hand.

"Give it to me quick," said Della.

Oh, and the next two hours tripped by on rosy wings. Forget the hashed metaphor. She was ransacking the stores for Jim's present.

She found it at last. It surely had been made for Jim and no one else. There was no other like it in any of the stores, and she had turned all of them inside out. It was a platinum fob chain simple and chaste in design, properly proclaiming its value by substance alone and not by meretricious ornamentation—as all good things should do. It was even worthy of The Watch. As soon as she saw it she knew that it must be Jim's. It was like him. Quietness and value—the description applied to both. Twenty-one dollars they took from her for it, and she hurried home with the 87 cents. With that chain on his watch Jim might be properly anxious about the time in any company. Grand as the watch was, he sometimes looked at it on the sly on account of the old leather strap that he used in place of a chain.

When Della reached home her intoxication gave way a little to prudence and reason. She got out her curling irons and lighted the gas and went to work repairing the ravages made by generosity added to love. Which is always a tremendous task, dear friends—a mammoth task.

Within forty minutes her head was covered with tiny, close-lying curls that made her look wonderfully like a truant schoolboy. She looked at her reflection in the mirror long, carefully, and critically.

"If Jim doesn't kill me," she said to herself, "before he takes a second look at me, he'll say I look like a Coney Island chorus girl. But what could I do—oh! what could I do with a dollar and eighty-seven cents?"

At 7 o'clock the coffee was made and the frying-pan was on the back of the stove hot and ready to cook the chops.

Jim was never late. Della doubled the fob chain in her hand and sat on the corner of the table near the door that he always entered. Then she heard his step on the stair away down on the first flight, and she turned white for just a moment. She had a habit for saying little silent prayers about the simplest everyday things, and now she whispered: "Please God, make him think I am still pretty."

The door opened and Jim stepped in and closed it. He looked thin and very serious. Poor fellow, he was only twenty-two—and to be burdened with a family! He needed a new overcoat and he was without gloves.

Jim stopped inside the door, as immovable as a setter at the scent of quail. His eyes were fixed upon Della, and there was an expression in them that she could not read, and it terrified her. It was not anger, nor surprise, nor disapproval, nor horror, nor any of the sentiments that she had been prepared for. He simply stared at her fixedly with that peculiar expression on his face.

Della wriggled off the table and went for him.

"Jim, darling," she cried, "don't look at me that way. I had my hair cut off and sold because I couldn't have lived through Christmas without giving you a present. It'll grow out again—you won't mind, will you? I just had to do it. My hair grows awfully fast. Say 'Merry Christmas!' Jim, and let's be happy. You don't know what a nice—what a beautiful, nice gift I've got for you."

"You've cut off your hair?" asked Jim, laboriously, as if he had not arrived at that patent fact yet even after the hardest mental labor.

"Cut it off and sold it," said Della. "Don't you like me just as well, anyhow? I'm me without my hair, ain't I?"

Jim looked about the room curiously.

"You say your hair is gone?" he said, with an air almost of idiocy.

"You needn't look for it," said Della. "It's sold, I tell you—sold and gone, too. It's Christmas Eve, boy. Be good to me, for it went for you. Maybe the hairs of my head were numbered," she went on with sudden serious sweetness, "but nobody could ever count my love for you. Shall I put the chops on, Jim?"

Out of his trance Jim seemed quickly to wake. He enfolded his Della. For ten seconds let us regard with discreet scrutiny some inconsequential object in the other direction. Eight dollars a week or a million a year—what is the difference? A mathematician or a wit would give you the wrong answer. The magi brought valuable gifts, but that was not among them. This dark assertion will be illuminated later on.

Jim drew a package from his overcoat pocket and threw it upon the table.

"Don't make any mistake, Dell," he said, "about me. I don't think there's anything in the way of a haircut or a shave or a shampoo that could make me like my girl any less. But if you'll unwrap that package you may see why you had me going awhile at first."

White fingers and nimble tore at the string and paper. And then an ecstatic scream of joy; and then, alas! a quick feminine change to hysterical tears and wails, necessitating the immediate employment of all the comforting powers of the lord of the flat.

For there lay The Combs—the set of combs, side and back, that Della had worshipped long in a Broadway window. Beautiful combs, pure tortoise shell, with jeweled rims—just the shade to wear in the beautiful vanished hair. They were expensive combs, she knew, and her heart had simply craved and yearned over them without the least hope of possession. And now, they were hers, but the tresses that should have adorned the coveted adornments were gone.

But she hugged them to her bosom, and at length she was able to look up with dim eyes and a smile and say: "My hair grows so fast, Jim!"

And then Della leaped up like a little singed cat and cried, "Oh, oh!"

Jim had not yet seen his beautiful present. She held it out to him eagerly upon her open palm. The dull precious metal seemed to flash with a reflection of her bright and ardent spirit.

"Isn't it a dandy, Jim? I hunted all over town to find it. You'll have to look at the time a hundred times a day now. Give me your watch. I want to see how it looks on it."

Instead of obeying, Jim tumbled down on the couch and put his hands under the back of his head and smiled.

"Dell," said he, "let's put our Christmas presents away and keep 'em awhile. They're too nice to use just at present. I sold the watch to get the money to buy your combs. And now suppose you put the chops on."

The magi, as you know, were wise men—wonderfully wise men—who brought gifts to the Babe in the manger. They invented the art of giving Christmas presents. Being wise, their gifts were no doubt wise ones, possibly bearing the privilege of exchange in case of duplication. And here I have lamely related to you the uneventful chronicle of two foolish children in a flat who most unwisely sacrificed for each other the greatest treasures of their house. But in a last word to the wise of these days let it be said that of all who give gifts these two were the wisest. O all who give and receive gifts, such as they are wisest. Everywhere they are wisest. They are the magi.

THE HARDY TIN SOLDIER

HANS CHRISTIAN ANDERSEN

There were once five and twenty tin soldiers. They were all brothers, for they had all been born of one old tin spoon. They shouldered their muskets and looked straight before them. Their uniforms were red and blue and very splendid. The first thing they had heard in the world when the lid was taken off their box had been the words "Tin Soldiers!" These words were uttered by a little boy, clapping his hands. The soldiers had been given to him, for it was his birthday, and now he put them upon the table. Each soldier was exactly like the rest. Only one of them was a little different—he had but one leg, for he had been cast last of all, and there had not been enough tin to finish him. But he stood as firmly upon his one leg as the others on their two—and it was just this soldier who became remarkable.

On the table on which they had been placed stood many other playthings, but the toy that attracted most attention was a neat castle of cardboard. Through the little windows one could see straight into the hall. Before the castle some little trees were placed round a little looking-glass, which was to represent a clear lake. Waxen swans swam on this lake and were mirrored in it. This was all very pretty; but the prettiest of all was a little lady who stood at the open door of the castle. She was also cut out in paper, but she had a dress of the clearest gauze and a little narrow blue ribbon over her shoulders that looked like a scarf. In the middle of this ribbon was a shining tinsel rose as big as her whole face. The little lady stretched out both her arms, for she was a dancer. Then she lifted one leg so high that the tin soldier could not see it at all, and thought that, like himself, she had but one leg.

That would be the wife for me, thought he; *but she is very grand. She lives in a castle, and I have only a box, and there are five and twenty of us in that. It is no place for her. But I must try to make acquaintance with her.*

And then he lay down at full length behind a snuff-box, which was on the table. There he could easily watch the little dainty lady, who continued to stand on one leg without losing her balance.

When the evening came, all the other tin soldiers were put into their box, and the people in the house went to bed. Now the toys began to play at "visiting," and at "war" and "giving balls." The tin soldiers rattled in their box, for they wanted to join but could not lift the lid. The nutcracker threw somersaults, and the pencil amused itself on the table. There was so much noise that the canary woke up and began to speak too—and even in verse. The only two who did not stir from their places were the tin soldier and the dancing lady. She stood straight up on the point of one of her toes and stretched out both her arms. And he was just as enduring on his one leg—he never turned his eyes away from her.

Now the clock struck twelve—and, bounce!—the lid flew off the snuff-box, but there was not snuff in it—just a little black goblin. You see it was a trick.

"Tin soldier!" said the goblin, "will you keep your eyes to yourself?"

But the tin soldier pretended not to hear him.

"Just wait until tomorrow!" said the goblin.

But when morning came and the children got up, the tin soldier was placed in the window. And whether it was the goblin or the draught that did it, all at once the window flew open, and the soldier fell head over heels out of the third story. That was a terrible passage! He put his leg straight up, and stuck with his helmet downward and his bayonet between the paving stones.

The servant-maid and the little boy came down directly to look for him, but though they almost trod upon him they could not see him. If the soldier had cried out "Here I am!" they would have found him; but he did not think it fitting to call out loudly because he was in uniform.

Now it began to rain. The drops soon fell thicker, and at last it came down in a complete stream. When the rain was past, two street boys came by.

"Just look!" said one of them, "there lies a tin soldier. He shall go out sailing."

They made a boat out of newspaper, and put the tin soldier in the middle of it. And so he sailed down the gutter, and the two boys ran beside him and clapped their hands. Goodness preserve us! How the waves rose in that gutter and how fast the stream ran! But then it had been a heavy rain. The paper boat rocked up and down, and sometimes turned around so rapidly that the tin soldier trembled. But he remained firm, and never changed countenance. He looked straight before him and shouldered his musket.

All at once the boat went into a long drain, and it became as dark as if he had been in his box.

Where am I going now? he thought. *Yes, yes, that's the goblin's fault. Ah! If the little lady only sat here with me in the boat, it might be twice as dark for what I should care.*

Suddenly there came a great water-rat, which lived under the drain.

"Have you a passport?" said the rat. "Give me your passport."

But the tin soldier kept silent and held his musket tighter than ever.

The boat went on, but the rat came after it. Ugh! How he gnashed his teeth, and called out to the bits of straw and wood.

"Hold him! Hold him! He hasn't paid toll—he hasn't shown his passport!"

But the stream became stronger and stronger. The tin soldier could see the bright daylight where the arch ended, but he heard a roaring noise, which might well frighten a bolder man. Only think—just where the tunnel ended, the drain ran into a great canal—for him that would have been as dangerous as for us to be carried down a great waterfall.

Now he was already so near it that he could not stop. The boat was carried out, the poor tin soldier stiffening himself as much as he could, and no one could say that he moved an eyelid. The boat whirled round three or four times, and was full of water to the very edge—it must sink. The tin soldier stood up to his neck in water, the boat sank deeper and deeper, and the paper was loosened more and more—until the water closed over the soldier's head. Then he thought of the pretty little dancer, and how he should never see her again. It sounded in the soldier's ears:

Farewell, farewell, thou warrior brave,

For this day thou must die!

And now the paper parted, and the tin soldier fell out. But at that moment he was snapped up by a great fish.

Oh, how dark it was in that fish's body! It was darker yet than in the drain tunnel and very narrow too. But the tin soldier remained unmoved, and lay at full length shouldering his musket.

The fish swam to and fro, making the most wonderful movements, and then became quite still. At last something flashed through him like lightning. The daylight shone quite clear, and a voice said aloud, "The tin soldier!" The fish had been caught, carried to market, bought, and taken into the kitchen, where the cook cut him open with a large knife. She seized the soldier round the body with both her hands and carried him into the room, where all were anxious to see the remarkable man who had traveled about in the inside of a fish—but the tin soldier was not at all proud. They placed him on a table, and there—no! What curious things may happen in the world! The tin soldier was in the very room in which he had been before! He saw the same children, and the same toys stood on the table. Over there was a pretty castle with the graceful little dancer. She was still balancing herself on one leg, while extending the other in the air. She was hardy too. That moved the tin soldier.

He was very nearly weeping tin tears, but that would not have been proper. He looked at her and she at him, but they said nothing to each other.

Then one of the little boys took the tin soldier and flung him into the stove. He gave no reason for doing this. It must have been the fault of the goblin in the snuff-box.

The tin soldier stood there quite illuminated and felt heat that was terrible. But whether this heat proceeded from the real fire or from love he did not know. The colors had quite gone off from him. But whether that had happened on the journey or had been caused by grief, no one could say. He looked at the little lady, she looked at him and he felt that he was melting, but he still stood firm, shouldering his musket. Then suddenly the door flew open, and the draught of air caught the dancer. She flew like a sylph just into the stove to the tin soldier and flashed up into a flame—she was gone. Then the tin soldier melted down into a lump, and when the servant-maid took the ashes out next day, she found him in the shape of a little tin heart. But of the dancer nothing remained but the tinsel rose, and that was burned as black as a coal.

CYRANO DE BERGERAC

EDMOND ROSTAND

AN EXCERPT

Poet Cyrano de Bergerac loves the beautiful Roxane, who in turn loves Christian, a handsome young soldier who is unable to express his love as poetically as Cyrano. In this scene Christian, with Cyrano lurking in the bushes, enters Roxane's garden to declare his love for her. A little while later, Christian—with Cyrano coaching—stands below Roxane's balcony and begs to climb up and give her a kiss. What results is the most enduring of romantic comedies.

⁂

SCENE 3. V.

ROXANE (suddenly seeing Christian): You!

(She goes to him): Evening falls. Let's sit. Speak on. I listen.

CHRISTIAN (sits by her on the bench. A silence): Oh! I love you!

ROXANE (shutting her eyes): Ay, speak to me of love.

CHRISTIAN: I love thee!

ROXANE: That's the theme—but vary it.

CHRISTIAN: I—

ROXANE: Vary it!

CHRISTIAN: I love you so!

ROXANE: Oh! Without doubt!—and then?

CHRISTIAN: And then—I should be—oh!—so glad—so glad if you would love me!—Roxane, tell me so!

ROXANE (with a little grimace): I hoped for cream—you give me gruel! Say how love possesses you?

CHRISTIAN: Oh utterly!

ROXANE: Come, come!—unknot those tangled sentiments!

CHRISTIAN: Your throat—I'd kiss it!

ROXANE: Christian!

CHRISTIAN: I love thee!

ROXANE (half-rising): Again!

CHRISTIAN (eagerly, detaining her): No, no! I love thee not!

ROXANE (reseating herself): 'Tis well!

CHRISTIAN: But I adore thee!

ROXANE (rising, and going further off): Oh!

CHRISTIAN: I am grown stupid!

ROXANE (dryly): And that displeases me, almost as much as 'twould displease me if you grew ill-favored.

CHRISTIAN: But—

ROXANE: Rally your poor eloquence that's flown!

CHRISTIAN: I—

ROXANE: Yes, you love me; that I know. Adieu.

(She goes toward her house.)

CHRISTIAN: Oh, go not yet! I'd tell you—

ROXANE (opening the door): You adore me? I've heard it very oft. No!—Go away!

CHRISTIAN: But I would fain—

(She shuts the door in his face.)

CYRANO (who has re-entered unseen): I' faith! It is successful!

SCENE 3. VI.

Christian, Cyrano, two pages.

CHRISTIAN: Come to my aid!

CYRANO: Not I!

CHRISTIAN: But I shall die unless at once I win back her fair favor.

CYRANO: And how can I, at once, i' th' devil's name, teach you—

CHRISTIAN (seizing his arm): Oh, she is there!

(The window of the balcony is now lighted up.)

CYRANO (moved): Her window!

CHRISTIAN: Oh! I shall die!

CYRANO: Speak lower!

CHRISTIAN (in a whisper): I shall die!

CYRANO: The night is dark—

CHRISTIAN: Well!

CYRANO: All can be repaired. Although you merit not, stand there, poor wretch! Fronting the balcony! I'll go beneath and prompt your words to you.

CHRISTIAN: But—

CYRANO: Hold your tongue!

THE PAGES (reappearing at back—to Cyrano): Ho!

CYRANO: Hush!

(He signs to them to speak softly.)

FIRST PAGE (in a low voice): We've played the serenade you bade to Montfleury!

CYRANO (quickly, in a low voice): Go! Lurk in ambush there—one at this street corner, and one at that. If a passer-by should here intrude, play you a tune!

SECOND PAGE: What tune, Sir Gassendist?

CYRANO: Gay, if a woman comes—for a man, sad!

(The pages disappear, one at each street corner. To Christian): Call her!

CHRISTIAN: Roxane!

CYRANO (picking up stones and throwing them at the window): Some pebbles! Wait awhile!

ROXANE (half-opening the casement): Who calls me?

CHRISTIAN: I!

ROXANE: Who's that?

CHRISTIAN: Christian!

ROXANE (disdainfully): Oh! You?

CHRISTIAN: I would speak with you.

CYRANO (under the balcony—to Christian): Good. Speak soft and low.

ROXANE: No, you speak stupidly!

CHRISTIAN: Oh, pity me!

ROXANE: No! You love me no more!

CHRISTIAN (prompted by Cyrano): You say—Great Heaven! I love no more?—when—I—love more and more!

ROXANE (who was about to shut the casement, pausing): Hold! 'Tis a trifle better! Ay, a trifle!

CHRISTIAN (same play): Love grew apace, rocked by the anxious beating of this poor heart, which the cruel wanton boy took for a cradle!

ROXANE (coming out on to the balcony): That is better! But if you deem that Cupid be so cruel, you should have stifled baby-love in its cradle!

CHRISTIAN (same play): Ah, Madame, I assayed, but all in vain. This new-born babe is a young Hercules!

ROXANE: Still better!

CHRISTIAN (same play): Thus he strangled in my heart the . . . serpents twain, of . . . Pride . . . and Doubt!

ROXANE (leaning over the balcony): Well said!—But why so faltering? Has mental palsy seized on your faculty imaginative?

CYRANO (drawing Christian under the balcony, and slipping into his place): Give place! This waxes critical!

ROXANE: Today your words are hesitating.

CYRANO (imitating Christian—in a whisper): Night has come. In the dusk they grope their way to find your ear.

ROXANE: But my words find no such impediment.

CYRANO: They find their way at once? Small wonder that! For 'tis within my heart they find their home; bethink how large my heart, how small your ear! And—from fair heights descending, words fall fast, but mine must mount, Madame, and that takes time!

ROXANE: Meseems that your last words have learned to climb.

CYRANO: With practice such gymnastic grows less hard!

ROXANE: In truth, I seem to speak from distant heights!

CYRANO: True, far above; at such a height 'twere death if a hard word from you fell on my heart.

ROXANE (moving): I will come down.

CYRANO (hastily): No!

ROXANE (showing him the bench under the balcony): Mount then on the bench!

CYRANO (starting back alarmed): No!

ROXANE: How, you will not?

CYRANO (more and more moved): Stay awhile! 'Tis sweet. The rare occasion, when our hearts can speak our selves unseen, unseeing!

ROXANE: Why—unseen?

CYRANO: Ay, it is sweet! Half hidden—half revealed—You see the dark folds of my shrouding cloak, and I, the glimmering whiteness of your dress. I but a shadow—you a radiance fair! Know you what such a moment holds for me? If ever I were eloquent.

ROXANE: You were!

CYRANO: Yet never till tonight my speech has sprung straight from my heart as now it springs.

ROXANE: Why not?

CYRANO: Till now I spoke haphazardly.

ROXANE: What?

CYRANO: Your eyes have beams that turn men dizzy!—But tonight methinks I shall find speech for the first time!

ROXANE: 'Tis true. Your voice rings with a tone that's new.

CYRANO (coming nearer, passionately): Ay, a new tone! In the tender, sheltering dusk I dare to be myself for once—at last! (He stops, falters:) What say I? I know not!—Oh, pardon me—it thrills me—'tis so sweet, so novel.

ROXANE: How? So novel?

CYRANO (off his balance, trying to find the thread of his sentence): Ay—to be at last sincere. Till now, my chilled heart feared to be mocked.

ROXANE: Mocked, and for what?

CYRANO: For its mad beating!—Ay, my heart has clothed itself with witty words, to shroud itself from curious eyes—impelled at times to aim at a star, I stay my hand, and, fearing ridicule—cull a wild flower!

ROXANE: A wild flower's sweet.

CYRANO: Ay, but to-night—the star!

ROXANE: Oh! never have you spoken thus before!

CYRANO: If, leaving Cupid's arrows, quivers, torches, we turned to seek for sweeter—fresher things! Instead of sipping in a pygmy glass, dull fashionable waters—did we try how the soul slakes its thirst in fearless draught by drinking from the river's flooding brim!

ROXANE: But wit?

CYRANO: If I have used it to arrest you at the first starting,—now, 'twould be an outrage, an insult—to the perfumed Night—to Nature—to speak fine words that garnish vain love-letters! Look up but at her stars! The quiet Heaven will ease our hearts of all things artificial; I fear lest, 'midst the alchemy we're skilled in, the truth of sentiment dissolve and vanish—the soul exhausted by these empty pastimes, the gain of fine things be the loss of all things!

ROXANE: But wit? I say—

CYRANO: In love 'tis crime—'tis hateful! Turning frank loving into subtle fencing! At last the moment comes, inevitable—Oh, woe for those who never know that moment! When feeling love exists in us, ennobling, each well-weighed word is futile and soul-saddening!

ROXANE: Well, if that moment's come for us—suppose it! What words would serve you?

CYRANO: All, all, all, whatever that came to me, e'en as they came, I'd fling them in a wild cluster, not a careful bouquet. I love thee! I am mad! I love, I stifle! Thy name is in my heart as in a sheep-bell, and as I ever tremble, thinking of thee, ever the bell shakes, ever thy name ringeth! All things of thine I mind, for I love all things. I know that last year on the twelfth of May-month, to walk abroad, one day you changed your hair-plaits! I am so used to take your hair for daylight that—like as when the eye stares on the sun's disk, one sees long after a red blot on all things—so, when I quit thy beams, my dazzled vision sees upon all things a blonde stain imprinted.

ROXANE (agitated): Why, this is love indeed!

CYRANO: Ay, true, the feeling which fills me, terrible and jealous, truly, love—which is ever sad amid its transports! Love—and yet, strangely, not a selfish passion! I for your joy would gladly lay mine own down—e'en though you never were to know it—never!—If but at times I might—far off and lonely—hear some gay echo of the joy I bought you! Each glance of thine awakes in me a virtue—a novel, unknown valor. Dost begin, sweet, to understand? So late, dost understand me? Feel'st thou my soul, here, through the darkness mounting? Too fair the night! Too fair, too fair the moment! That I should speak thus, and that you should hearken! Too fair! In moments when my hopes rose proudest, I never hoped such guerdon. Naught is left me but to die now! Have words of mine the power to make you tremble—throned there in the branches? Ay, like a leaf among the leaves, you tremble! You tremble! For I feel—and if you will it, or will it not—your hand's beloved trembling thrill through the branches, down your sprays of jasmine!

(He kisses passionately one of the hanging tendrils.)

ROXANE: Ay! I am trembling, weeping!—I am thine! Thou hast conquered all of me!

CYRANO: Then let death come! 'Tis I, 'tis I myself, who conquered thee! One thing, but one, I dare to ask—

CHRISTIAN (under the balcony): A kiss!

ROXANE (drawing back): What?

CYRANO: Oh!

ROXANE: You ask?

CYRANO: I—

(To Christian, whispering): Fool! you go too quick!

CHRISTIAN: Since she is moved thus—I will profit by it!

CYRANO (to Roxane): My words sprang thoughtlessly, but now I see—shame on me!—I was too presumptuous.

ROXANE (a little chilled): How quickly you withdraw.

CYRANO: Yes, I withdraw without withdrawing! Hurt I modesty? If so—the kiss I asked—oh, grant it not.

CHRISTIAN (to Cyrano, pulling him by his cloak): Why?

CYRANO: Silence, Christian! Hush!

ROXANE (leaning over): What whisper you?

CYRANO: I chide myself for my too bold advances, said, 'Silence, Christian!'

(The lutes begin to play):

Hark! Wait awhile. Steps come!

(Roxane shuts the window. Cyrano listens to the lutes, one of which plays a merry, the other a melancholy, tune): Why, they play sad—then gay—then sad! What? Neither man nor woman?—oh! A monk!

(Enter a capuchin friar, with a lantern. He goes from house to house, looking at every door.)

Scene 3. VII.

Cyrano, Christian, a capuchin friar.

CYRANO (to the friar): What do you, playing at Diogenes?

THE FRIAR: I seek the house of Madame—

CHRISTIAN: Oh! Plague take him!

THE FRIAR: Madeleine Robin—

CHRISTIAN: What would he?

CYRANO (pointing to a street at the back): This way! Straight on.

THE FRIAR: I thank you, and, in your intention will tell my rosary to its last bead.

(He goes out.)

CYRANO: Good luck! My blessings rest upon your cowl!

(He goes back to Christian.)

SCENE 3. VIII.

Cyrano, Christian.

CHRISTIAN: Oh! win for me that kiss—

CYRANO: No!

CHRISTIAN: Soon or late!

CYRANO: 'Tis true! The moment of intoxication—of madness—when your mouths are sure to meet thanks to your fair mustache—and her rose lips!

(To himself): I'd fainer it should come thanks to—

(A sound of shutters reopening. Christian goes in again under the balcony.)

SCENE 3. IX.

Cyrano, Christian, Roxane.

ROXANE (coming out on the balcony): Still there? We spoke of a—

CYRANO: A kiss! The word is sweet. I see not why your lip should shrink from it. If the word burns it—what would the kiss do? Oh! let it not your bashfulness affright. Have you not, all this time, insensibly, left badinage aside, and unalarmed glided from smile to sigh—from sigh to weeping? Glide gently, imperceptibly, still onward—from tear to kiss—a moment's thrill!—a heartbeat!

ROXANE: Hush! hush!

CYRANO: A kiss, when all is said—what is it?
An oath that's ratified—a sealed promise,
A heart's avowal claiming confirmation—

A rose-dot on the 'i' of 'adoration'—
A secret that to mouth, not ear, is whispered—

Brush of a bee's wing, that makes time eternal—
Communion perfumed like the spring's wild flowers—
The heart's relieving in the heart's outbreathing, when to the lips the soul's flood rises, brimming!

ROXANE: Hush! hush!

CYRANO: A kiss, Madame, is honorable. The Queen of France, to a most favored lord did grant a kiss—the Queen herself!

ROXANE: What then?

CYRANO (speaking more warmly): Buckingham suffered dumbly—so have I—adored his Queen, as loyally as I—was sad, but faithful—so am I.

ROXANE: And you are fair as Buckingham!

CYRANO (aside—suddenly cooled): True—I forgot!

ROXANE: Must I then bid thee mount to cull this flower?

CYRANO (pushing Christian toward the balcony): Mount!

ROXANE: This heart-breathing!

CYRANO: Mount!

ROXANE: This brush of bee's wing!

CYRANO: Mount!

CHRISTIAN (hesitating): But I feel now, as though 'twere ill done!

ROXANE: This moment infinite!

CYRANO (still pushing him): Come, blockhead, mount!

(Christian springs forward, and by means of the bench, the branches, and the pillars, climbs to the balcony and strides over it.)

CHRISTIAN: Ah, Roxane!

(He takes her in his arms, and bends over her lips.)

CYRANO: Aie! Strange pain that wrings my heart! The kiss, love's feast, so near! I, Lazarus, lie at the gate in darkness. Yet to me falls still a crumb or two from the rich man's board—Ay, 'tis my heart receives thee, Roxane—mine! For on the lips you press you kiss as well the words I spoke just now!—my words—my words!

A LETTER
FROM ELIZABETH BARRETT TO
ROBERT BROWNING

Elizabeth Barrett, a thirty-two-year-old semi-invalid English poet, had recently published a collection of her verse, in which she included a tribute to the poetry of renowned Robert Browning. He enthusiastically wrote back, "I love your verses," and near the end of the letter declared, "and I love you too." So began a two-year correspondence that resulted in an exchange of some 600 letters. One year after Robert's initial missive, Elizabeth writes:

January 10, 1846

Do you know, when you have told me to think of you, I have been feeling ashamed of thinking of you so much, of thinking only of you—which is too much, perhaps. Shall I tell you? It seems to me to myself, that no man was ever before to any woman what you are to me—the fullness must be in proportion, you know, to the vacancy . . . and only I know what was behind—the long wilderness without the blossoming rose . . . and the capacity for happiness, like a black gaping hole, before this silver flooding. Is it wonderful that I should stand as in a dream, and disbelieve—not you—but my own fate? Was ever any one taken suddenly from a lampless dungeon and placed upon the pinnacle of a mountain, without the head turning round and the heart turning faint, as mine do? And you love me more, you say? Shall I thank you or God? Both—indeed—and there is no possible return from me to either of you! I thank you as the unworthy may . . . and as we all thank God. How shall I ever prove what my heart is to you? How will you ever see it as I feel it? I ask myself in vain.

Have so much faith in me, my only beloved, as to use me simply for your own advantage and happiness, and to your own ends without a thought of any others—May God bless you!

Your

· B. A.

LINCOLN'S PROPOSAL

ABRAHAM LINCOLN

This remarkable love letter, written by one of our dearest presidents, does not contain a word about love, and though it serves as a marriage proposal, does not propose.

My dear Mary,

You must know that I cannot see you or think of you with entire indifference; and yet it may be that you are mistaken in regard to what my real feelings toward you are. If I knew that you were not, I should not trouble you with this letter. Perhaps any other man would know enough without further information, but I consider it my peculiar right to plead ignorance and your bounden duty to allow the plea. I want in all cases to do right, and most particularly so in all cases with women. I want at this particular time more than anything else to do right with you, and if I knew it would be doing right, as I rather suspect it would, to let you alone, I would do it. And for the purpose of making the matter as plain as possible, I now say you can drop the subject, dismiss your thoughts—if you ever had any—from me forever, and leave this letter unanswered without calling forth one accusing murmur from me. And I will even go further and say that if it will add to your comfort and peace of mind to do so, it is my sincere wish that you should.

Do not understand by this that I wish to cut your acquaintance. I mean no such thing. What I do wish is that our further acquaintance should depend upon yourself. If such further acquaintance would contribute nothing to your happiness, I am sure it would not to mine. If you feel yourself in any degree bound to me, I am now willing to release you, provided you wish it; while, on the other hand, I am willing and even anxious to bind you faster, if I can be convinced that it will in any degree add to your happiness. This indeed is the whole question with me. Nothing would make me more miserable than to believe you miserable; nothing more happy than to know you were so.

In what I have now said I cannot be misunderstood; and to make myself understood is the only object of this letter. If it suits you best not to answer this, farewell. A long life and a merry one attend you. But if you conclude to write back, speak as plainly as I do. There can be neither harm nor danger in saying to me anything you think just in the manner you think it.

Your friend,

A. Lincoln

CINDERELLA

CHARLES PERRAULT

Once there was a gentleman who married—for his second wife—the proudest and most haughty woman that was ever seen. She had, by a former husband, two daughters of her own, who were, indeed, exactly like her in all things. He had likewise, a young daughter, but of unparalleled goodness and sweetness of temper, which she took from her mother, who was the best creature in the world.

No sooner were the ceremonies of the wedding over but the stepmother began to show her true colors. She could not bear the good qualities of this pretty girl, and the less because they made her own daughters appear the more repugnant. She employed her in the meanest work of the house—scouring the dishes, tables, floors, and scrubbing madam's room, as well as those of her daughters. She slept in a sorry garret on a wretched straw bed, while her sisters slept in fine rooms with inlaid floors, on fashionable, new beds. Their mirrors were so large that they could see themselves at their full length from head to foot.

The poor girl bore it all patiently and dared not tell her father, who would have scolded her—for his wife governed him entirely. When she had finished her work for the day, she would go to the chimney corner and sit down there in the cinders and ashes. For this reason, she was called Cinderwench. Only the younger sister, who was not so rude and uncivil as the older one, called her Cinderella. Cinderella was a hundred times more beautiful than her sisters, although they were always dressed in the finest fabrics.

It happened that the king's son gave a ball and invited all persons of fashion to it. The two sisters were also invited, for they cut a very grand figure among those of quality. They were delighted at this invitation and quickly got busy selecting the gowns, petticoats, and hair dressing that would best become them. This was a new difficulty for Cinderella; for it was she who ironed her sisters' linen and pleated their ruffles. They talked all day long of nothing but how they should be dressed.

"For my part," said the eldest, "I will wear my red velvet suit with French trimming."

"And I," said the youngest, "shall have my usual petticoat. But then, to make amends for that, I will put on my gold-flowered cloak and diamond stomacher, which is far from being the most ordinary one in the world."

They sent for the best hairdresser they could get to make up their headpieces and adjust their hairdos, and they had their red brushes and patches from Mademoiselle de la Poche.

They also consulted Cinderella in all these matters, for she had excellent ideas, and her advice was always good. Indeed, she even offered her services to fix their hair, which they very willingly accepted. As she was doing this, they said to her, "Cinderella, would you not like to go to the ball?"

"Alas!" said she, "you only jeer me. It is not for such as I to go to such a place."

"You are quite right," they replied. "It would make the people laugh to see a Cinderwench at a ball."

Anyone but Cinderella would have fixed her sisters' hair awry, but she was very good and dressed them perfectly well. They were so excited that they hadn't eaten a thing for almost two days. Then they broke more than a dozen laces trying to have themselves laced up tightly enough to give them a fine slender shape. They were continually in front of their mirrors. At last the happy day came. They went to the ball, and Cinderella followed them with her eyes as long as she could. When she lost sight of them, she started to cry.

Her godmother, who saw her all in tears, asked her what was the matter.

"I wish I could—I wish I could—" She was not able to speak the rest, being interrupted by her tears and sobbing.

This godmother of hers, who was a fairy, said to her, "You wish that you could go to the ball; is it not so?"

"Yes," cried Cinderella, with a great sigh.

"Well," said her godmother, "be but a good girl, and I will contrive that you shall go." Then she took her into her chamber and said to her, "Run into the garden, and bring me a pumpkin."

Cinderella went immediately to gather the finest she could get, and brought it to her godmother—not being able to imagine how this pumpkin could help her go to the ball. Her godmother scooped out all the inside of it, leaving nothing but the rind. Having done this, she struck the pumpkin with her wand, and it was instantly turned into a fine coach, gilded all over with gold.

She then went to look into her mousetrap, where she found six mice—all alive—and told Cinderella to lift up the little trapdoor. She gave each mouse, as it went out, a little tap with her wand, and the mouse was that moment turned into a fine horse, which altogether made a very fine set of six horses of a beautiful mouse-colored gray.

Being at a loss for a coachman, Cinderella said, "I will go and see if there is not a rat in the rat trap that we can turn into a coachman."

"You are right," replied her godmother, "Go and look."

Cinderella brought the trap to her, and in it were three huge rats. The fairy chose the one that had the largest beard, touched him with her wand, and turned him into a fat, jolly coachman, who had the smartest whiskers that eyes ever beheld.

After that, she said to her, "Go again into the garden, and you will find six lizards behind the watering pot. Bring them to me."

She had no sooner done so than her godmother turned them into six footmen, who skipped up immediately behind the coach with their liveries all bedaubed with gold and silver, and clung as close behind each other as if they had done nothing else their whole lives. The fairy then said to Cinderella,

"Well, you see here an equipage fit to go to the ball with—are you not pleased with it?"

"Oh, yes," she cried; "but must I go in these nasty rags?"

Her godmother then touched her with her wand, and, at the same instant, her clothes turned into cloth of gold and silver, all beset with jewels. This done, she gave her a pair of glass slippers, the prettiest in the whole world. Being thus decked out, she got up into her coach; but her godmother, above all things, commanded her not to stay past midnight, telling her, at the same time, that if she stayed one moment longer, the coach would be a pumpkin again, her horses mice, her coachman a rat, her footmen lizards, and her clothes would become just as they were before.

She promised her godmother to leave the ball before midnight and then drove away, scarcely able to contain herself for joy. The king's son, who was told that a great princess—whom nobody knew—had arrived, ran out to receive her. He gave her his hand as she alighted from the coach and led her into the hall among all the company. Immediately, a profound silence fell over the place. Everyone stopped dancing, and the violins ceased to play, so entranced was everyone with the singular beauties of the unknown newcomer.

Nothing was then heard but a confused noise of, "How beautiful she is! How beautiful she is!"

The king himself, old as he was, could not help watching her, and telling the queen softly that it was a long time since he had seen so beautiful and lovely a creature.

All the ladies were busied in considering her clothes and headdress, hoping to have some made next day after the same pattern—provided they could find such fine materials and able hands to make them.

The king's son led her to the most honorable seat, and afterward took her out to dance with him. She danced so very gracefully that everyone admired her more and more. A fine meal was served up, but the young prince ate not a morsel, so intently was he busied in gazing on her.

She went and sat down by her sisters, showing them a thousand civilities, giving them part of the oranges and citrons the prince had presented to her. This very much surprised them, for they did not know her. While Cinderella was thus amusing her sisters, she heard the clock strike eleven and three-quarters, whereupon she immediately made a courtesy to the company and hurried away as fast as she could.

Arriving home, she ran to seek out her godmother, and, after having thanked her, she said she could not but heartily wish she might go to the ball the next day as well, because the king's son had invited her.

As she was eagerly telling her godmother everything that had happened at the ball, her two sisters knocked at the door. Cinderella ran and opened it for them.

"You stayed such a long time!" she cried, gaping, rubbing her eyes and stretching herself as if she had been sleeping. Of course, she had not had any inclination to sleep while they were away.

"If you had been at the ball," said one of her sisters, "you would not have been tired with it. The finest princess was there—the most beautiful that mortal eyes have ever seen. She showed us a thousand civilities and gave us oranges and citrons."

Cinderella seemed very indifferent in the matter. Indeed, she asked them the name of the princess; but they told her they did not know. "In fact," they continued, "the king's son was very uneasy on her account and would give all the world to know who she was."

At this Cinderella, smiling, replied, "She must, then, be very beautiful indeed. How happy you have been! Could not I see her? Ah, dear Charlotte, do lend me your yellow dress that you wear every day."

"Yes, to be sure!" cried Charlotte; "lend my clothes to such a dirty Cinderwench as you! I should be such a fool."

Cinderella, indeed, well expected such an answer and was very glad of the refusal. She would have been sadly put to it, if her sister had lent her what she asked for jestingly.

The next day the two sisters were at the ball—as was Cinderella—but dressed even more magnificently than before. The king's son was always by her, and never ceased his compliments and kind speeches to her. All this was so far from being tiresome to her, and, indeed, she quite forgot what her godmother had told her. She thought that it was no later than eleven when she counted the clock striking twelve. She jumped up and fled, as nimble as a deer. The prince followed, but could not overtake her. She left behind one of her glass slippers, which the prince picked up most carefully. When she reached home, she was quite out of breath and in her old clothes, having nothing left of all her finery but one little slipper—the mate to the one she had dropped.

The guards at the palace gate were asked if they had not seen a princess go out. They replied that they had seen nobody leave but a young girl, very shabbily dressed, and who had more the air of a poor country wench than a gentlewoman.

When the two sisters returned from the ball, Cinderella asked them if they had been well entertained, and whether the fine lady had been there once more.

They told her, yes, but added that she had hurried away immediately when the clock struck twelve. Her leaving was so hasty that she had dropped one of her little glass slippers—the prettiest in the world—which the king's son had picked up. He had done nothing but look at her all the time at the ball. They were certain that he was very much in love with the beautiful person who owned the glass slipper.

What they said was very true; for a few days later, the king's son had it proclaimed by sound of trumpet that he would marry the woman whose foot fit with ease into this slipper. They began with the princesses—each trying on the slipper—then each duchess in the king's court. But to no avail. When the search was expanded to include the commoners, the king's men soon arrived at Cinderella's home. Each of the two stepsisters tried on the shoe. They did all they possibly could to force their feet into the slipper, but they did not succeed.

Cinderella, who saw all this and knew that it was her slipper, said to them, laughing, "Let me see if it will not fit me."

Her sisters burst out laughing and began to banter with her. But the gentlemen who were sent to try the slipper looked earnestly at Cinderella, and finding her very beautiful, said that she should try as well—they had orders to let everyone try.

Cinderella sat down, and as the king's representative put the slipper to her foot, he found that it went on very easily, fitting her as if it had been made of wax. Her two sisters were greatly astonished—but even more so when Cinderella pulled the other slipper from her pocket and put it on her other foot. Then in came her godmother and touched her wand to Cinderella's clothes, making them richer and more magnificent than any of those she had worn before.

Cinderella's sisters then realized that she was the fine, beautiful lady whom they had seen at the ball. They threw themselves at her feet to beg pardon for all the ill treatment they had made her undergo. Cinderella pulled them up and embraced them, saying that she forgave them with all her heart and wanted them always to love her.

She was taken to the young prince, dressed as she was. He thought her more charming than before, and, a few days later, married her. Cinderella, who was no less good than beautiful, gave her two sisters lodgings in the palace, and that very same day matched them with two great lords of the court.

THE PICKWICK PAPERS

CHARLES DICKENS

AN EXCERPT TITLED "THE BAGMAN'S STORY"

"My uncle, gentlemen," said the bagman, "was one of the merriest, pleasantest, cleverest fellows who ever lived. I wish you had known him. On second thought, gentlemen, I don't wish you had known him, for, if you had, you would have been all, by this time, in the ordinary course of nature, if not dead, at all events so near it, as to have taken to stopping at home and giving up company: which would have deprived me of the inestimable pleasure of addressing you at this moment. Gentlemen, I wish your fathers and mothers had known my uncle. They would have been amazingly fond of him, especially your respectable mothers—I know they would. If any two of his numerous virtues predominated over the many that adorned his character, I should say they were his mixed punch and his after-supper song. Excuse my dwelling on these melancholy recollections of departed worth. You won't see a man like my uncle every day in the week.

"In personal appearance, my uncle was a trifle shorter than the middle size. He was a thought stouter too, than the ordinary run of people, and perhaps his face might be a shade redder. He had the jolliest face you ever saw, gentleman, with a handsome nose and chin. His eyes were always twinkling and sparkling with good-humor, and a smile—not one of your unmeaning wooden grins, but a real, merry, hearty, good-tempered smile—was perpetually on his countenance. He was pitched out of his gig once, and knocked, head first, against a milestone. There he lay, stunned, and so cut about the face with some gravel that had been heaped up alongside it, that, to use my uncle's own strong expression, his mother could have revisited the earth, she wouldn't have known him.

"Indeed, when I come to think of the matter, gentlemen, I feel pretty sure she wouldn't, for she died when my uncle was two years and seven months old, and I think it's very likely that, even without the gravel, his top-boots would have puzzled the good lady not a little—to say nothing of his jolly red face. However, there he lay, and I have heard my uncle say many a time that the man said who picked him up that he was smiling as merrily as if he had tumbled out for a treat. They also said that after they had bled him, the first faint glimmerings of returning animation were his jumping up in bed, bursting out into a loud laugh, kissing the young woman who held the basin, and demanding a mutton chop and a pickled walnut. He was very fond of pickled walnuts, gentlemen.

"My uncle's great journey was in the fall of the leaf, at which time he collected debts and took orders in the north, going from London to Edinburgh, from Edinburgh to Glasgow, from Glasgow back to Edinburgh, and thence to London. You are to understand that his second visit to Edinburgh was for his own pleasure. He used to go back for a week just to look up his old friends; and what with breakfasting with this one, lunching with that one, dining with the third, and supping with another, he made a pretty tight week of it. I don't know whether any of you gentlemen ever partook of a real substantial hospitable Scotch breakfast. If you ever did, you will agree with me that it requires a pretty strong head to go out to dinner and supper afterward.

"But bless your hearts and eyebrows, all this sort of thing was nothing to my uncle! He was so well seasoned, that it was mere child's play. I have heard him say that he could see the Dundee people out, any day, and walk home afterward without staggering. And yet the Dundee people have as strong heads and as strong punch, gentlemen, as you are likely to meet with, between the poles.

"One night, within twenty-four hours of when he had determined to take a ship for London, my uncle supped at the house of a very old friend of his, a Baillie Mac (Scottish Municipal Officer) something and four syllables after it, who lived in the old town of Edinburgh. There were the baillie's wife, and the baillie's three daughters, and the baillie's grown-up son, and three or four stout, bushy eye-browed, canny old Scotch fellows, which the baillie had got together to do honor to my uncle and help make merry. It was a glorious supper. There was kippered salmon and Finnan haddocks, a lamb's head, and a haggis—a celebrated Scotch dish, gentlemen.

"It was a wild, gusty night when my uncle closed the baillie's door, and settling his hat firmly on his head to prevent the wind from taking it, thrust his hands into his pockets, and looking upward, took a short survey of the state of the weather. The clouds were drifting over the moon at their giddiest speed—at one time wholly obscuring her, at another, suffering her to burst forth in full splendor and shed her light on all the objects around, and then, driving over her again with increased velocity and shrouding everything in darkness. 'Really, this won't do,' said my uncle, addressing himself to the weather, as if he felt himself personally offended. 'This is not at all the kind of thing for my voyage. It will not do, at any price,' said my uncle, very impressively. Having repeated this, several times, he recovered his balance with some difficulty—for he was rather giddy with looking up into the sky so long—and walked merrily on. The baillie's house was in the Canongate, and my uncle was going to the other end of Leith Walk, rather better than a mile's journey. On either side of him, there shot up against the dark sky, tall gaunt straggling houses, with time-stained fronts, and windows that seemed to have shared the lot of eyes in mortals and grown dim and sunken with age. The houses were six, seven, eight stories high, story piled above story as children build with cards—throwing their dark shadows over the roughly paved road, and making the dark night darker. A few oil lamps were scattered at long distances, but they only served to mark the dirty entrance to some narrow close, or to show where a common stair communicated, by steep and intricate windings, with the various flats above. Glancing at all these things with the

air of a man who had seen them too often before to think them worthy of
much notice now, my uncle walked up the middle of the street with a thumb
in each waistcoat pocket, indulging from time to time in various snatches of
song, chanted forth with such good will and spirit that the quiet honest folk
started from their first sleep and lay trembling in bed till the sound died away
in the distance. Having satisfied themselves that it was only some drunken
ne'er-do-well finding his way home, they covered themselves up warm and fell
asleep again.

"I am particular in describing how my uncle walked up the middle of
the street with his thumbs in his waistcoat pocket, gentlemen, because, as he
often used to say (and with great reason too) there is nothing at all extraordinary in this story, unless you distinctly understand at the beginning that he
was not by any means of a marvelous or romantic turn.

"Gentlemen, my uncle walked on with his thumbs in his waistcoat
pocket, taking the middle of the street to himself, and singing, now a verse
of a love song, and then a verse of something else, and when he was tired of
both, whistling melodiously, until he reached the North Bridge, which, at
this point, connects the old and new towns of Edinburgh. Here he stopped
for a minute to look at the strange irregular clusters of lights piled one above
the other and twinkling afar off so high that they looked like stars gleaming
from the castle walls on the one side and the Calton Hill on the other. It was
as if they illuminated veritable castles in the air, while the old picturesque
town slept heavily on in gloom and darkness below. Its palace and chapel of
Holyrood, were guarded day and night, as a friend of my uncle's used to say,
by old Arthur's Seat, towering, surly and dark, like some gruff genius, over
the ancient city he has watched so long. I say, gentlemen, my uncle stopped
here, for a minute to look about him; and then, paying a compliment to the
weather, which had a little cleared up though the moon was sinking, walked
on again as royally as before. He kept to the middle of the road with great
dignity, looking as if he would very much like to meet with somebody who

would dispute possession of it with him. There was nobody at all disposed to contest the point, as it happened; and so on he went with his thumbs in his waistcoat pocket, like a lamb.

"When my uncle reached the end of Leith Walk, he had to cross a pretty large piece of waste ground that separated him from a short street, which he had to turn down to go direct to his lodging. Now, in this piece of waste ground, there was at that time, an enclosure belonging to some wheelwright who contracted with the Post-office for the purchase of old worn-out mail coaches. My uncle, being very fond of coaches, old, young, or middle-aged, all at once took it into his head to step out of his road for no other purpose than to peep between the palings at these mail coaches—about a dozen of which he remembered to have seen, crowded together in a very forlorn and dismantled state, inside. My uncle was a very enthusiastic, emphatic sort of person, gentlemen; so, finding that he could not obtain a good peep between the palings he climbed over them, and sitting himself quietly down on an old axletree, began to seriously contemplate the mail coaches.

"There might be a dozen of them, or there might be more—my uncle was never quite certain on this point, and being a man of very scrupulous veracity about numbers, didn't like to say—but there they stood, all huddled together in the most desolate condition imaginable. The doors had been torn from their hinges and removed. The linings had been stripped off—only a shred hanging here and there by a rusty nail. The lamps were gone, the poles had long since vanished, the ironwork was rusty, the paint was worn away; the wind whistled through the chinks in the bare woodwork, and the rain, which had collected on the roofs, fell, drop by drop, into the insides with a hollow and melancholy sound. They were the decaying skeletons of departed mail coaches, and in that lonely place, at that time of night, they looked chill and dismal.

"My uncle rested his head upon his hands, and thought of the busy, bustling people who had rattled about, years before, in the old coaches, and were now as silent and changed. He thought of the numbers of people to whom one of these crazy, moldering vehicles had borne, night after night, for many years and through all weathers, the anxiously expected information, the eagerly looked-for remittance, the promised assurance of health and safety, the sudden announcement of sickness and death. The merchant, the lover, the wife, the widow, the mother, the school-boy, the very child who tottered to the door at the postman's knock—how had they all looked forward to the arrival of the old coach. And where were they all now?

"Gentlemen, my uncle used to say that he thought all this at the time, but I rather suspect he learned it out of some book afterward, for he distinctly stated that he fell into a kind of doze as he sat on the old axletree looking at the decayed mail coaches, and that he was suddenly awakened by some deep church-bell striking two. Now, my uncle was never a fast thinker, and if he had thought all these things, I am quite certain it would have taken him till full half-past two o'clock at the very least. I am, therefore, decidedly of opinion, gentlemen, that my uncle fell into a kind of doze without having thought about anything at all.

"Be this, as it may, a church bell struck two. My uncle woke, rubbed his eyes, and jumped up in astonishment.

"In one instant after the clock struck two, the whole of this deserted and quiet spot had become a scene of most extraordinary life and animation. The mail coach-doors were on their hinges, the lining was replaced, the ironwork was as good as new, the paint was restored, the lamps were alight, cushions and greatcoats were on every coach-box, porters were thrusting parcels into every boot, guards were stowing away letter-bags, hostlers were dashing pails of water against the renovated wheels. Numbers of men were pushing about, fixing poles into every coach; passengers arrived, baggage was handed up, horses were put to. In short, it was perfectly clear that every mail coach there was to be off directly. Gentlemen, my uncle opened his eyes so wide at all this, that, to the very last moment of his life, he used to wonder how it happened that he had ever been able to shut 'em again.

"'Now then!' said a voice, as my uncle felt a hand on his shoulder, 'you're booked for one inside. You'd better get in.'

"'I booked!' said my uncle, turning round.

"'Yes, certainly.'

"My uncle, gentlemen, could say nothing he was so very much astonished. The strangest thing of all was that although there was such a crowd of persons and although fresh faces were pouring in every moment, there was no telling where they came from. They seemed to start up in some strange manner from the ground, or the air, and disappear in the same way. When a porter had put his luggage in the coach, and received his fare, he turned round and was gone; and before my uncle had well begun to wonder what had become of him, half a dozen fresh ones started up and staggered along under the weight of parcels that seemed big enough to crush them. The passengers were all dressed so oddly too! Large, broad-skirted, laced coats with great cuffs and no collars, and wigs, gentlemen—great formal wigs with a tie behind. My uncle could make nothing of it.

"'Now, are you going to get in?' said the person who had addressed my uncle before. He was dressed as a mail guard with a wig on his head and most enormous cuffs to his coat. He had a lantern in one hand and a huge blunder-buss [muzzle-leading firearm] in the other, which he was going to stow away in his little arm-chest. 'Are you going to get in, Jack Martin?' said the guard, holding the lantern to my uncle's face.

"'Hallo!' said my uncle, falling back a step or two. 'That's familiar!'

"'It's so on the way-bill,' said the guard.

"'Isn't there a "Mister" before it?' said my uncle. For he felt, gentlemen, that for a guard he didn't know to call him Jack Martin was a liberty which the Post-office wouldn't have sanctioned if they had known it.

"'No, there is not,' rejoined the guard coolly.

"'Is the fare paid?' inquired my uncle.

"'Of course it is,' rejoined the guard.

"'It is, is it?' said my uncle. 'Then here goes! Which coach?'

"'This,' said the guard, pointing to an old-fashioned Edinburgh and London Mail Coach, which had the steps down and the door open. 'Stop! Here are the other passengers. Let them get in first.'

"As the guard spoke, there all at once appeared right in front of my uncle, a young gentleman in a powdered wig and a sky-blue coat trimmed with silver. The coat was made very full and broad in the skirts, which were lined with buckram. Tiggin and Welps were in the printed calico and waistcoat piece line, gentlemen, so my uncle knew all the materials at once. He wore knee breeches and a kind of leggings rolled up over his silk stockings, and shoes with buckles; he had ruffles at his wrists, a three-cornered hat on his head, and a long taper sword by his side. The flaps of his waist-coat came half-way down his thighs, and the ends of his cravat reached to his waist. He stalked gravely to the coach-door, pulled off his hat, and held it above his head at arm's length, cocking his little finger in the air at the same time as some affected people do when they take a cup of tea. Then he drew his feet together, and made a low grave bow, and then put out his left hand. My uncle was just going to step forward and shake it heartily, when he perceived that these attentions were directed not toward him but to a young lady who just then appeared at the foot of the steps. She was attired in an old-fashioned green velvet dress with a long waist and stomacher. She had no bonnet on her head, gentlemen, which was muffled in a black silk hood, but she looked round for an instant as she prepared to get into the coach. Such a beautiful face as she disclosed, my uncle had never seen—not even in a picture. She got into the coach, holding up her dress with one hand; and as my uncle always said when he told the story, he wouldn't have believed it possible that legs and feet could have been brought to such a state of perfection unless he had seen them with his own eyes.

"But, in this one glimpse of the beautiful face, my uncle saw that the

young lady cast an imploring look upon him, and that she appeared terrified
and distressed. He noticed, too, that the young fellow in the powdered wig,
notwithstanding his show of gallantry, which was all very fine and grand,
clasped her tight by the wrist when she got in and followed himself immediately afterward. An uncommonly ill-looking fellow in a close brown wig
and plum-colored suit, wearing a very large sword and boots up to his hips,
belonged to the party. When he sat himself down next to the young lady, who
shrunk into a corner at his approach, my uncle was confirmed in his original
impression that something dark and mysterious was going on or as he always
said himself, 'there was a screw loose somewhere.' It's quite surprising how
quickly he made up his mind to help the lady at any peril—if she needed any
help.

'"Death and lightning!' exclaimed the young gentleman, laying his hand
upon his sword as my uncle entered the coach.

'"Blood and thunder!' roared the other gentleman. With this, he whipped
his sword out and made a lunge at my uncle without further ceremony. My
uncle had no weapon about him, but with great dexterity, he snatched the
ill-looking gentleman's three-cornered hat from his head, and, receiving the
point of his sword right through the crown, squeezed the sides together, and
held it tight.

'"Get him from behind!' cried the ill-looking gentleman to his
companion, as he struggled to regain his sword.

'"He had better not,' cried my uncle, displaying the heel of one of his
shoes, in a threatening manner. 'I'll kick his brains out, if he has any—or
fracture his skull if he hasn't.' Exerting all his strength, at this moment, my
uncle wrenched the ill-looking man's sword from his grasp and flung it clean
out of the coach-window, upon which the younger gentleman shouted 'Death
and lightning!' again and laid his hand upon the hilt of his sword in a very
fierce manner, but didn't draw it. Perhaps, gentlemen, as my uncle used to
say with a smile, perhaps he was afraid of alarming the lady.

"'Now, gentlemen,' said my uncle, taking his seat deliberately, 'I don't want to have any death, with or without lightning, in a lady's presence. We have had quite blood and thundering enough for one journey; so, if you please, we'll sit in our places quietly. Here, guard, pick up that gentleman's carving-knife.'

"As quickly as my uncle said the words, the guard appeared at the coach-window with the gentleman's sword in his hand. He held up his lantern, and looked earnestly in my uncle's face, as he handed it in. By its light my uncle saw, to his great surprise, that an immense crowd of mail-coach guards swarmed round the window, every one of whom with his eyes earnestly fixed upon him. He had never seen such a sea of white faces, red bodies, and earnest eyes, in all his born days.

"'This is the strangest sort of thing I ever had anything to do with,' thought my uncle. 'Allow me to return you your hat, sir.'

"The ill-looking gentleman received his three-cornered hat in silence, looked at the hole in the middle with an inquiring air, and finally stuck it on the top of his wig quite solemnly—the effect of which was a trifle impaired by his sneezing violently at the moment and jerking it off again.

"'All right!' cried the guard with the lantern, mounting into his little seat behind. Away they went. My uncle peeped out of the coach window as they emerged from the yard, and observed that the other mail coaches, with coachmen, guards, horses, and passengers, complete, were driving round and round in circles at a slow trot of about five miles an hour. My uncle burned with indignation, gentlemen. As a commercial man, he felt that the mail-bags were not to be trifled with, and he resolved to address the Post-office on the subject the very instant he reached London.

"At present, however, his thoughts were occupied with the young lady who sat in the farthest corner of the coach with her face muffled closely in her hood. The gentleman with the sky-blue coat sat opposite her, and the other man in the plum-colored suit, sat by her side—both were watching her intently. If she so much as rustled the folds of her hood, he could hear the ill-looking man clap his hand upon his sword, and could tell by the other's breathing (it was so dark he couldn't see his face) that he was looking as big as if he were going to devour her at a mouthful. This baffled my uncle more and more, and he resolved, come what might, to see the end of it. He had a great admiration for bright eyes, sweet faces, and pretty legs and feet. In short, he was fond of the whole sex. It runs in our family, gentleman—so am I.

"'Many were the devices that my uncle practiced to attract the lady's attention or, at all events, to engage the mysterious gentlemen in conversation. They were all in vain. The gentlemen wouldn't talk, and the lady didn't dare. He thrust his head out of the coach-window at intervals, and bawled out to know why they weren't going faster. But he called till he was hoarse, and nobody paid the least attention to him. He leaned back in the coach and thought of the beautiful face, feet, and legs. This was better. It whiled away the time and kept him from wondering where he was going and how it was that he found himself in such an odd situation. Not that this would have worried him much anyway—my uncle was a mighty free and easy, roving, devil-may-care sort of person, gentlemen.

"All of a sudden the coach stopped. 'Hallo!' said my uncle, 'what's in the wind now?'

"'Alight here,' said the guard, letting down the steps.

"'Here!' cried my uncle.

"'Here,' rejoined the guard.

"'I'll do nothing of the sort,' said my uncle.

"'Very well, then stop where you are,' said the guard.

"'I will,' said my uncle.

"'Do,' said the guard.

"The passengers had regarded this colloquy with great attention, and finding that my uncle was determined not to alight, the younger man squeezed past him to hand the lady out. At this moment, the ill-looking man was inspecting the hole in the crown of his three-cornered hat. As the young lady brushed past, she dropped one of her gloves into my uncle's hand, and softly whispered, with her lips so close to his face that he felt her warm breath on his nose, the single word 'Help!' Gentlemen, my uncle leaped out of the coach at once, with such violence that it rocked on the springs again.

"'Oh! you've thought better of it, have you?' said the guard when he saw my uncle standing on the ground.

"My uncle looked at the guard for a few seconds in some doubt whether it wouldn't be better to wrench his blunderbuss from him, fire it in the face of the man with the big sword, knock the rest of the company over the head with the stock, snatch up the young lady, and go off in the smoke. On second thought, however, he abandoned this plan as being a shade too melodramatic in the execution and followed the two mysterious men, who, keeping the lady between them, were now entering an old house in front of which the coach had stopped. They turned into the passage, and my uncle followed.

"Of all the ruinous and desolate places my uncle had ever beheld, this was the most so. It looked as if it had once been a large house of entertainment; but the roof had fallen in in many places, and the stairs were steep, rugged, and broken. There was a huge fireplace in the room into which they walked, and the chimney was blackened with smoke. But no warm blaze lighted it up now. The white feathery dust of burned wood was still strewed over the hearth, but the stove was cold, and all was dark and gloomy.

"'Well,' said my uncle, as he looked about him, 'a mail coach traveling at the rate of six and a half miles an hour and stopping for an indefinite time at such a hole as this is rather an irregular sort of proceeding, I fancy. This shall be made known. I'll write to the papers.'

"My uncle said this in a pretty loud voice and in an open, unreserved sort of manner, with the view of engaging the two strangers in conversation if he could. But, neither of them took any more notice of him than whispering to each other and scowling at him as they did so. The lady was at the farther end of the room, and once she ventured to wave her hand as if beseeching my uncle's assistance.

"At length the two strangers advanced a little, and the conversation began in earnest.

"'You don't know this is a private room, I suppose, fellow?' said the gentleman in sky-blue.

"'No, I do not, fellow,' rejoined my uncle. 'Only if this is a private room specially ordered for the occasion, I should think the public room must be a very comfortable one.' With this, my uncle sat himself down in a high-backed chair and took such an accurate measure of the gentleman with his eyes that Tiggin and Welps could have supplied him with printed calico for a suit and not an inch too much or too little from that estimate alone.

"'Leave this room,' said both men together, grasping their swords.

"'Eh?' said my uncle, not at all appearing to comprehend their meaning.

"'Leave the room or you are a dead man,' said the ill-looking fellow with the large sword, drawing it at the same time and flourishing it in the air.

"'Down with him!' cried the gentleman in sky-blue, drawing his sword also, and falling back two or three yards. 'Down with him!' The lady gave a loud scream.

"Now, my uncle was always remarkable for great boldness and great presence of mind. All the time that he had appeared so indifferent to what was going on, he had been looking slyly about for some missile or weapon of defence, and at the very instant when the swords were drawn, he saw, standing in the chimney-corner, an old basket-hilted rapier in a rusty scabbard. At one bound, my uncle caught it in his hand, drew it, flourished it gallantly above his head, called aloud to the lady to keep out of the way, hurled the chair at the man in sky-blue and the scabbard at the man in plum-color, and taking advantage of the confusion, fell upon them both pell-mell.

"Gentlemen, there is an old story—none the worse for being true—

regarding a fine young Irish gentleman, who being asked if he could play the fiddle, replied he had no doubt he could, but he couldn't exactly say, for certain, because he had never tried. This is not inapplicable to my uncle and his fencing. He had never had a sword in his hand before—except once when he played Richard the Third at a private theatre, upon which occasion it was arranged with Richmond that he was to be run through from behind without showing fight at all. But here he was, cutting and slashing with two experienced swordsmen—thrusting and guarding and poking and slicing, and acquitting himself in the most manful and dexterous manner possible, although up to that time he had never been aware that he had the least notion of the science. It only shows how true the old saying is, that a man never knows what he can do until he tries, gentlemen.

"The noise of the combat was terrific, each of the three combatants swearing like troopers and their swords clashing with as much noise as if all the knives and steels in Newport market were rattling together at the same time. When it was at its very height, the lady (most probably to encourage my uncle) withdrew her hood entirely from her face and disclosed a countenance of such dazzling beauty that he would have fought against fifty men to win one smile from it and die. He had done wonders before, but now he began to powder away like a raving mad giant.

"At this very moment, the gentleman in sky-blue turning round and seeing the young lady with her face uncovered vented an exclamation of rage and jealousy, and turning his weapon against her beautiful bosom pointed a thrust at her heart. This caused my uncle to utter a cry of apprehension that made the building ring. The lady stepped lightly aside, and snatching the young man's sword from his hand—before he had recovered his balance—drove him to the wall, and running it through him and the paneling up to the very hilt, pinned him there, hard and fast. It was a splendid example. My uncle, with a loud shout of triumph and a strength that was irresistible, made his adversary retreat in the same direction, and plunging the old rapier into the very centre of a large red flower in the pattern of his waistcoat, nailed him beside his friend.

"'The mail coach!' cried the lady, running up to my uncle and throwing her beautiful arms round his neck; 'we may yet escape.'

"'May!' cried my uncle; 'why, my dear, there's no one else here, is there?'

"'We have not an instant to lose,' said the young lady. 'He (pointing to the young gentleman in sky-blue) is the only son of the powerful Marquess of Filletoville.'

"'Well then, my dear, I'm afraid he'll never come to the title,' said my uncle, looking coolly at the young gentleman as he stood fixed up against the wall.

"'I have been torn from my home and my friends by these villains,' said the young lady, her features glowing with indignation. 'That wretch would have married me by violence in another hour.'

"'Confound his impudence!' said my uncle, bestowing a very contemptuous look on the heir of Filletoville.

"'As you may guess from what you have seen,' said the young lady, 'these men were prepared to murder me if I appealed to any one for assistance. If their accomplices find us here, we are lost. Two minutes hence may be too late. The mail coach!' With these words, overpowered by her feelings and the exertion of fighting the young Marquess of Filletoville, she sank into my uncle's arms. My uncle caught her up and bore her to the house-door. There stood the mail coach, with four long-tailed, flowing-maned, black horses, ready harnessed; but no coachman, no guard, no hostler even, at the horses' heads.

"Gentlemen, I hope I do no injustice to my uncle's memory when I express my opinion that although he was a bachelor—he had held some ladies in his arms before this time—I believe, indeed, that he had rather a habit of kissing barmaids; and I know, that in one or two instances, he had been seen by creditable witnesses, to hug a landlady in a very perceptible manner. I mention the circumstance to show what a very uncommon sort of person this beautiful young lady must have been to have affected my uncle in the way she did. He used to say, that as her long dark hair trailed over his arm and her beautiful dark eyes fixed themselves upon his face as she recovered, he felt so strange and nervous that his legs trembled beneath him. But, who can look in a sweet, soft pair of dark eyes, without feeling strange? I can't, gentlemen. I am afraid to look at some eyes I know, and that's the truth of it.

"'You will never leave me?' murmured the young lady.

"'Never,' said my uncle. And he meant it too.

"'My dear preserver!' exclaimed the young lady. 'My dear, kind, brave preserver!'

"'Don't,' said my uncle, interrupting her.

"'Why?' inquired the young lady.

"'Because your mouth looks so beautiful when you speak,' rejoined my uncle, 'that I'm afraid I shall be rude enough to kiss it.'

"'The young lady put up her hand as if to caution my uncle not to do so, and said—no, she didn't say anything—she smiled. When you are looking at a pair of the most delicious lips in the world and see them gently break into a roguish smile—if you are very near them and nobody else nearby—you cannot better testify your admiration of their beautiful form and color than by kissing them at once. My uncle did so, and I honor him for it.

"'Hark!' cried the young lady, starting. 'The noise of wheels and horses!'

"'So it is,' said my uncle, listening. He had a good ear for wheels and the trampling of hoofs. But there appeared to be so many horses and carriages rattling toward them from a distance that it was impossible to form a guess at their number. The sound was like that of fifty wagons, with six cattle in each.

"'We are pursued!' cried the young lady clasping her hands. 'We are pursued. I have no hope but in you!'

'There was such an expression of terror in her beautiful face that my uncle made up his mind at once. He lifted her into the coach, told her not to be frightened, pressed his lips to hers once more, and then advising her to draw up the window to keep the cold air out, climbed to the box.

"'Stay, love,' cried the young lady.

"'What's the matter?' said my uncle from the coach-box.

"'I want to speak to you,' said the young lady; 'only a word. Only one word, dearest.'

"'Must I get down?' inquired my uncle. The lady made no answer, but she smiled again. Such a smile, gentlemen! It beat the other one all to nothing. My uncle descended from his perch in a twinkling.

"'What is it, my dear?' said my uncle, looking in at the coach window. The lady happened to move at the same time, and my uncle thought she looked more beautiful than she had done yet. He was very close to her just then, gentlemen, so he really ought to know.

"'What is it, my dear?' said my uncle.

"'Will you never love any one but me—never marry any one beside?' said the young lady.

"My uncle swore a great oath that he never would marry anybody else, and the young lady drew in her head and pulled up the window. He jumped upon the box, squared his elbows, adjusted the reins, seized the whip which lay on the roof, gave one flick to the off leader, and away went the four long-tailed, flowing-maned black horses at fifteen good English miles an hour, with the old mail coach behind them. Whew! How they tore along!

"The noise behind grew louder. The faster the old mail coach went, the faster came the pursuers—men, horses, dogs, were together in the pursuit. The noise was frightful—but above all rose the voice of the young lady, urging my uncle on and shrieking, 'Faster! Faster!'

"They whirled past the dark trees, as feathers would be swept before a hurricane. They shot by houses, gates, churches, haystacks, objects of every kind with a velocity and noise like roaring waters suddenly let loose. But still the noise of pursuit grew louder, and still my uncle could hear the young lady wildly screaming, 'Faster! Faster!'

"My uncle plied whip and rein, and the horses flew onward till they were white with foam—and yet the noise behind increased and the young lady cried, 'Faster! Faster!' My uncle gave a loud stamp on the boot in the energy of the moment and—found that it was grey morning, and he was sitting in the wheelwright's yard, on the box of an old Edinburgh mail coach, shivering with the cold and wet and stamping his feet to warm them! He got down and looked eagerly inside for the beautiful young lady. Alas! There was neither door nor seat to the coach. It was a mere shell.

"Of course, my uncle knew very well that there was some mystery in the matter, and that everything had passed exactly as he used to relate it. He remained staunch to the great oath he had sworn to the beautiful young lady, refusing several eligible landladies on her account, and dying a bachelor at last. He always said what a curious thing it was that he should have found out, by such a mere accident as his clambering over the palings, that the ghosts of mail-coaches and horses, guards, coachmen, and passengers, were in the habit of making journeys regularly every night. He used to add, that he believed he was the only living person who had ever been taken as a passenger on one of these excursions. And I think he was right, gentlemen—at least I never heard of any other."

MORE THAN A HEART CAN HOLD:
Ruth and Boaz

THE BOOK OF RUTH

RETOLD BY VICKI J. KUYPER

How can one heart hold so many tears? Ruth's mind chose to question the "how" instead of the "why" of this new heartbreak. It was easier that way. She'd already struggled with the "why" of not being able to conceive a child. The "why" of her brother-in-law's sudden death. The "why" of the loss of Mahlon, the man she loved, her husband and friend. Now, she found herself standing at a crossroad, physically and emotionally.

A warm afternoon wind whipped the cloth of the black mourning clothes across the face of her widowed mother-in-law, but not before Ruth saw that Naomi's eyes were as filled with tears as her own. They'd all lost so much. Three women in black—Ruth, Naomi, and Orpah, Naomi's other daughter-in-law. All of them were widows. All of them left without heirs, without provision for their needs, without hope.

Ruth knew that's why Naomi was asking her daughters-in-law to return home to their own families. Naomi hoped she and Orpah might still have a chance to find other husbands, to secure a different future for themselves. As for Naomi, she'd already accepted that her future had but one path. She'd return to Bethlehem, the land she and her husband left years before when the famine forced them south to Moab. There she'd call on the generosity of her relatives. Perhaps their faith, and their pity, would move them to care for a poor widow. But for three widows? Naomi knew better than to pray for miracles. She'd tried it before. *And look what God's done!* Naomi said angrily to herself. *He's abandoned me, like all the rest.*

Ruth studied Naomi's face, hardened by years of grief, through her own tear-filled eyes. She knew Naomi loved her and Orpah as deeply as if they'd been her daughters by birth. She knew it was love that compelled Naomi to say good-bye, even though it meant another loss, another heartbreak. But still Ruth couldn't let go. She held onto Naomi's frail shoulders with the tender care of a child rescuing a bird that had fallen from its nest. Naomi tried to pull away, but Ruth grabbed the cloth of her mother-in-law's shawl and fell to her knees in the dirt.

"Look!" Naomi pleaded with Ruth, pointing toward Orpah who was stumbling slowly back toward town, the young woman's shoulders racked with sobs. "Your sister-in-law is going back to her people and her gods. Go back with her."

"Don't urge me to leave you or to turn back from you!" Ruth pleaded. "Where you go I will go, and where you stay I will stay. Your people will be my people and your God my God."

For a moment Naomi stood as still as a stone, staring down at her daughter-in-law crumpled at her feet in the dusty road. Then ever so slowly, Naomi took Ruth's hand in her own and pulled it toward her heart. Ruth rose to look her beloved mother-in-law in the eye.

"Then let us go," Naomi said softly. Ruth couldn't tell whether it was sorrow or gratitude she heard beneath her words.

Their walk to Judah was long, dusty, and dry. It was the most distant, most desolate journey Ruth has ever taken. Some days she wondered if her mother-in-law would even survive the trip. But as their supply of food drew near an end, Naomi began to recognize long-forgotten landmarks. She became more animated as she told Ruth stories of her childhood and about the early days of her marriage to Elimelech. Suddenly, she grew quiet.

"Naomi," Ruth tried to reassure her, "It will be alright. We're almost there."

"Don't call me Naomi," her mother-in-law said with a cold edge to her voice. "That means 'pleasant.' From now call me Mara . . . 'bitter.' For I left this land full and now I'm returning empty."

Though Naomi seemed to warm a bit at the welcome her relatives extended as she and Ruth settled into town, Ruth worried about the bitter seed that seemed to have taken root in her mother-in-law's heart. Determined to provide for Naomi in any way she could, Ruth rose early the next day to glean in a nearby barley field. It was the work of the poor, picking up grain that paid harvest workers miss. But Ruth's love for Naomi was stronger than her pride.

Ruth's back began to ache as the sun rose high in the sky. She balanced a small basket of barley on her hip as she made her way up and down the rows of grain. Suddenly Ruth noticed she was alone in the field. The other harvesters had made their way toward the shade of a leafy tree where the field's foreman was talking with a well-dressed man.

Even from where she stood, Ruth could hear the deep rumble of the man's voice greeting the harvesters. "The Lord be with you!" he said.

"The Lord bless you!" one after another responded in reply.

Ruth lowered her eyes and got back to work. Naomi was depending on her. She couldn't stop for small talk.

"Welcome!" a man's voice startled Ruth, almost sending a shower of barley from her basket back onto the ground. She looked up into the eyes of the well-dressed man, now close to her side. Though the man's hair was sprinkled with gray, his broad shoulders showed the strength of someone who was not a stranger to physical labor. But the man's face didn't show the deep lines of those who spend their lives working under the hot sun. Instead, it was smooth and lightly bronzed, with finely cut features offset by a slightly crooked smile.

"I'm so glad you've come to work in my fields," he said softly. "I hope you'll continue working here as long as you'd like. I've told the men to leave you alone, but do stay close to the other women. And feel free to drink from the water jars whenever you're thirsty."

Ruth dropped to her knees in a sign of respect, placing her face low to the ground. "Sir, I'm a foreigner here. Why have I found such kind favor in your eyes?"

"Please call me Boaz," the man replied. He bent down to help Ruth to her feet and then continued, "I've heard of what you've done for my relative Naomi. How you left your father and your mother and your home and came to live with people you've never met. May the Lord repay you for what you've done. May you be richly rewarded by the Lord, the God of Israel, under whose wings you've come to take refuge." Boaz paused, then asked softly, "Are you hungry?"

Ruth was at a loss for what to say. She mumbled out a soft, "yes," to which the man replied, "Please join us for some food."

As Ruth seated herself in the shade with the other women, Boaz walked over to where the men were resting. Under his breath, he told his foreman, "Let this woman gather wherever she wants. Drop a few stalks of barley along the way for her to glean with the heads of grain. Don't embarrass her. Just be generous. Just as God has been to us."

Boaz returned to Ruth with bread and some roasted grain. Then with a smile and a nod of his head, Boaz turned and walked back through the fields toward the threshing floor. The rest of the afternoon passed quickly, as Ruth's hands seemed to keep pace with the thoughts tumbling through her mind.

I can't wait to show Naomi all of the grain I've gathered! I must have gleaned over half a bushel already—on my first day! Boaz seems like such a kind man . . . and a handsome man. His smile seemed to say more to me than his words . . . But what am I thinking? Of course, he's just helping me to help Naomi. Isn't he? I haven't felt this way since my parents arranged my marriage to Mahlon . . . Stop daydreaming, you foolish woman! Don't let your emotions run away with you. . . .

But that night Naomi's emotions seemed as filled with girlish daydreams as Ruth's. "The Lord hasn't abandoned us!" Naomi said with a joyful clap of her wrinkled hands. "He's led you straight to one of our kinsmen-redeemers! Boaz is one of my closest relatives. Therefore by law he has the choice of purchasing your husband's property and marrying you. Now here's what you need to do . . ."

Weeks passed as Ruth and Naomi waited for just the right time to put Naomi's plan into action. One evening when Ruth returned from working in the fields, Naomi greeted her at the door with a wide smile. It was a smile Ruth had grown to look forward to over the last few weeks, a smile that showed God was gleaning the bitterness from Naomi's heart.

"Tonight Boaz will be winnowing barley on the harvesting floor," Naomi said with delight. "Go get washed up! Use that last bit of perfume. Put on your best clothes. The Lord will be with you as you go."

The plan was finally in motion.

***

Startled, Boaz awoke from a sound sleep. He lifted his head up from his makeshift bed beside a pile of grain. Every year at winnowing time this was his bedroom, his outer robe thrown on the threshing floor. But tonight, his feet were cold. He must have kicked the robe off during the night. He peered into the darkness, straining to see if anything was out of place. That's when something moved at his feet.

"Who's there? Who is it?" Boaz cried out in the night.

"Don't be afraid!" Ruth reassured Boaz. "It's your servant, Ruth. Please, sir, spread the corner of your garment over me. You're my kinsman-redeemer."

For a moment, there was silence. Then, Boaz said softly, "The Lord bless you . . . Not only have you honored your mother-in-law by loving her as faithfully as any true daughter ever could, but now you've honored me with your request! Instead of running after younger relatives, you've chosen to come to me. I'll cover you with the garment of my protection and provision. And I'll gladly take you as my wife so that your husband's name won't be forgotten or erased from our family.

***

The barley was ripening. Even the slightest breeze set the grain dancing in the fields. Soon, the harvesters would return to their work under the hot sun. But Ruth was no longer in the fields. Instead, she watched Naomi lift her new grandson into her arms, nuzzling the soft chestnut fuzz on his head close to her cheek. Ruth's eyes filled with tears. But this time they overflowed from a heart filled with joy, instead of sorrow.

"Your daughter-in-law's love is better than seven sons!" a neighbor shouted to Naomi when she noticed the old woman cradling the newborn in her arms.

"It's true," Naomi replied, looking Ruth in the eyes. "I returned to this land empty and now my life is once again full. How the Lord has blessed me through you!"

How can one heart hold so much love? Ruth looked at the joy on Naomi's face and then took a quick look back over the last few years. Love lost and then found again. Naomi, Boaz, and now Obed, a son. This land and this faith that at first felt so foreign, now felt like the only home Ruth ever longed for.

"The Lord is with me!" she whispered, lifting her eyes to the azure skies. "And Lord I am with you. Forever yours."

THE SON'S VETO

THOMAS HARDY

To the eyes of a man viewing it from behind, the nut-brown hair was a
wonder and a mystery. Under the black beaver hat, surmounted by its tuft of
black feathers, the long locks, braided and twisted and coiled like the rushes
of a basket, composed a rare, if somewhat barbaric, example of ingenious art.
One could understand such weavings and coilings being wrought to last intact
for a year or even a calendar month, but that they should be all demolished
regularly at bedtime, after a single day of permanence, seemed a reckless
waste of successful fabrication.

And she had done it all herself, poor thing. She had no maid, and it was
almost the only accomplishment she could boast of. Hence the unstinted
pains.

She was a young invalid lady—not so very much of an invalid—sitting
in a wheeled chair, which had been pulled up in the front part of a green
enclosure, close to a band-stand where a concert was going on during a warm
June afternoon. It had place in one of the minor parks or private gardens that
are to be found in the suburbs of London, and was the effort of a local association to raise money for some charity. There are worlds within worlds in the
great city, and though nobody outside the immediate district had ever heard
of the charity or the band or the garden, the enclosure was filled with an
interested audience sufficiently informed on all these.

As the strains proceeded many of the listeners observed the chaired
lady, whose back hair, by reason of her prominent position, so challenged
inspection. Her face was not easily discernible, but the aforesaid cunning
tress-weavings, the white ear and poll, and the curve of a cheek that was
neither flaccid nor sallow, were signals that led to the expectation of good
beauty in front. Such expectations are not infrequently disappointed as soon

as the disclosure comes; and in the present case, when the lady, by a turn of the head, at length revealed herself, she was not so handsome as the people behind her had supposed, and even hoped—they did not know why.

For one thing (alas! the commonness of this complaint), she was less young than they had fancied her to be. Yet her face was unquestionably attractive, and not at all sickly. The revelation of its details came each time she turned to talk to a boy of twelve or thirteen who stood beside her, and the shape of whose hat and jacket implied that he belonged to a well-known public school. The immediate by-standers could hear that he called her "Mother."

When the end of the program was reached and the audience withdrew, many chose to find their way out by passing at her elbow. Almost all turned their heads to take a full and near look at the interesting woman, who remained stationary in the chair till the way should be clear enough for her to be wheeled out without obstruction. As if she expected their glances and did not mind gratifying their curiosity, she met the eyes of several of her observers by lifting her own, showing these to be soft, brown, and affectionate orbs, a little plaintive in their regard.

She was conducted out of the garden and passed along the pavement till she disappeared from view, the school-boy walking beside her. To inquiries made by some persons who watched her away, the answer came that she was the second wife of the incumbent of a neighboring parish and that she was lame. She was generally believed to be a woman with a story—an innocent one, but a story of some sort or other.

In conversing with her on their way home, the boy who walked at her elbow said that he hoped his father had not missed them.

"He have been so comfortable these last few hours that I am sure he cannot have missed us," she replied.

"Has, dear mother—not have!" exclaimed the public-school boy with an impatient fastidiousness that was almost harsh. "Surely you know that by this time!"

His mother hastily adopted the correction, and did not resent his making it, nor did she retaliate, as she might well have done by bidding him to wipe that crumby mouth of his, whose condition had been caused by surreptitious attempts to eat a piece of cake without taking it out of the pocket wherein it lay concealed. After this the pretty woman and the boy went onward in silence.

That question of grammar bore upon her history, and she fell into reverie—of a somewhat sad kind to all appearance. It might have been assumed that she was wondering if she had done wisely in shaping her life as she had shaped it, to bring out such a result as this.

In a remote nook in North Wessex, forty miles from London, near the thriving county-town of Aldbrickham, there stood a pretty village with its church and parsonage, which she knew well enough, but her son had never seen. It was her native village, Gaymead, and the first event bearing upon her present situation had occurred at that place when she was only a girl of nineteen.

How well she remembered it, that first act in her little tragi-comedy, the death of her reverend husband's first wife. It happened on a spring evening, and she who now and for many years had filled that first wife's place was then parlor-maid in the parson's house.

When everything had been done that could be done, and the death was announced, she had gone out in the dusk to visit her parents, who were living in the same village, to tell them the sad news. As she opened the white swing-gate and looked toward the trees which rose westward, shutting out the pale light of the evening sky, she discerned, without much surprise, the figure of a man standing in the hedge, though she roguishly exclaimed as a matter of form, "Oh, Sam, how you frightened me!"

He was a young gardener of her acquaintance. She told him the particulars of the late event, and they stood silent, these two young people, in that elevated, calmly philosophic mind that is engendered when a tragedy has happened close at hand, and has not happened to the philosophers themselves. But it had its bearing upon their relations.

"And will you stay on now at the Vicarage, just the same?" asked he.

She had hardly thought of that. "Oh, yes—I suppose," she said. "Everything will be just as usual, I imagine."

He walked beside her toward her mother's. Presently his arm stole round her waist. She gently removed it; but he placed it there again, and she yielded the point. "You see, dear Sophy, you don't know that you'll stay on. You may want a home; and I shall be ready to offer one some day, though I may not be ready just yet."

"Why, Sam, how can you be so fast! I've never even said I liked 'ee, and it is all your own doing, coming after me!"

"Still, it is nonsense to say I am not to have a try at you, like the rest." He stooped to kiss her a farewell, for they had reached her mother's door.

"No, Sam; you sha'n't!" she cried, putting her hand over his mouth. "You ought to be more serious on such a night as this." And she bade him adieu without allowing him to kiss her or to come indoors.

The vicar just left a widower was at this time a man about forty years of age, of good family, and childless. He had led a secluded existence in this college living, partly because there were no resident landowners, and his loss now intensified his habit of withdrawal from outward observation. He was still less seen than heretofore, kept himself still less in time with the rhythm and racket of the movements called progress in the world without. For many months after his wife's decease, the economy of his household remained as before. The cook, the housemaid, the parlour-maid, and the man out-of-doors performed their duties or left them undone, just as nature prompted them—the vicar knew not which. It was then represented to him that his servants seemed to have nothing to do in his small family of one. He was struck with the truth of this representation and decided to cut down his establishment. But he was forestalled by Sophy, the parlour-maid, who said one evening that she wished to leave him.

"And why?" said the parson.

"Sam Hobson has asked me to marry him, sir."

"Well—do you want to marry?"

"Not much. But it would be a home for me. And we have heard that one of us will have to leave."

A day or two after, she said: "I don't want to leave just yet, sir, if you don't wish it. Sam and I have quarreled."

He looked up at her. He had hardly ever observed her before, though he had been frequently conscious of her soft presence in the room. What a kitten-like, flexuous, tender creature she was! She was the only one of the servants with whom he came into immediate and continuous contact. What should he do if Sophy were gone?

Sophy did not go, but one of the others did, and things went on quietly again.

When Mr. Twycott, the vicar, was ill, Sophy brought up his meals to him, and she had no sooner left the room one day than he heard a noise on the stairs. She had slipped down with the tray, and so twisted her foot that she could not stand. The village surgeon was called in. The vicar got better, but Sophy was incapacitated for a long time. She was informed that she must never again walk much or engage in any occupation that required her to stand long on her feet. As soon as she was comparatively well, she spoke to him alone. Since she was forbidden to walk and bustle about, and, indeed, could not do so, it became her duty to leave. She could very well work at something sitting down, and she had an aunt who was a seamstress.

The parson had been very greatly moved by what she had suffered on his account, and he exclaimed, "No, Sophy, lame or not lame, I cannot let you go. You must never leave me again."

He came close to her, and, though she could never exactly tell how it happened, she became conscious of his lips upon her cheek. He then asked her to marry him. Sophy did not exactly love him, but she had a respect for him that almost amounted to veneration. Even if she had wished to get away from him, she hardly dared refuse a personage so reverend and august in her eyes, and she assented forthwith to be his wife.

Thus it happened that one fine morning, when the doors of the church were naturally open for ventilation, and the singing birds fluttered in and alighted on the tie-beams of the roof, there was a marriage-service at the communion-rails, which hardly a soul knew of. The parson and a neighboring curate had entered at one door and Sophy at another, followed by two necessary persons. Whereupon in a short time there emerged a newly-made husband and wife.

Mr. Twycott knew perfectly well that he had committed social suicide by this step, despite Sophy's spotless character, and he had taken his measures accordingly. An exchange of livings had been arranged with an acquaintance who was incumbent of a church in the south of London, and as soon as possible the couple removed thither, abandoning their pretty country home with trees and shrubs and glebe for a narrow, dusty house in a long, straight street, and their fine peal of bells for the most wretched one-tongued clangor that ever tortured mortal ears. It was all on her account. They were, however, away from every one who had known her former position; and also under less observation from without than they would have had to put up with in any country parish.

Sophy—the woman—was as charming a partner as a man could possess, though Sophy—the lady—had her deficiencies. She showed a natural aptitude for little domestic refinements, so far as related to things and manners. But in what is called culture, she was less intuitive. She had now been married more than fourteen years, and her husband had taken much trouble with her education. But she still held confused ideas on the use of "was" and "were," which did not beget a respect for her among the few acquaintances she made. Her great grief in this relation was that her only child, on whose education no expense had been and would be spared, was now old enough to perceive these deficiencies in his mother, and not only to see them but to feel irritated at their existence.

Thus she lived on in the city, and wasted hours in braiding her beautiful hair, till her once apple cheeks waned to pink of the very faintest. Her foot had never regained its natural strength after the accident, and she was mostly obliged to avoid walking altogether. Her husband had grown to like London for its freedom and its domestic privacy, but he was twenty years his Sophy's senior, and had latterly been seized with a serious illness. On this day, however, he had seemed to be well enough to justify her accompanying her son Randolph to the concert.

The next time we get a glimpse of her is when she appears in the mournful attire of a widow.

Mr. Twycott had never rallied, and now lay in a well-packed cemetery to the south of the great city, where, if all the dead it contained had stood erect and alive, not one would have known him or recognized his name. The boy had dutifully followed him to the grave, and was now again at school.

Throughout these changes, Sophy had been treated like the child she was in nature though not in years. She was left with no control over anything that had been her husband's beyond her modest personal income. In his anxiety lest her inexperience should be overreached, he had safeguarded with trustees all he possibly could. The completion of the boy's course at the public school, to be followed in due time by Oxford and ordination, had been all previsioned and arranged. She really had nothing to occupy her in the world but to eat and drink, make a business of indolence, and go on weaving and coiling the nut-brown hair, merely keeping a home open for the son whenever he came to her during vacations.

Foreseeing his probable decease long years before her, her husband in his lifetime had purchased for her use a semi-detached villa in the same long, straight road whereon the church and parsonage faced, which was to be hers as long as she chose to live in it. Here she now resided, looking out upon the fragment of lawn in front and through the railings at the ever-flowing traffic, or, bending forward over the window-sill on the first floor, stretching her eyes far up and down the vista of sooty trees, hazy air, and drab house-facades, along which echoed the noises common to a suburban main thoroughfare.

Somehow, her boy with his aristocratic school-knowledge, his grammars, and his aversions, was losing those wide infantine sympathies, extending as far as to the sun and moon themselves, with which he, like other children, had been born, and which his mother, a child of nature herself, had loved in him. He was reducing their compass to a population of a few thousand wealthy and titled people, the mere veneer of a thousand million or so of others who did not interest him at all. He drifted further and further away from her. Sophy's milieu being a suburb of minor tradesmen and under-clerks, and her almost only companions the two servants of her own house, it was not surprising that after her husband's death, she soon lost the little artificial tastes she had acquired from him, and became—in her son's eyes—a mother whose mistakes and origin it was his painful lot as a gentleman to blush for. As yet he was far from being man enough—if he ever would be—to rate these sins of hers at their true infinitesimal value beside the yearning fondness that welled up and remained penned in her heart till it should be more fully accepted by him or by some other person or thing. If he had lived at home with her, he would have had all of it; but he seemed to require so very little in present circumstances, and it remained stored.

Her life became insupportably dreary—she could not take walks, and had no interest in going for drives, or, indeed, in traveling anywhere. Nearly two years passed without an event, and still she looked on that suburban road, thinking of the village in which she had been born and whither she would have gone back—O how gladly!—even to work in the fields.

Taking no exercise, she often could not sleep, and would rise in the night or early morning and look out upon the then vacant thoroughfare, where the lamps stood like sentinels waiting for some procession to go by. An approximation to such a procession was indeed made early every morning about one o'clock when the country vehicles passed up with loads of vegetables for Covent Garden market. She often saw them creeping along at this silent and dusky hour—wagon after wagon, bearing green bastions of cabbages nodding to their fall, yet never falling; walls of baskets enclosing masses of beans and peas; pyramids of snow-white turnips, swaying howdahs of mixed produce— creeping along behind aged night-horses, who seemed ever patiently wondering between their hollow coughs why they had always to work at that still hour when all other sentient creatures were privileged to rest. Wrapped in a cloak, it was soothing to watch and sympathize with them when depression and nervousness hindered sleep, and to see how the fresh green-stuff brightened to life as it came opposite the lamp, and how the sweating animals steamed and shone with their miles of travel.

They had an interest, almost a charm, for Sophy, these semi-rural people and vehicles moving in an urban atmosphere, leading a life quite distinct from that of the daytime toilers on the same road. One morning a man who accompanied a wagon-load of potatoes gazed rather hard at the house fronts as he passed, and with a curious emotion she thought his form was familiar to her. She looked out for him again. His being an old-fashioned conveyance with a yellow front, it was easily recognizable, and on the third night after, she saw it a second time. The man alongside was, as she had fancied, Sam Hobson, formerly gardener at Gaymead, who would at one time have married her.

She had occasionally thought of him, and wondered if life in a cottage with him would not have been a happier lot than the life she had accepted. She had not thought of him passionately, but her now dismal situation lent an interest to his resurrection—a tender interest that it is impossible to exaggerate. She went back to bed and began thinking. When did these market-gardeners, who traveled up to town so regularly at one or two in the morning, come back? She dimly recollected seeing their empty wagons, hardly noticeable amid the ordinary day-traffic, passing down at some hour before noon.

It was only April, but that morning after breakfast, she had the window opened, and sat looking out, the feeble sun shining full upon her. She affected to sew, but her eyes never left the street. Between ten and eleven, the desired wagon, now unladen, reappeared on its return journey. But Sam was not looking round him then and drove on in a reverie.

"Sam!" cried she.

Turning with a start, his face lighted up. He called to him a little boy to hold the horse, alighted, and came and stood under her window.

"I can't come down easily, Sam, or I would!" she said. "Did you know I lived here?"

"Well, Mrs. Twycott, I knew you lived along here somewhere. I have often looked out for 'ee."

He briefly explained his own presence on the scene. He had long since given up his gardening in the village near Aldbrickham, and was now manager at a market-gardener's on the south side of London, it being part of his duty to go up to Covent Garden with wagon-loads of produce two or three times a week. In answer to her curious inquiry, he admitted that he had come to this particular district because he had seen in the Aldbrickham paper, a year or two before, the announcement of the death in South London of the aforetime vicar of Gaymead, which had revived an interest in her dwelling-place that he could not extinguish, leading him to hover about the locality till his present post had been secured.

They spoke of their native village in dear old North Wessex, the spots in which they had played together as children. She tried to feel that she was a dignified personage now, that she must not be too confidential with Sam. But she could not keep it up, and the tears hanging in her eyes were indicated in her voice.

"I'm afraid you are not happy, Mrs. Twycott," he said.

"Oh, of course not! I lost my husband only the year before last."

"Ah! I meant in another way. You'd like to be home again?"

"This is my home—for life. The house belongs to me. But I understand"—She let it out then. "Yes, Sam. I long for home—our home! I should like to be there, and never leave it, and die there." But she remembered herself. "That's only a momentary feeling. I have a son, you know, a dear boy. He's at school now."

"Somewhere handy, I suppose? I see there's lots on 'em along this road."

"Oh no! Not in one of these wretched holes! At a public school—one of the most distinguished in England."

"Chok' it all! of course! I forget, ma'am, that you've been a lady for so many years."

"No, I am not a lady," she said sadly. "I never shall be. But he's a gentleman, and that—makes it—oh how difficult for me!"

The acquaintance thus oddly reopened proceeded apace. She often looked out to get a few words with him, by night or by day. Her sorrow was that she could not accompany her one old friend on foot a little way and talk more freely than she could do while he paused before the house. One night, at the beginning of June, when she was again on the watch after an absence of some days from the window, he entered the gate and said softly, "Now, wouldn't some air do you good? I've only half a load this morning. Why not ride up to Covent Garden with me? There's a nice seat on the cabbages, where I've spread a sack. You can be home again in a cab before anybody is up."

She refused at first, and then, trembling with excitement, hastily finished her dressing, and wrapped herself up in cloak and veil, afterward sidling downstairs by the aid of the handrail, in a way she could adopt in an emergency. When she had opened the door, she found Sam on the step, and he lifted her bodily on his strong arm across the little forecourt into his vehicle. Not a soul was visible or audible in the infinite length of the straight, flat highway, with its ever-waiting lamps converging to points in each direction. The air was fresh as country air at this hour, and the stars shone, except to the north-eastward, where there was a whitish light—the dawn. Sam carefully placed her in the seat, and drove on.

They talked as they had talked in old days, Sam pulling himself up now and then when he thought himself too familiar. More than once she said with misgiving that she wondered if she ought to have indulged in the freak. "But I am so lonely in my house," she added, "and this makes me so happy!"

"You must come again, dear Mrs. Twycott. There is no time o' day for taking the air like this."

It grew lighter and lighter. The sparrows became busy in the streets, and the city waxed denser around them. When they approached the river, it was day, and on the bridge they beheld the full blaze of morning sunlight in the direction of St. Paul's, the river glistening toward it, and not a craft stirring.

Near Covent Garden he put her into a cab, and they parted, looking into each other's faces like the very old friends they were. She reached home without adventure, limped to the door, and let herself in with her latch-key unseen.

The air and Sam's presence had revived her; her cheeks were quite pink—almost beautiful. She had something to live for in addition to her son. A woman of pure instincts, she knew there had been nothing really wrong in the journey, but supposed it conventionally to be very wrong indeed.

Soon, however, she gave way to the temptation of going with him again, and on this occasion their conversation was distinctly tender. Sam said he never should forget her, notwithstanding that she had served him rather badly at one time. After much hesitation he told her of a plan it was in his power to carry out, and one he should like to take in hand, since he did not care for London work—it was to set up as a master greengrocer down at Aldbrickham, the county-town of their native place. He knew of an opening— a shop kept by aged people who wished to retire.

"And why don't you do it, then, Sam?" she asked with a slight heart-sinking.

"Because I'm not sure if—you'd join me. I know you wouldn't—couldn't! Such a lady as ye've been so long, you couldn't be a wife to a man like me."

"I hardly suppose I could!" she assented, also frightened at the idea.

"If you could," he said eagerly, "you'd on'y have to sit in the back parlor and look through the glass partition when I was away sometimes—just to keep an eye on things. The lameness wouldn't hinder that. I'd keep you as genteel as ever I could, dear Sophy—if I might think of it," he pleaded.

"Sam, I'll be frank," she said, putting her hand on his. "If it were only myself I would do it and gladly, though everything I possess would be lost to me by marrying again."

"I don't mind that! It's more independent."

"That's good of you, dear, dear Sam. But there's something else. I have a son. I almost fancy when I am miserable sometimes that he is not really mine, but one I hold in trust for my late husband. He seems to belong so little to me personally, so entirely to his dead father. He is so much educated and I so little that I do not feel dignified enough to be his mother. Well, he would have to be told."

"Yes. Unquestionably." Sam saw her thought and her fear. "Still, you can do as you like, Sophy—Mrs. Twycott," he added. "It is not you who is the child, but he."

"Ah, you don't know! Sam, if I could, I would marry you, some day. But you must wait a while, and let me think."

It was enough for him, and he was blithe at their parting. Not so she. To tell Randolph seemed impossible. She could wait till he had gone up to Oxford, when what she did would affect his life but little. But would he ever tolerate the idea? And if not, could she defy him?

She had not told him a word when the yearly cricket-match came on at Lord's between the public schools, though Sam had already gone back to

Aldbrickham. Mrs. Twycott felt stronger than usual. She went to the match with Randolph, and was able to leave her chair and walk about occasionally. The bright idea occurred to her that she could casually broach the subject while moving round among the spectators, when the boy's spirits were high with interest in the game, and he would weigh domestic matters as feathers in the scale beside the day's victory. They promenaded under the lurid July sun, this pair, so wide apart, yet so near, and Sophy saw the large proportion of boys like her own, in their broad white collars and dwarf hats, and all around the rows of great coaches under which was jumbled the debris of luxurious luncheons—bones, pie-crusts, champagne-bottles, glasses, plates, napkins, and the family silver; while on the coaches sat the proud fathers and mothers—but never a poor mother like her. If Randolph had not appertained to these, had not centered all his interests in them, had not cared exclusively for the class they belonged to, how happy would things have been! A great huzza at some small performance with the bat burst from the multitude of relatives, and Randolph jumped wildly into the air to see what had happened. Sophy fetched up the sentence that had been already shaped, but she could not get it out. The occasion was, perhaps, an inopportune one. The contrast between her story and the display of fashion to which Randolph had grown to regard himself as akin would be fatal. She awaited a better time.

It was on an evening when they were alone in their plain suburban residence, where life was not blue but brown, that she ultimately broke silence, qualifying her announcement of a probable second marriage by assuring him that it would not take place for a long time to come, when he would be living quite independently of her.

The boy thought the idea a very reasonable one, and asked if she had chosen anybody. She hesitated, and he seemed to have a misgiving. He hoped his step-father would be a gentleman, he said.

"Not what you call a gentleman," she answered, timidly. "He'll be much as I was before I knew your father;" and by degrees she acquainted him with the whole. The youth's face remained fixed for a moment; then he flushed, leant on the table, and burst into passionate tears.

His mother went up to him, kissed all of his face that she could get at, and patted his back as if he were still the baby he once had been, crying herself the while. When he had somewhat recovered from his paroxysm, he went hastily to his own room and fastened the door.

Parleyings were attempted through the keyhole, outside which she waited and listened. It was long before he would reply, and when he did it was to say sternly at her from within: "I am ashamed of you! It will ruin me! A miserable boor! a churl! a clown! It will degrade me in the eyes of all the gentlemen of England!"

"Say no more—perhaps I am wrong! I will struggle against it!" she cried miserably.

Before Randolph left her that summer a letter arrived from Sam to inform her that he had been unexpectedly fortunate in obtaining the shop. He was in possession. It was the largest in the town, combining fruit with vegetables, and he thought it would form a home worthy even of her some day. Might he not run up to town to see her?

She met him by stealth, and said he must still wait for her final answer. The autumn dragged on, and when Randolph was home at Christmas for the holidays, she broached the matter again. But the young gentleman was inexorable.

It was dropped for months, renewed again, abandoned under his repugnance, again attempted, and thus the gentle creature reasoned and pleaded till four or five long years had passed. Then the faithful Sam revived his suit with some peremptoriness. Sophy's son, now an undergraduate, was down from Oxford one Easter, when she again opened the subject. As soon as he was ordained, she argued, he would have a home of his own, wherein she, with her bad grammar and her ignorance, would be an encumbrance to him. Better obliterate her as much as possible.

He showed a more manly anger now, but would not agree. She on her side was more persistent, and he had doubts whether she could be trusted in his absence. But by indignation and contempt for her taste, he completely maintained his ascendancy; and finally taking her before a little cross and altar that he had erected in his bedroom for his private devotions, there bade her kneel and swear that she would not wed Samuel Hobson without his consent. "I owe this to my father!" he said.

The poor woman swore, thinking he would soften as soon as he was ordained and in full swing of clerical work. But he did not. His education had by this time sufficiently ousted his humanity to keep him quite firm, though his mother might have led an idyllic life with her faithful fruiterer and greengrocer and nobody have been anything the worse in the world.

Her lameness became more confirmed as time went on, and she seldom or never left the house in the long southern thoroughfare, where she seemed to be pining her heart away. "Why mayn't I say to Sam that I'll marry him? Why mayn't I?" she would murmur plaintively to herself when nobody was near.

Some four years after this date, a middle-aged man was standing at the door of the largest fruiterer's shop in Aldbrickham. He was the proprietor, but to-day, instead of his usual business attire, he wore a neat suit of black, and his window was partly shuttered. From the railway-station a funeral procession was seen approaching: it passed his door and went out of the town toward the village of Gaymead. The man, whose eyes were wet, held his hat in his hand as the vehicles moved by, while from the mourning coach a young smooth-shaven priest in a high waistcoat looked black as a cloud at the shop keeper standing there.

ROMEO AND JULIET

WILLIAM SHAKESPEARE

ADAPTED FROM CHARLES AND MARY LAMB'S NARRATIVE

BY REBECCA CURRINGTON

The Capulets and the Montagues were the two most prominent families in Verona. They might have been comfortable friends were it not for an old quarrel that had grown to a terrible height and spawned a deadly enmity between them—a hatred so deep that it extended to the remotest kindred and the followers and retainers of both sides. A servant of the house of Montague could not meet a servant of the house of Capulet, nor a Capulet encounter a Montague—even by chance—without fierce words and sometimes bloodshed ensuing; and there were frequent brawls from such accidental meetings, which disturbed the happy quiet of Verona's streets.

It happened that old Lord Capulet planned a great dinner to which many beautiful women and noble guests were invited. All the admired beauties of Verona were present. In fact, all comers were welcome—as long as they were not of the house of Montague.

A young woman named Rosaline was expected to attend this grand event hosted by the Capulets. As it happened, Rosaline was loved by Romeo, the son of Lord Capulet's bitter enemy—Lord Montague. Though it was dangerous for a Montague to be seen at a Capulet dinner, Benvolio, a friend of Romeo, persuaded the young lord to attend disguised in a mask. Benvolio suggested that this would be a good way for Romeo to see his Rosaline and compare her to some of the other choice beauties of Verona. This he felt would cause Romeo to think Rosaline to be more of a crow than a swan.

Romeo had small faith in Benvolio's words; nevertheless, for the love of Rosaline, he was persuaded to go.

Romeo was a sincere and passionate lover—one who was known to lose sleep when in love. Of late, he had secluded himself, thinking only of Rosaline, despite the fact that she had scorned him and never requited his love with the least show of courtesy or affection. Benvolio wished to cure his friend of this misguided love by showing him that there were indeed many other lovely women who would welcome his company. Convinced, Romeo, his friend Benvolio, and their mutual friend Mercutio donned their masks and left for the Capulet's grand feast.

The old Lord Capulet welcomed them when they arrived and invited them to dance with all those who were able. The old man was light-hearted and merry. He even confided to the men that when he was young, he had once worn a mask to a similar affair, hoping to find the chance to whisper anonymously into the ear of some beautiful woman.

The men soon began to dance and that's when Romeo suddenly laid his eyes on a young woman of exceeding beauty. It seemed to him that her beauty glowed in the light of the brightly burning torches like a rich jewel—beauty too rich for use, too dear for earth! He felt her beauty and perfections were so much greater than that of her companions that she was as a snowy dove trooping with crows.

While he uttered these praises, he was overheard by Tybalt, a nephew of Lord Capulet, who recognized his voice. Tybalt possessed a fiery and passionate temper. He was angry to think that a Montague would hide himself behind a mask in order to make fun of the Capulet's feast. He stormed about, enraged, and would have struck young Romeo dead—if he could have. But his uncle, the old Lord Capulet, would not allow Tybalt to cause a scene in front of his guests. In fact, if it had not been for the fact that Romeo was a Montague, the old man might have considered him fondly. The young man had always behaved like a gentleman, and everyone in Verona spoke of him as a virtuous and self-controlled youth. Tybalt, forced to be patient against his will, was not so gracious. Though he restrained himself, he swore that this vile Montague should at another time dearly pay for his intrusion.

The dancing being done, Romeo watched the place where the lady stood and, under the cover of his mask, presumed in the gentlest manner to take her by the hand, calling it a shrine, which, he declared, if it were profaned by his touching it, he would consider himself a blushing pilgrim and would kiss it for atonement.

"Good pilgrim," answered the lady, "your devotion is by far too mannerly and too courtly. Even saints have hands, which pilgrims may touch but not kiss."

"Saints have lips and so do pilgrims, do they not?" said Romeo.

"Ay," said the lady, "lips which they must use in prayer."

"Oh then, my dear saint," said Romeo, "hear my prayer and grant it, or else I will despair."

They were in the middle of this pleasant conversation when the lady was called away by her mother. Romeo, inquiring who her mother was, discovered that the lady whose peerless beauty he was so stricken with, was young Juliet, daughter and heir to the Lord Capulet—the great enemy of the Montagues. He had unknowingly engaged his heart to his foe. This troubled him, but it could not discourage him from loving.

Juliet found herself in the same position when she discovered the gentleman whom she had been talking with was Romeo—a Montague. She, too, had been suddenly smitten with the same hasty and unfortunate passion for Romeo that he had felt for her. It was a prodigious birth of love—it seemed to her—that she must love her enemy and that her affections should settle where family considerations should induce her chiefly to hate.

It being midnight, Romeo departed with his companions, but soon they noticed that he was no longer with them. Unable to stay away from the place where he had left his heart, Romeo leaped the wall of an orchard at the back of Juliet's house. Here he was waiting, thinking about his new love, when

Juliet appeared at an upstairs window. Her exceeding beauty seemed to break like the light of the sun in the east. The moon, which shone in the orchard with a faint light, appeared to Romeo as if sick and pale with grief at the superior luster of this new sun. As she leaned her cheek upon her hand, he passionately wished himself a glove upon that hand that he might touch her cheek.

She—all the while—was thinking to herself and with a deep sigh exclaimed, "Ah me!"

Romeo, enraptured to hear her speak, said so softly that the lady could not hear, "O speak again, bright angel, for such you appear, being above my head like a winged messenger from heaven whom mortals fall back to gaze upon."

Full of the new passion which that night's adventure had given birth to, Juliet called upon her lover by name (though she had no idea he was near), "O Romeo, Romeo!" she said, "wherefore art thou Romeo? Deny thy father and refuse thy name for my sake. Or if thou wilt not, be but my sworn love, and I no longer will be a Capulet."

Encouraged by her words, Romeo would have spoken, but he wanted to hear more, and the lady seemed ready to continue her passionate discourse with herself. She began again to chide him for being Romeo and a Montague at that. She wished him to have some other name or be willing to put away such a hated name for that name which was no part of himself so that he could take her for his wife.

Romeo, listening carefully to her words, could not keep himself from responding, as if the words had purposely been addressed to him and not just spoken in fancy. He asked her to call him "Love" or by any other words she liked, for he was no longer Romeo, if that name was displeasing to her.

Juliet, alarmed to hear a man's voice in the garden, did not at first know who it was—it seemed that the night had somehow stumbled upon her secret. But then, Romeo spoke again. Though she had heard fewer than a hundred words from his tongue, yet the voice was so sweet to her ears that she immediately knew it was young Romeo. First, she scolded him about exposing himself to danger by climbing the orchard wall. If any of her kinsmen had found him there, they would have killed him just because he was a Montague, she pointed out.

"Alack," said Romeo, "there is more peril in your eye than in twenty of their swords. Should you but look kindly upon me, lady, their enmity cannot touch me. Besides, I would rather my life be ended by their hatred than that I should live long without your love."

"What brings you here," said Juliet, "and by whose direction?"

"Love directed me," answered Romeo, "I am no pilot, yet if you were as far away from me as that vast shore that is washed by the farthest sea, I should still think it worthwhile."

A crimson blush came over Juliet's face, though the night was too dark for Romeo to see. She reflected for a moment on the discovery she had now made—though she had had no intention of doing so. She was in love with Romeo. She might have recalled her words, but that was impossible. She might also have stood upon form and kept her lover at a distance, as is the custom of discreet ladies who like to give their suitors harsh denials at first, standing aloof and affecting an attitude of coyness and indifference—even where love is strong—in order that their lovers not think them too lightly or too easily won, believing that the difficulty of attainment increases the value of the object. But there was no room in this case for denials or putting off or any of the customary games of delay and protracted courtship. Romeo had heard a confession of her love from her own tongue—when she did not dream he was even near. So with an honest frankness, which the novelty of her situation excused, she confirmed the truth of what he had heard. Addressing him by the name of "fair Montague" (love can sweeten a sour name), she begged him not to impute her easy yielding to levity or an unworthy mind, but that he must lay the fault of it (if it were a fault) upon the accident of the night that had so strangely discovered her thoughts. And she added, that though her behavior to him might not be sufficiently prudent, measured by the custom of her sex, she would yet prove more true than many whose prudence was false and modesty artificial cunning.

Romeo was beginning to call the heavens to witness that nothing was farther from his thoughts than to impute a shadow of dishonor to such an honored lady, when she stopped him. Juliet begged him not to swear; for although she took joy in his words, yet she was apprehensive about that night's contract—it was too rash, too unadvised, too sudden. But he did not back away and urged her to exchange a vow of love with him that night. She reminded him that she already had given him hers before he requested it. She was referring to the confession he had overheard. However, she expressed her willingness to retract what she had bestowed for the pleasure of giving it again—for her bounty was as infinite as the sea and her love as deep.

Juliet was then called away from this loving conference by her nurse, who slept with her and thought it time for her to be in bed—it was, after all, nearly daybreak. She left the window but hastily returned and spoke a few more words to Romeo. This is the gift of the words she spoke: "If your love is indeed honorable and you are proposing marriage, I will send a messenger to you tomorrow to appoint a time for our marriage. At that time I will lay all my fortunes at your feet and follow you as my lord through the world." While they were settling this point, Juliet was repeatedly called by her nurse and went back and forth many times. She seemed as reluctant to see Romeo go from her as a young girl of her bird, which she lets hop a little from her hand and then pulls it back with a silken thread—and Romeo was just as loathe to depart from her, for the sweetest music to a lover is the sound of his lover's voice at night. Nevertheless, they parted at last, wishing mutually sweet sleep and rest for the remainder of the night.

The day was breaking by the time Romeo departed, but he was too full of thoughts of Juliet to sleep, so instead of going home, he went to a nearby monastery to find Friar Lawrence. The good friar was already up, engaged in his devotions, but seeing young Romeo about so early, he wondered if the young man had even been to bed that night. *What manner of youthful affection has kept him awake,* he wondered. The friar was right to assign the cause of Romeo's wakefulness to love, but he made a wrong guess at the object, thinking it had been Rosaline. But when Romeo revealed his new passion for Juliet and requested the assistance of the friar to marry them that day, the holy man lifted up his eyes and hands in a sort of wonder at the sudden change in Romeo's affections. He had known of Romeo's love for Rosaline and heard his many complaints about how badly she had treated him. He reminded Romeo that young men's love lay not truly in their hearts but in their eyes. But Romeo answered that the friar himself had often chided him for doting on Rosaline, who could not love him in return, whereas Juliet both loved and was beloved by him. The friar assented in some measure to Romeo's reasoning. Besides, he couldn't help thinking that a matrimonial alliance between young Juliet and Romeo might be the means of making up the long breach between the Capulets and the Montagues. No one lamented this feud more than this good friar, who was a friend to both families and had often urged them to make up—though to no avail. Moved partly by this motive and partly by his fondness for young Romeo—to whom he could deny nothing—the old man consented to join their hands in marriage.

Now Romeo was blessed indeed, and Juliet, who knew his intent from a messenger whom she had dispatched just as she had promised, went early to the cell of Friar Lawrence, where her hand was joined with Romeo's in holy marriage. The good friar prayed the heavens would smile upon that act and that in the union of this young Montague and young Capulet, their families would be able to bury the old strife and dissensions between them.

When the ceremony was over, Juliet hurried home and waited impatiently for the coming of night. At that time, Romeo had promised to come and meet her in the orchard, where they had met the night before. For

Juliet, the night passed as slowly as the night before some great festival seems to an impatient child who has new clothes that cannot be put on until morning.

That same day, about noon, Romeo's friends Benvolio and Mercutio, walking through the streets of Verona, were met by a group of the Capulets with the impetuous Tybalt leading the way. This was the same angry Tybalt who had wanted to fight with Romeo at old Lord Capulet's feast. He, seeing Mercutio, accused him bluntly of associating with Romeo—a Montague. Mercutio, who had as much fire and youthful blood in him as Tybalt, replied sharply to this accusation. Benvolio tried to calm them both down, but the quarrel was quickly escalating when Romeo happened to pass by. The fiercely angry Tybalt turned from Mercutio to Romeo and called him a villain.

Romeo did not want to quarrel with Tybalt, because Tybalt was Juliet's kinsman and much beloved by her. Besides, Romeo was by nature wise and gentle. He had never thoroughly entered into the family quarrel, and the Capulet name was now his dear lady's name, so it seemed now to be more of a charm to allay resentment than a watchword to excite fury. For these reasons, Romeo tried to reason with Tybalt, whom he saluted mildly by the name of "good Capulet." It was as if he, though a Montague, had some secret pleasure in uttering that name. But Tybalt, who hated all Montagues as he hated hell, would hear no reason and drew his weapon.

Mercutio knew nothing of his friend's secret motive for desiring peace with Tybalt, however. He interpreted Romeo's actions as a sort of calm, dishonorable submission, and, therefore, began to further provoke Tybalt with many disdainful words, until he had drawn the quarrel back to himself and away from Romeo.

Romeo and Benvolio tried in vain to part the combatants, but Tybalt and Mercutio were determined to fight—and fight they did until

Mercutio fell dead from his wounds. When Romeo saw that Mercutio was dead, he could no longer control his temper. He began to call Tybalt by the same disparaging name he had at first called him—villain. They fought bitterly until Romeo had slain Tybalt—and this deadly fight happened in the middle of Verona in broad daylight. News traveled quickly and a group of citizens gathered on the spot. Among them were the old lords Capulet and Montague and their wives. Soon the prince himself arrived. He was related to Mercutio, whom Tybalt had slain, and besides, he had grown impatient with the frequent brawls between the Capulets and the Montagues. He was determined, this time, to prosecute the offenders to the full extent of the law. Benvolio, an eyewitness to the fray, was commanded by the prince to relate what had happened, which he did, keeping as near the truth as he could without implicating Romeo, and he also softened the part that his friends had played in it.

Lady Capulet, grieving for the loss her kinsman Tybalt to the point of vengeance, urged the prince to bring strict justice upon the head of the murderer and disregard Benvolio's version of the events, since he was Romeo's friend and, after all, a Montague. She pleaded long and hard, never realizing that Romeo was her new son-in-law and Juliet's husband. Lady Montague was equally as passionate in pleading for her child's life and arguing, with some truth, that Romeo had done nothing worthy of punishment in taking the life of Tybalt, who was already a murderer himself, having slain Mercutio. The prince was unmoved by the passionate exclamations of the women, however. He made a careful examination of the facts and pronounced his sentence that Romeo was to be banished from Verona.

This was heart-breaking news for young Juliet. She had been a new bride for no more than a few hours, and now by this decree, it seemed she would be everlastingly divorced! When the tidings reached her, she at first gave way to rage against Romeo. He had slain her dear cousin, whom she called a beautiful tyrant, a fiend angelical, a ravenous dove, a lamb with a wolf's nature, a serpent-heart hid with a flowering face, and other similar contradictory names, which denoted the struggles in her mind between her love and her anger. In the end, love got the mastery—the tears of grief she had shed for her cousin Tybalt turned to drops of joy that her husband had not been slain. Then came fresh tears—altogether tears of grief for Romeo's banishment. That word was more terrible to her than the death of many Tybalts.

Romeo, after the deadly battle, had taken refuge in Friar Lawrence's cell, where he first learned of the prince's sentence—to him it seemed far more terrible than death. Romeo could see no world outside Verona's walls, no living without Juliet. Heaven was where Juliet lived, and everything beyond was purgatory, torture, hell. The good friar would have consoled the young man with philosophy, but Romeo was far too frantic to listen. He became like a madman, tearing his hair and throwing himself on the ground. He exclaimed that he might as well be dead.

Romeo was in this very state when he received a message from his dear lady. Hearing from Juliet revived him a little, enough for the friar to let him know that his actions were showing him to be weak and unmanly. He had slain Tybalt—now was he ready to slay himself and his dear lady as well? The noble form of man, he said, was but a shape of wax, when it lacked the courage needed to keep it firm. In truth, the law had been lenient to him. Instead of pronouncing a death sentence, the prince had only chosen to banish him, noting that had he not slain Tybalt, he would himself have been slain. There was, the friar reminded Romeo, a sort of happiness in that. Juliet was alive and (beyond all hope) had become his dear wife, and that also was a happy circumstance. The sullen, misbehaving Romeo dismissed all these blessings, however. At this, the friar warned Romeo that those who languish in despair end up dying miserably.

When Romeo was a little calmed, the friar counseled him that he should go that night and secretly say good-bye to Juliet. From there, he should head for Mantua and stay there until the friar found a good opportunity to reveal the news of his marriage, which might be a joyful means of reconciling their families. He added that it might also be that the prince, at that time, might choose to pardon him, allowing him to return with twenty times more joy than the grief with which he departed.

Romeo was convinced by the friar's arguments and left to find Juliet. He hoped to stay with her that night and leave for Mantua in the morning. The good friar promised to send him letters from time to time, acquainting him with the state of affairs at home.

Romeo spent that night with his dear wife, gaining secret admission to her chamber from the orchard in which he had heard her confession of love only the night before. That had been a night of unmixed joy and rapture; but the pleasures of this night, and the delight these lovers took in each other's company, were sadly diminished by the prospect of parting and the fatal adventures of the past day. The unwelcome daybreak seemed to come too soon, and when Juliet heard the morning song of the lark, she would have persuaded herself that it was the nightingale, which sings by night. But it was too truly the lark that sang, and a discordant and unpleasing note it seemed to her. The streaks of day in the east too certainly pointed out that it was time for these lovers to part. Romeo took his leave of his dear wife with a heavy heart, promising to write her from Mantua every hour in the day. When he had descended from her chamber window, Juliet looked down at him below her on the ground, and in that sad foreboding state of mind in which she was, he appeared to her as one dead in the bottom of a tomb. Romeo's mind was unsettled in like manner, but now he was forced to depart quickly. It would have been death for him to be found within the walls of Verona after daybreak.

This was but the beginning of the tragedy of this pair of star-crossed lovers. Romeo had not been gone many days before the old Lord Capulet proposed a match for Juliet. The husband he had chosen for her, not dreaming that she was married already, was Count Paris, a gallant, young, and noble gentleman. He would have been a worthy suitor to the young Juliet—if only she had never seen Romeo.

The terrified Juliet was sadly perplexed by her father's offer. She pleaded her youth unsuitable to marriage and argued that the recent death of Tybalt had left her spirits too weak to meet a husband with any joy on her face. It would reflect badly on the Capulets to be celebrating a nuptial feast when their kinsman's funeral services were barely over. She raised every argument she could think of against the match, without mentioning the true one, namely, that she was already married. But Lord Capulet was deaf to all her excuses and in a peremptory manner ordered her to get ready, for by the following Thursday she should be married to Paris. Thinking her putting on an affected coyness, as was the custom, he insisted that she should stop throwing up obstacles to her good fortune and be thankful that a rich, young, and noble husband, such as the proudest maid in Verona might joyfully accept, had been found for her.

At last, Juliet applied to the friendly friar, always her counselor in distress. He asked if she would agree to undertake a desperate remedy, to which she answered that she would go into the grave alive rather than marry Paris, while her own dear husband was living. He directed her to go home, appear merry, and give her consent to marry Paris, according to her father's desire. On the next night, which was the night before the marriage, he instructed her to drink of the contents of a phial, which he then gave her. The effect would be that for forty-two hours after drinking it, she should appear cold and lifeless. When the bridegroom came to fetch her in the morning, he would think her dead. She would be carried, as the manner in that country was, uncovered on a bier to be buried in the family vault. He urged her that if she could put off womanish fear and consent to this terrible trial, she would in forty-two hours after

swallowing the liquid (such was its certain operation) awaken, as from a
dream. Before that time, the friar promised to send a message to Romeo
letting him know of the plan and telling him to come in the night and carry
her back to Mantua. Love—and the dread of marrying Paris—gave young
Juliet strength to undertake this horrible adventure. She took the phial of the
friar and promised to observe his directions.

Going from the monastery, she met the young Count Paris and modestly
playing along, promised to become his bride. This was joyful news to the Lord
Capulet and his wife. It seemed to put new life into the old man; and Juliet,
who had displeased him exceedingly by her refusal of the count, became his
darling again by promising to be obedient. All things in the house were in
a bustle in anticipation of the approaching wedding. No cost was spared to
prepare for the most lavish event Verona had ever witnessed.

On the Wednesday night agreed upon, Juliet drank the potion from the
phial. She had many misgivings, wondering if the friar, anxious to avoid the
blame for marrying her to Romeo, might have given her poison. But, she
reasoned, he had always been known as a holy man. She also worried that she
might awaken before the time Romeo was to come for her and find herself
lying terrified in a vault of dead Capulets' bones, including those of Tybalt,
who would be still bloody and festering in his shroud. And if that wasn't
enough to drive her to distraction, she thought of all the stories she had heard
of spirits haunting the places where their bodies were kept. But then her love
for Romeo and her aversion to marrying Paris returned, and she desperately
swallowed the potion and lapsed unconscious.

When young Paris came early in the morning with music to awaken his
bride, her chamber presented the dreary spectacle of a lifeless corpse rather
than a living Juliet. What death to his hopes! What confusion then reigned
through the whole house! Poor Paris, lamenting his bride whom death had
taken from him, had divorced from him even before their hands were joined.
But it was still more piteous to hear the mourning of the old Lord and Lady

Capulet, who had but this one poor loving child to rejoice and solace in. Now, cruel death had snatched her from their sight, just as these careful parents were on the point of seeing her become the recipient (as they thought) of a promising and advantageous match. Now everything that had been planned for the marriage party would have to be used for a black funeral instead. The wedding cheer changed to sadness as the wedding dinner became a burial feast, the bridal hymns were exchanged for sullen dirges, the sprightly instruments gave way to melancholy bells, and the flowers that should have been strewed in the bride's path, were now strewn about her corpse. Now, instead of a priest to marry her, a priest was needed to bury her, and she was borne to church indeed, not to add to the cheerful hopes of the living, but to swell the dreary numbers of the dead.

Bad news, which always travels faster than good, now brought the dismal story of Juliet's death to Romeo at Mantua before the messenger—sent by Friar Lawrence—could arrive to apprise him that this was a mock funeral only—just the shadow and representation of death—and that his dear lady lay in the tomb but for a short while, expecting Romeo to come and release her from that dreary mansion.

Just before, Romeo had been unusually joyful and light-hearted. He had dreamed in the night that he was dead (a strange dream that gave a dead man leave to think) and that his lady came and found him dead and breathed such life with kisses in his lips that he revived and was an emperor! When the messenger came from Verona, he thought surely it was to confirm some good news, of which his dreams had been a premonition. But when the contrary appeared and he read that his lady was dead in truth, whom he could not revive by any kisses, he ordered horses to be got ready, for he was determined to visit Verona that very night and see his lady in her tomb.

Mischief being swift to enter into the thoughts of desperate men, he called to mind a poor pharmacist, whose shop in Mantua he had lately passed. From the beggarly appearance of the man, who seemed famished, and the condition of his shop—rows of empty boxes arranged on dirty shelves and other tokens of financial desperation—he had said at the time (perhaps because he worried he might become desperate in his own disastrous life), "If a man were to need poison, which by the law of Mantua it is death to sell, this poor man might be desperate enough to sell it him." These words of his now came into his mind, and he sought out the pharmacist. The man pretended at first that the task was against his scruples, but when Romeo offered him gold—a commodity his poverty could not resist—he willingly sold him a poison that he warned was so strong that should it be swallowed, it would easily kill even a man with the strength of twenty.

With this poison, he set out for Verona to visit the tomb of his dear lady. He intended to view Juliet's body and then swallow the poison, hoping to be buried by her side. He reached Verona at midnight and located the church-yard, in the midst of which was situated the ancient tomb of the Capulets. Romeo had brought along a light, a shovel, and a crowbar and had started breaking up the monument, when he was interrupted by a voice, which referring to Romeo by the name of "vile Montague," ordered him to desist from his unlawful business. It was the young Count Paris. He had come to Juliet's tomb at that unseasonable time of night to strew flowers and weep over the grave of the woman who should have been his bride. He had no idea what Romeo's interest was in the dead. He only knew him to be a Montague and (as he supposed) a sworn enemy of all the Capulets, intending perhaps to inflict some villainous shame on the dead bodies. Therefore, in an angry tone, he ordered Romeo to desist; and since Romeo was a criminal condemned by the laws of Verona to die if he were found within the walls of the city, Count Paris moved to apprehend him. Romeo urged the man to leave him alone and warned him by the fate of Tybalt, who lay buried there, not to provoke his anger or draw down another sin upon his head by forcing Romeo to kill him. But the count in scorn refused his warning and laid hands on him as a felon. Romeo resisted, the two men fought, and Paris fell.

When Romeo, by the help of a light, came to see that it was Paris he had slain—the one he learned on his way from Mantua should have married Juliet—he took the dead youth by the hand, as one whom misfortune had made a companion, and determined that he would bury him in a triumphal grave—meaning Juliet's—which he now opened. There lay his lady, as one whom death had no power upon to change a feature or complexion, preserved in her matchless beauty, or as if Death, the lean abhorred monster, kept her there for its own delight. She lay yet fresh and blooming, as if she had only fallen asleep when she swallowed that benumbing potion. Near her lay Tybalt in his bloody shroud. When Romeo saw him, he begged pardon of his lifeless corpse and for Juliet's sake called him "cousin" and said that he was about to do him a favor by putting his enemy to death. Here Romeo kissed his lady's lips one last time and shaking the burden of his cross stars from his weary body, swallowed the poison that the pharmacist had sold him. This poison was indeed fatal and real, not like that deceptive potion Juliet had swallowed. Romeo was now dying—just as Juliet was about to awaken to complain that her beloved had come on time or that he had come too soon.

Now the hour arrived at which the friar had promised that Juliet should awaken. Desperate after learning that the letters he had sent to Mantua, by some unlucky delay of the messenger, had never reached Romeo, went himself to the tomb with a pickaxe and lantern to deliver the lady from her prison. He was surprised to find a light already burning in the Capulets' monument, swords and blood nearby, and Romeo and Paris lying breathless on the ground.

Before he could imagine how all this could have happened, Juliet awoke out of her trance, and seeing the friar near her remembered where she was and why she was there. She asked for Romeo, but the friar, hearing a noise, told her to come out of that place of death and unnatural sleep, for a greater power than they could imagine had thwarted their plans. Then the friar, frightened by the noise of people coming, fled. When Juliet saw the cup closed in her true love's hand, she guessed that poison had killed him. She would have swallowed the last of the cup had there been any. She kissed his still warm lips to see if any poison clung to them, then hearing people coming, she quickly unsheathed the dagger she was wearing and stabbed herself. There she died by her true Romeo's side.

The crowd by this time had made its way to the tomb. They had been alerted by a page belonging to Count Paris, who had witnessed the fight between his master and Romeo. The alarm spread quickly among the citizens, who went up and down the streets of Verona confusedly exclaiming, "A Paris! A Romeo! A Juliet!" as the rumor had imperfectly reached them. The uproar soon brought Lord Montague and Lord Capulet out of their beds, as well as the prince, to inquire into the cause of the disturbance. The friar had been apprehended by some of the people coming from the churchyard. He was trembling, sighing, and weeping in a suspicious manner. A great crowd assembled at the Capulets' monument, and the prince demanded that the friar explain what he knew of these strange and disastrous deaths.

So there in the presence of the old Lord Montague and Lord Capulet and the town's people, he faithfully related the story of Romeo and Juliet's fatal love, his part in promoting their marriage in the hope that their union would end the long quarrels between their families, and how Romeo, there dead, was the husband of Juliet and Juliet, there dead, was Romeo's faithful wife. He explained to them that before he could find an opportunity to reveal their marriage, another match was made for Juliet, who, in order to avoid the crime of a second marriage, swallowed the sleeping potion (as he advised). He told them that when all thought her dead, he had written to Romeo, telling him to come and take her away with him once the force of the potion had worn off, and how, unfortunately, the messenger was delayed and the letter never reached Romeo. More than this, the friar said that he did not know. He had himself come to deliver Juliet from the tomb when he found Count Paris and Romeo slain. The remainder of the story was provided by the page who had seen Paris and Romeo fight and by the servant who came with Romeo from Verona, to whom this faithful lover had given letters to be delivered to his father in the event of his death. These confirmed the friar's words, confessing his marriage with Juliet, imploring the forgiveness of his parents, acknowledging the buying of the poison from the poor pharmacist, and describing his intent in coming to the monument to die and lie with Juliet. All these circumstances agreed together to clear the friar from any hand he could be supposed to have had in these complicated deaths, further than the unintended consequences of his own well-intended, yet flawed intrigue.

The prince, turning to the old Lord Montague and Lord Capulet, rebuked them for their brutal and irrational hatred and pointed out what a scourge Heaven had laid upon such offences, that it had found means even through the love of their children to punish their unnatural hate. And these old rivals, no longer enemies, agreed to bury their long strife in their children's graves. Lord Capulet requested that Lord Montague give him his hand, calling him by the name of brother as if in acknowledgment of the union of their families by the marriage of the young Capulet and Montague. He stated that Lord Montague's hand (in token of reconcilement) was all he demanded for his daughter's estate; but Lord Montague said he would give him more. He was in fact determined to raise a statue to her of pure gold. As long as Verona kept its name, he asserted, no figure would be so esteemed for its richness and workmanship as that of the true and faithful Juliet. And Lord Capulet in return said that he would raise another statue to Romeo. So did these poor old lords—when it was too late—strive to outdo each other in mutual courtesies. So deadly had been their rage and enmity in past times that nothing but the fearful overthrow of their children (poor sacrifices to their quarrels and dissensions) could remove the rooted hates and jealousies of these noble families.

C. S. LEWIS: THROUGH THE SHADOWLANDS

BRIAN SIBLEY

AN EXCERPT

The story of the love between C. S. Lewis and Joy Davidman Gresham is a curious one. At first glance, it seems hard to imagine two less likely lovers than they: Lewis, a sixty-year-old British bachelor don with a reputation for being the greatest Christian thinker, teacher, and writer of our time, and Joy, an American Jewish divorcée who had been a youthful member of the Communist party and who later became an adult convert to Christianity.

There is, however, no doubt at all that they were deeply, passionately in love. "We feasted on love," said Lewis, "every mode of it—solemn and merry, romantic and realistic, sometimes as dramatic as a thunderstorm, sometimes as comfortable and unemphatic as putting on your soft slippers."

Joy Davidman Gresham had sought every avenue of spiritual enlighten-ment before God met her in a time of severe crisis. "All my defenses—the walls of arrogance and cocksureness and self-love behind which I had hid from God—went down momentarily. And God came in," she said. Along with her husband, Bill, Joy began rereading authors whose beliefs they had previously shunned or dismissed, and in particular the writings of C. S. Lewis. She began to write to C. S. (Jack) Lewis, and but for the remarkably cogent nature of her letters, she might have been considered "just another American fan."

Lewis was in the habit of responding to all his mail personally, and he maintained a lifelong correspondence with a number of those who wrote to him. The same became the case with Joy Davidman. The two finally met in person when Joy traveled to London on vacation with another of her pen *pals, Phyllis Williams. Together, they invited Lewis to have lunch with them, and a deep friendship quickly developed.*

It was on that very vacation that Joy's marriage came apart at the seams. Her husband, also a writer, had greeted his professional disappointments with drink and risky living, but this was even worse. A letter arrived stating that he had fallen in love with someone else. He wanted a divorce so that they could be married. He hoped she would also find "some really nice guy." A short time later, Joy sailed for America to try to mend her troubled marriage, but her husband was determined. He filed for divorce in 1954 and married his other woman on the day it was final.

Joy, in hope of starting a new life for herself and her boys, decided to move to London permanently. It was there that she had experienced the first true happiness in many years. Her friendship with Jack Lewis grew over time. Eventually they fell in love.

But there was another problem for the couple. Lewis belonged to the Church of England, which did not approve marriage to a divorced person. Would God find a way?

In 1956, Joy faced a crisis. The British Home Office refused to renew her visitor's visa, which meant that she and the boys would have to uproot themselves once more and return to America.

There was only one way in which Joy's expulsion could be avoided and that was if she could somehow acquire British citizenship. The obvious way in which she could do that was to marry a British subject. It is not known how Jack found out about this solution—whether he made legal enquiries himself, or whether Joy informed him. Whichever was the case, Jack decided to marry Joy.

Jack may have been anticipating the likelihood of such an event for some months, for in the autumn of 1955, he wrote enigmatically to his old friend

Arthur Greeves, ". . . The other affair remains where it did. I don't feel the point about a 'false position.' Everyone whom it concerned would be told. The 'reality' would be from my point of view, adultery and therefore mustn't happen. (An easy resolution when one doesn't in the least want it!)"

On 23 April 1956, Jack and Joy were married at the Registry Office in Oxford. Two days later, Jack told Roger Lancelyn Green about the marriage, saying that it was "a pure matter of friendship and expediency" and that his solicitor had drawn up a legal document stating the reasons for the marriage having taken place.

Writing later, in his diary, about the secret wedding, Warnie [Jack's brother] noted that Jack had assured him "Joy would continue to occupy her own house as 'Mrs. Gresham,' and that the marriage was a pure formality designed to give Joy the right to go on living in England: and I saw the uselessness of disabusing him."

Then a fresh problem arose. For some reason, Joy was given notice to quit her house. Although Jack didn't really regard the civil ceremony they had gone through as, in any sense, a Christian marriage (and despite the concern that his relationship with Joy should not become an adulterous one), he decided that Joy and her sons would have to live with him. "All arrangements had been made," wrote Warnie, "for the installation of the family at The Kilns, when disaster overtook us."

Late on the evening of 18 October 1956, Katherine Farrer had a sudden premonition that something was wrong with Joy. She dashed to the telephone and began to dial her friend's number. Before it could ring, Joy—who was carrying a tray of tea things in from the kitchen—tripped over the telephone wire and fell. Joy felt the bone in her leg snap and a surge of excruciating pain. She was incapable of moving, but beside her on the floor was the telephone receiver and at the other end the anxious voice of Katherine Farrer.

Joy was rushed to the Wingfield-Morris Orthopaedic Hospital and her broken leg was examined. For some while Joy had been in pain with what she presumed to be rheumatism. As the months had passed, the pain had worsened. But it was not, she now discovered, rheumatism. It was cancer.

The disease had eaten through her left femur and so weakened the bone that, when she fell, it had snapped like a dry stick. There was also a malignant lump in her breast.

For Jack it marked the return of a grisly spectre from the past. Listening to the doctor's doomful diagnosis, all the anguish and terror of his mother's illness and death must have come flooding back to him.

"No one," Jack once observed, "can mark the exact moment at which friendship becomes love." This however, was as good a moment as any; as he tried to take in the fact that he might soon be parted from Joy, so he began to realize just how agonizing that parting would be for him.

Jack insisted that the seriousness of Joy's condition should not be kept from her: "I would allow no lies to be told to a grown-up and a Christian. As you may imagine," he wrote to a friend, "new beauty and new tragedy have entered my life. You would be surprised (or perhaps you would not?) to know how much of a strange sort of happiness and even gaiety there is between us."

Now, when Joy was physically at her least attractive, she won Jack's heart. "Years ago," Jack wrote, "when I wrote about medieval love-poetry and described its strange, half make-believe, 'religion of love,' I was blind enough to treat this as an almost purely literary phenomenon. I know better now."

Jack's love for Joy—and the pain which was part of it—deepened with every passing day. He wrote to his old friend Arthur Greeves: "It will be a great tragedy for me to lose her," and to another friend: "I can hardly describe to you the state of mind I live in at present—except that all emotion, with me, is periodically drowned in sheer tiredness, deep lakes of stupor."

Shortly before the storm had broken, Jack had published *The Last Battle*, the seventh and final Chronicle of Narnia; in it the characters come, at last, to a paradise garden:

". . . They found themselves facing great golden gates. And for a moment none of them was bold enough to try if the gates would open. . . . 'Dare we? Is it right? Can it be meant for us?'

"But while they were standing thus, a great horn, wonderfully loud and sweet, blew from somewhere inside that walled garden and the gates swung open."

***

"A marriage has taken place between Professor C. S. Lewis, of Magdalene College, Cambridge, and Mrs. Joy Gresham, now a patient in the Churchill Hospital, Oxford. It is requested that no letters be sent."

This announcement appeared in the personal column of the Times on Christmas Eve, 1956.

Joy had been moved to the Churchill Hospital earlier in December after having three major operations. Jack began to prepare for whatever might follow. David and Douglas were moved into the Kilns, and Jack decided that he wanted to publicly confirm the private formality of his marriage to Joy.

It was probably around this time (although Warnie recalls it as happening earlier) that the Bishop of Oxford was approached and asked to grant the necessary permission for Jack and Joy to receive a Christian marriage.

In November, while Joy was still undergoing operations, Jack told the American lady with whom he regularly corresponded: "I may soon be, in rapid succession, a bridegroom and a widower. There may, in fact, be a deathbed marriage."

But the bishop of Oxford refused to sanction the marriage. . . . The official position of the Church of England was, as it still is, that remarriage by a divorced person is, according to Scripture, an act of adultery. It is, therefore, impossible for the church to approve of such a union, let alone bless it with the sacrament of marriage.

However insensitive—even intolerant—such a ruling may seem, the

Bishop of Oxford had no choice but to refuse. To make an exception in the case of so eminent a Christian as C. S. Lewis was obviously unthinkable.

Jack was left with no alternative but to make public the fact that he was, anyway, legally married to Joy. In a letter to Arthur Greeves, Jack explained, "If she gets over this bout, and emerges from the hospital, she will no longer be fit to live alone so she must come and live here. That means (in order to avoid scandal) that our marriage must shortly be published." A few weeks later, Jack placed his carefully worded announcement to the Times.

Concluding his letter to Arthur, Jack wrote: "I know you will pray for her and for me: and for Warnie, to whom also, the loss if we lose her, will be great."

Warnie had, some time before, overcome his reservations about Joy and now felt a strong brotherly affection for her. "I have never loved her more," he wrote in his diary, "than since she was struck down; her pluck and cheerfulness are beyond praise, and she talks to her disease and its fluctuations as if she was describing the experiences of a friend of hers. God grant that she may recover."

But Joy did not recover. By the following March, when she was once again in the Wingfield Hospital undergoing radiation treatment, her condition had so far deteriorated that Warnie recorded in his diary, "One of the most painful days of my life. Sentence of death has been passed on Joy, and the end is only a matter of time."

Joy now had feelings of terrible despair: "I am in rather a bad state of mind as yet," she wrote to friends, "they had promised me definitely that the x-rays would work; I'd pinned all my hopes to having a year or so of happiness with Jack at least—and indeed it seems I shall lie about in the hospital with my broken femur waiting for death, and unable to do anything to make my last shred of life useful or bearable. . . . I am trying very hard to hold on to my faith, but I find it difficult; there seems such a gratuitous and merciless cruelty in this. . . . I hope all we have believed is true. I dare not now hope for anything in this world."

Encouraged and supported by Jack, Joy rallied a little; enough, in fact, to write again to her friends: "I feel now that I can bear, not too unhappily, whatever is to come, and the problem of pain just doesn't loom so large—I'm not at all sure I didn't deserve it after all, and I'm pretty sure that in some way I need it. . . . Jack pointed out to me that we were wrong in trying to accept utter hopelessness; uncertainty is what God has given us for a cross."

Although Joy described everything as looking "much brighter than it did before," her condition was still worsening. Since there was nothing that the doctors could now do for Joy, and since Jack was determined that she should not have to face death in a hospital, he asked for permission to take her home. The request was granted.

There remained, however, the question of whether or not they were married in the sight of God. It has been suggested (by Warnie among others) that the civil marriage ceremony had meant far more to Jack at the time than a mere act of charity. But if this had been the case, then the couple would have seen no obstacle to their now living together as man and wife. As it was, they both considered it essential that their union be blessed by God.

A solution to the problem came quiet unexpectedly, when Jack invited a friend and former student, Peter Bide, to visit the Kilns. As a priest, Peter Bide had several times had experiences that led him to believe that he possessed the gift of Christian healing. He had confided these experiences to Jack and discussed with him the concept of faith healing.

Jack had an open mind on the subject. He considered praying for the sick to be "unquestionably right," but was cautious about prayers accompanied by anointing or laying on of hands: "Whether any individual Christian who attempts Faith Healing," he once wrote, "is prompted by genuine faith and charity or by spiritual pride is, I take it, a question we cannot decide. That is between God and him. Whether the cure occurs in any given case is clearly a question for the doctor."

What led him to the opinion that Peter Bide possessed a God-given gift was that the young man was extremely reticent about claiming to have performed miracles and had such a strong sense of his own unworthiness that he could not possibly have been accused of spiritual pride. Jack asked him to lay hands on Joy and pray for her recovery.

When Peter Bide agreed, Jack raised the question of the marriage. He had no right, of course, to ask Father Bide to perform a service the bishop himself had refused to conduct, but Jack was desperate to make what looked like Joy's final days as bearable as possible.

Writing, many years later, to Joy's biographer, Father Bide explained: "It did not seem to me in the circumstances, possible to refuse her the outward and visible sign of grace which she so ardently desired and which might lead to a peaceful end to a fairly desperate situation." The decision to marry Jack and Joy according to the service of the Church of England prayer book was, as Warnie described it, "a notable act of charity." If for no other reason than because Peter Bide must have known that the action would earn the severe displeasure not only of his own bishop, but of a bishop to whose diocese he did not even belong.

The marriage took place in the stark, sanitized setting of the Wingfield Hospital at eleven o'clock in the morning of Thursday, 21 March 1957. The bride lay propped up on pillows and the bridegroom sat on the side of the bed while the sad little ceremony was conducted by Father Bide and watched by Warnie and one of the nursing sisters who attended Joy.

There was a terrible poignancy about the exchange of vows, as Jack and Joy promised to be faithful to each other "for better for worse, for richer for poorer, in sickness and in health, to love and to cherish, till death us do part."

"I found it heartrending," wrote Warnie, "especially Joy's eagerness for the pitiable consolation of dying under the same roof as Jack; though to feel pity for anyone so magnificently brave as Joy is almost an insult." After the marriage, Father Bide laid his hands on Joy and prayed for her recovery.

Jack knew just how hopeless Joy's condition was, but he would not have been human if he hadn't entertained a hope, however feeble, that she might be healed. Did he perhaps recall the words he'd written ten years before in *Miracles*? "We must not picture destiny as a film unrolling for the most part on its own, but in which our prayers are sometimes allowed to insert additional items. On the contrary; what the film displays to us as it unrolls already contains the results of our prayers and of all our other acts. There is no question *whether* an event has happened because of your prayer. When the event you prayed for occurs your prayer has always contributed to it. When the opposite event occurs your prayer has never been ignored; it has been considered and refused, for your ultimate good and the good of the whole universe."

A week after the marriage, Joy was taken home to the Kilns by ambulance and installed in the sitting room. "Every moment," wrote Jack, "is spent at her bedside," despite the fact that a resident hospital nurse was in attendance. A month later, Jack was writing to a friend that he was leading "the life of a hospital orderly, and have hardly time to say my prayer or eat my meals."

A few weeks after Joy's homecoming, Jack was writing to Roger Lancelyn Green: "Joy is completely bedridden . . . but, thank God, no pain, sleeping well, and often in good spirits." Jack, however, was in pain. He had prayed that God would let him bear some of Joy's discomfort for her. Not long afterwards, Joy began to find relief while Jack developed excruciating pains in his legs. The doctors diagnosed Jack to be suffering from calcium deficiency: "No one suggests that the disease is either curable or fatal. It normally accompanies that fatal disease we call senility, but no one knows why I have got it so early in life," at the same time Joy—who needed calcium badly—was found to be making more.

But Jack remained cautious about Joy's slight improvement in condition. "Though the doctors hold out no ultimate hope," he wrote in May, "the progress of the disease does seem to be temporarily arrested to a degree they never expected. There is little pain, often none, her strength increases and she eats and sleeps well. This has the paradoxical result of giving her lower spirits and less peace. The more general health, of course, the stronger the instinctive will to live. Forbidden and torturing hopes will intrude on us both. In short, a dungeon is never harder to bear than when the door is open and the sunshine and birdsong float in."

As the months passed, their hopes continued to build: "Joy is to all appearances (blessedly or heartbreakingly) well and anyone but a doctor would feel sure she was recovering."

Soon, however, the doctors themselves were wondering whether Joy's condition might not be improving. The cancer, it seemed, had been arrested: the diseased spots in the bone were no longer multiplying. Then, as Jack put it, "the tide began to turn," the cancerous spots began to disappear, and new bone was being made.

By September, Joy was up and sitting in an invalid chair. Two months later she wrote, in a letter to Bill [her former husband], that she could "now climb two or three stairs, walk fifty feet or so, sit nearly normally, and use the John like the big folks—and no small triumph that!" She was given a raised shoe and by December was walking about the house and garden: "limping," wrote Jack, "and with a stick, but walking." This was real, undoubted progress and Jack was forced to accept that, however unlikely, Joy was recovering. "She even found herself getting up unconsciously to answer the telephone the other day. It is the unconsciousness that is the real triumph—the body that would not obey the most planned volition now begins to act on its own. Of course, the sword of Damocles still hangs over us; or should I say, we are forced to be aware of the sword which really hangs over all mortals?"

By March 1958, Joy's condition was still improving. Roger Lancelyn Green dined at the Kilns and recorded in his diary that Joy was "up and about, miraculous as it seems."

In a letter to friends, Joy wrote: "My case is now arrested for the time being. I may be alright for three or four years. . . . Jack and I are managing to be surprisingly happy considering the circumstances: you'd think we were a honeymooning couple in our early twenties, rather than our middle-aged selves." They took a few days away together, about which Jack happily remarked: "I'm such a confirmed bachelor that I couldn't help feeling I was being rather naughty ('staying with a woman at a hotel!' Just like people in the newspapers!)"

Just as their love for each other had been heightened by the threat of separation, so now it was given a new intensity by Joy's reprieve. "Do you know," Jack told friends, "I am experiencing what I thought would never be mine. I never thought I would have in my sixties the happiness that passed me by in my twenties." Joy simply observed that "the movies and the poets are right: it does exist!"

"There were never two people alive in the history of the world," says Douglas Gresham [Joy's son], "who were more in love than Jack and Joy."

Joy also gave Jack the benefit of her sharp mind: in conversation, to his great delight, she would often deflate his pomposity and cut him down to size. Douglas Gresham recalls one occasion when Jack was holding forth at great length at the dinner table and Joy cut in with a request that he "shut up and pass the pedanticide!"

To Jack's writing she brought a fresh, incisive critical approach that, on his own admission, helped him greatly with both *Reflections on the Psalms* and *The Four Loves.*

Reflections, Jack's first "religious" book in ten years, particularly benefited from the insights into Judaism which Joy gave him, and in a sense he could never have written *The Four Loves* if he had not fallen in love with, and married, Joy. Of *Reflections,* the *Church Times* said: "He has never written better. Nearly every page scintillates with observations which are illuminating, provocative and original." Certainly, Jack had never written with more maturity, tempering intellect with emotion, reason with experience:

"Our quarrels provide a very good example of the way in which the

Christian and Jewish conceptions differ, while yet both should be kept in mind. As Christians we must of course repent of all this anger, malice and self-will which allowed the discussion to become, on our side, a quarrel at all. But there is also the question on a far lower level: Did we pretend to be angry about one thing when we knew, or could have known, that our anger had a different and much less presentable cause? Did we pretend to be 'hurt' in our sensitive and tender feelings when envy, ungratified vanity, or thwarted self-will was our real trouble? Such tactics often succeed. The other parties give in. They give in not because they have long known it only too well, and that sleeping dog can be roused, that skeleton brought out of its cupboard, only at the cost of imperiling their whole relationship with us—and so we win; by cheating. But the unfairness is very deeply felt. Indeed what is commonly called 'sensitiveness' is the most powerful engine of domestic tyranny, sometimes a lifelong tyranny."

There was, of course, nothing new about Joy showing an interest in Jack's work: she had done that from the time she had first come to live in England. Now, out of love (and gratitude) she extended that interest to the rest of Jack's life. She took over the management of his finances which—since he was hopeless at dealing with money—were utterly disorganized. Although he had no great fortune, Jack would often lose track of income from royalties, and be quite convinced that he was practically destitute while large forgotten sums (once as much as £900) were lying, unprofitably, in a current account at the bank.

Joy also began to improve the quality of life at the Kilns. For years the Lewises' bachelor premises had been so disreputable they had been referred to by Oxford friends as "the Midden" (a Middle-English word literally meaning "dung heap"): "Nothing has been done for thirty years," wrote Joy. "The walls and floors are full of holes; the carpets are tattered rags—in fact, the house is being held up by the books that line the walls and if we ever move a bookcase All Fall Down!"

But all did not fall down. Joy was soon having some "cautious painting and repair done." Holes in the roof were mended, and the central heating system, which had not been used since the war, was gotten going again. Joy spent a little money on furnishings and curtains (always pretending that they had cost vast sums in order to outrage Jack, when they had invariably been purchased at sales), and generally made the Kilns not merely habitable, but homey.

Writing to Roger Lancelyn Green in May 1958, Joy told him: "The Kilns is now a real home, with paint on the walls, ceiling properly repaired, clean sheets on the beds—we can receive and put up several guests. . . . I've got a fence round the woods and all the trespassers chased away! We'd love a visit."

Joy's renovations were also extended to Jack's wardrobe, which was purged of the torn jackets, battered hats, and elbowless pullovers which he was wont to wear. Although Jack occasionally feigned irritation and annoyance, he was secretly delighted by the transformation wrought by Joy. For the first time in years, he and Warnie were living in comfort.

Most of Jack's old friends accepted this new lifestyle of his because they could see the happiness and fulfillment it had brought him. However, some felt that in marrying Joy Gresham, Jack had betrayed their friendship and his own principles. Tolkien, particularly, found the whole thing "very strange." As a devout Catholic, he was deeply shocked to hear that his closest friend had entered into a marriage with a divorced person. He was also hurt at hearing the news from someone other than Jack himself, especially since he had taken Jack into his confidence about problems within his own marriage.

In July, Jack took Joy on a belated honeymoon to Wales and then to see the green hills and misty mountains of Ireland. They went by air (sea travel being thought too hazardous for Joy). "It was the first flight either of us had ever experienced," wrote Jack, "and we found it—after our initial moment of terror—enchanting. The cloudscape seen from above is a new world of beauty—and then the rifts in the clouds through which one sees 'a glimpse of that dark world where I was born'. . . ."

Joy adored Ireland. "We had a heavenly time," she told Bill in a letter, "beautiful sunny weather, miraculous golden light over everything, clear air in which the mountains glowed like jewels . . . there's a good deal of austerity in its beauty, but it is the most beautiful place I've ever seen."

They visited Louth, Down, and Donegal and returned, wrote Jack, "drunk with blue mountains, yellow beaches, dark fuchsia, breaking waves, braying donkeys, peat-smell, and the heather just beginning to bloom."

The days following Joy's recovery were filled with happiness—made all the sweeter for having been pried from the clutches of death. For both of them, life and love had been touched and transformed by a Deeper Magic from before the Dawn of Time.

***

In January 1959, readers of *The Atlantic Monthly* would have come across an article by C. S. Lewis on "The Efficacy of Prayer": "I have stood," he wrote, "by the bedside of a woman whose thigh-bone was eaten through with cancer and who had thriving colonies of disease in many other bones as well. It took three people to move her in bed. The doctors predicted a few months of life: the nurses (who often know better), a few weeks. A good man laid his hands on her and prayed. A year later the patient was walking (uphill, too, through rough woodland) and the man who took the last x-ray photos was saying, 'These bones are as solid as rock. It's miraculous.'"

And so, indeed, it seemed. By the autumn Joy was walking distances of up to a mile with relative ease. There were still a few small holes in her bones, and the pain was invariably present. "It's not easy," she explained, "walking about with one thigh more than three inches shorter than the other." Yet she was "miraculously well and active." The hospital, she told Bill, "tell me I'm one of their great triumphs and exhibit me to visiting doctors. . . ."

In October 1959, almost two years after the cancer had begun to disappear, Joy went to the hospital for a routine x-ray. "This last check," wrote

Jack, "is the only one we approached without dread. Her health seemed so complete." But, in fact, the x-rays showed that the cancer had returned.

The recovery, it appeared, was not really a recovery at all. It was, Jack wrote to his American lady friend, "only a reprieve, not a pardon. There seems," he continued, "to be some hope of a few years life still and there are still things the doctors can do. But they are in the nature of 'rear-guard actions.' We are in retreat." Then, using a phrase he had used so differently only months before: "The tide has turned. Of course, God can do again what He did before. The sky is not now so dark as when I married her in hospital. Her courage is wonderful and she gives me more support than I can give her."

The cancerous spots and lumps were in evidence again—so much so that Joy jokingly observed: "I've got so many cancers at work on me that I expect them to start organizing a union." And by March 1960, three years after the hospital wedding ceremony, those cancers were no longer responding to the radiation treatment.

Jack had once described his and Joy's existence as being lived under the sword of Damocles—the sword which, according to legend, was suspended by nothing more than a human hair. It was now only a matter of time before the hair snapped.

**

Although the cancer was continuing to spread throughout her body, Joy fought hard against it. A combination of faith and willpower drove her on. She had also one burning ambition still to be fulfilled: to recapture the happiness of her honeymoon with Jack on another holiday. This holiday, however, would be somewhat further afield than the Emerald Isle—Joy wanted, more than anything, to visit Greece.

"Fair Greece!" wrote Byron, "sad relic of departed worth! Immortal, though no more; though fallen, great!" A fitting place, perhaps, for a final odyssey.

In 1959, the Lewises' friends June and Roger Lancelyn Green had toured

Greece and, on their return, enthused so much that Jack said if they were
to go again, he and Joy would like to go with them. Later that year, Roger
booked the four of them onto a "Wings" tour for the following spring.

Although Jack had loved the tales of Ancient Greece since boyhood, he
had never felt any desire to visit the land of their origin; to do so might detract
from his imagined conception of the place. He had, in fact, shunned foreign
travel altogether and had left the British Isles only twice in his life: once for
a holiday near Dieppe when he was eight, and later during his war service in
France. Now, however, Jack wanted to do everything he could to make what he
felt sure were Joy's dying days as happy and memorable as he could.

Although careful not to communicate it, Jack must have felt consider-
able anxiety at the prospect of taking a very sick person on such a strenuous
journey. Since he was himself suffering from osteoporosis and high blood
pressure, he was hardly in any condition to cope if Joy were to be taken
suddenly ill. It was of the greatest importance, therefore, that the holiday
was going to be taken in company with understanding friends who would be
willing and able to help if the need arose. Jack could scarcely have chosen two
better traveling companions.

Roger Lancelyn Green had first visited Greece when he was an
undergraduate at Merton College. He had fallen under the spell of the land
and its literature and later wrote novels for children set in Ancient Greece
as well as publishing his own masterly retelling of the great myths, Tales of
the Greek Heroes. Roger's vivacious wife, June, a well-read and entertaining
conversationalist, was an ideal companion for Joy.

With the return of the cancer, the holiday became less certain. Jack
tried to remain hopeful, and in the same letter in which he had described
to Roger Joy's recapture by the Giant, he wrote: "Whether a second miracle
will be vouchsafed us, or, if not, when the sentence will be inflicted, remains
uncertain. It is quite possible she may be able to do the Greek trip next
spring. Pray for us."

By March 1960, Jack was clearly very worried. He told Arthur Greeves, in a letter that "cancer is returning in almost every part of her skeleton. They do something with radiotherapy, but as soon as they have silenced an ache in one place, one breaks out in another. The doctors hold out no hope of a cure. We hope to do a lightning trip to Greece by air this vacation. We hardly dare to look as far ahead as next summer."

Although the odds were now heavily stacked against her, Joy struggled on. When spring came round, it found her all the more determined to make the visit. Cheerfully disregarding the doctors' warning that to go to Greece would be taking "a big chance," she wrote to Bill: "I'd rather go out with a bang than a whimper, particularly on the steps of the Parthenon!"

On Sunday, 3 April 1960, the Lewises and the Greens were seen off at London Airport by Douglas. In a small Viking plane, they traveled via Lyon, Naples, and Brindisi to Athens.

***

Shortly before his death, Jack reflected on the time in Greece, telling Father Walter Hooper: "Joy knew she was dying, I knew she was dying, and she knew I knew she was dying—but when we heard the shepherds playing their flutes in the hills, it seemed to make no difference."

Here in this earthly paradise garden, they stood upon the very frontier of Aslan's country; how effortless it seemed to contemplate saying farewell to the shadowlands.

The holiday drew to an end, and the four friends flew home via Pisa, arriving in London on 14 April. Concluding his diary of the holiday, Roger Lancelyn Green wrote: "My last sight of Joy was of Jack wheeling her briskly in an invalid chair towards the waiting car."

Despite the anxieties and some problems, the trip had been a great success. In a letter to his publisher, Jocelyn Gibb, Jack wrote: "Greece was wonderful. We badly need a word meaning 'the-exact-opposite-of-a-disappointment.' Appointment won't do!" Five days after their return, Jack wrote to his American lady correspondent saying how difficult he found it to describe Greece: "Attica is hauntingly beautiful and Rhodes is an earthly paradise—all orange and lemon orchards and wild flowers and vines and olives, and the mountains of Asia on the horizon. . . ." Joy he described as being "very exhausted and full of aches. But I would not have had her denied it. The condemned man is allowed his favorite breakfast even if it is indigestible. She was absolutely enraptured by what she saw. But pray for us: the sky grows very dark. . . ."

Joy's condition now began to deteriorate quickly, making their time in Greece all the more precious to them. Writing to Chad Walsh, Jack said that Joy had come back "in a nunc dimittis frame of mind, having realized, beyond hope, her greatest, lifelong, this-worldly desire." There had been, however, "a heavy price to pay in increased lameness and leg-pains: not that her exertions had or could have any effect on the course of cancer, but that the muscles etc, had been overtaxed. Since then there has been a recrudescence of the original growth in the right breast which started the whole trouble. It had to be removed last Friday—or, as she characteristically put it, she was 'made an Amazon.' This operation went through, thank God, with greater ease than we had dared to hope."

Joy's mastectomy was carried out on 30 May, just five weeks after she and Jack returned from Greece. Two weeks later she was home again and, as her jesting description of the operation suggests, was in good sprits. Warnie described her as having "emerged from the ordeal radiant," and the surgeons spoke in encouraging terms of her condition.

Although confined once more to a wheelchair, Joy refused to sit back and wait to die. She kept up her correspondence, giving helpful advice to Bill, who was planning a visit to Oxford in the autumn, and got Warnie to push her to the library and out into the Kilns' garden so that she could inspect the flower beds and greenhouse.

Then, suddenly, Joy was taken ill once more. For several days she had been complaining of indigestion. When it got worse and was accompanied by retching and vomiting, the doctor was called in and diagnosed her suffering as a gastric infection. During the night of Sunday, 19 June, she became much worse and by the middle of the next morning told her nurse "This is the end, I know now I'm dying. Telegraph for Doug."

The end, it seemed, had finally come. A week later however, Warnie was writing: "Once again Joy has made fools of the doctors and nurses." She had recovered and was home again, "but all the time there is the grim knowledge that it cannot be more than a reprieve." Nevertheless, Douglas returned to school where, as head prefect, he had to take part in the end-of-term service.

A few days later, Joy and Jack had Sunday lunch at Studley Priory Hotel. The following day she was taken for a car ride into the Cotswolds. For Jack and Warnie, anxiety was tempered with the kind of optimism that is so often born of desperation.

On the night of 12 July, Warnie took tea in to Jack and Joy in the downstairs room that had become Joy's bedroom: "I found her looking remarkably better, and she herself said she felt much more comfortable . . . when I left her she was playing Scrabble with Jack; and before I dropped off to sleep they sounded as if they were reading a play together."

Later Jack was to write: "How long, how tranquilly, how nourishingly, we talked together the last night!" Joy had once said to Jack, "Even if we both died at exactly the same moment, as we lie here side by side, it would be just as much a separation as the one you're so afraid of." Later, perhaps on this very night, Jack asked her: "If you can—if it is allowed—come to me when I too am on my death bed." "Allowed!" she replied, "heaven would have a job to hold me; and as for hell, I'd break it into bits." "She knew," wrote Jack, "she was speaking a kind of mythological language, with an element of comedy in it. There was a twinkle as well as a tear in her eye. But there was no myth and no joke about the will, deeper than any feeling, that flashed through her."

At 6:15 on the morning of Wednesday, 13 July, Warnie was awakened by terrible screams. Downstairs, he found Joy writhing in agony. He roused Jack, and the doctor was called. Within an hour, drugs were being pumped into her but, due to her tremendous resistance, did little more than make her drowsy.

The next few hours were a frenzy of activity as Jack tried unsuccessfully to get Joy admitted to a hospital. Finally, he succeeded in persuading her surgeon to give her a bed in his private ward at the Radcliffe Infirmary. At 1:30, the ambulance arrived, and Jack traveled with Joy to the hospital.

What a rabble of memories must have crowded into Jack's mind during that journey. Was this really the man who, just a handful of years before, had remarked that he could not understand why anyone should choose to marry a woman, since every topic of conversation would be used up in the first six months? Strange then that but a few days ago he should have written with such passion and such anguish:

> All this rhetoric about loving you.
> I never had a selfless thought since I was born.
> I am mercenary and self-seeking through and through:
> I want God, you, all friends, merely to serve my turn.
>
> Peace, re-assurance, pleasure, are the goals I seek,
> I cannot crawl one inch outside my proper skin:
> I talk of love—a scholar's parrot may talk Greek—
> But, self-imprisoned, always end where I begin.
>
> Only that now you have taught me (but how late) my lack.
> I see the chasm. And everything you are was making
> My heart into a bridge by which I might get back
> From exile, and grow a man. And now the bridge is breaking. . . .

He called the poem, "As the Ruin Falls." It ends:

> For this I bless you as the ruin falls. The pains
> You give me are more precious than all other gains.

The afternoon and evening passed gently with Joy dozing. When she was awake, however, she was fully aware of all that was happening. She asked Jack to give her fur coat as a parting gift to Katherine Farrer, and told him that she wanted Austin Farrer to read her funeral service. She asked to be cremated, adding, "Don't get me a posh coffin; posh coffins are all rot."

As the evening wore on, the surgeon called Jack from the room. Joy, he told him, was now rapidly dying. When Jack went back to her, he told her that the end was near; it was, she replied, the best news they could now have.

Then Austin Farrer gave Joy final Absolution: "Almighty God, our heavenly Father, who of his great mercy hath promised forgiveness of sins to all them that with hearty repentance and true faith turn unto him: Have mercy upon you; pardon and deliver you from all your sins; confirm and strengthen you in all goodness; and bring you to everlasting life; through Jesus Christ our Lord. . . ."

Turning to Jack, Joy told him, 'You have made me happy." Then, a little while after, "I am at peace with God."

Joy died at 10:15 that evening.

"She smiled," Jack later recalled, "but not at me."

***

Monday, 18 July 1960—the day of Joy's funeral—was, wrote Warnie, "a sunny, blustering day, with big white clouds." It was, as Warnie recalled it, in "a nice, simple, sunlit chapel, with 'thank God' no music." . . . It was a heartbreaking affair, and a pathetic exit for such a vibrant, courageous soul. "At the end," concluded Warnie, "the coffin was withdrawn and curtains, pulled invisibly, hid it from us for ever. There is no doubt that cremation is the most dignified ending; Joy really has become dust, returned to dust in clean sunlight.

They left the chapel at Headington Crematorium and made their way back to the cars; past the trees and flower beds of the garden of remembrance. Years earlier Jack had written, in answer to a question from one of his correspondents, that he preferred "trees to flowers in the sense that if I had to live in a world without one or the other, I'd choose to keep the trees. I certainly prefer tree-like people to flower-like people—the staunch and knotty and storm-enduring kind to the frilly and fragrant and easily withered." In Joy he had endured the storms while other friends had withered away.

Jack began to try to go on living. It was anything but easy. He had once glibly remarked, "There is nothing discreditable in dying: I've know the most respectable people to do it!" But with his grief," says Douglas, "he suffered his grief—he suffered enormously with it. Sometimes, someone would bring up a reference to Mrs. Lewis, and Jack would burst into floods of uncontrollable tears."

"I not only live each endless day in grief," he wrote, "but I live each day thinking about living each day in grief . . . what am I to do?" The answer, for a writer, was to write. Day by day he began to record his feelings and emotions: "By writing it all down (all?—no: one thought in a hundred) I believe I get a little outside it."

Here, in the anonymous pages of a child's exercise book, the Christian apologist was free to express his doubts, the great teacher able to ask unanswerable questions:

"I look up at the night sky. Is anything more certain than that in all those vast times and spaces, if I were allowed to search them, I should nowhere find her face, her voice, her touch? She died. She is dead. Is the word so difficult to learn?"

But it was difficult to learn, and except for his work—"Where the machine seems to run on much as usual"—the difficulty of accepting Joy's death left him physically and mentally exhausted. Except for his jottings about grief, he was unable to write. He found it impossible to read, and simple daily tasks, such as shaving, seemed burdensome and unnecessary.

Then, suddenly, there would be times when it seemed to Jack that he might get over his grief, when the voice of common sense reminded him that he had been happy before he had met Joy, and insisted that he would, one day soon, be happy again. But the memory of what he had lost always returned: the commonsense arguments vanished "like an ant in the mouth of a furnace" and Jack was once more reduced to "a whimpering child."

"My heart and body are crying out, come back, come back—but I know this is impossible. I know that the thing I want I can never get. The old life, the jokes, the arguments, the love-making, the tiny, heartbreaking commonplace."

It was this desperate yearning that he wrote of in a poem, cryptically titled "Joys That Sting":

> To take the old walks alone, or not at all,
> To order one pint where I ordered two,
> To think of, and then not to make, the small
> Time-honored joke (senseless to all but you);
> To laugh (oh, one'll laugh), to talk upon
> Themes that we talked upon when you were there,
> To make some poor pretence of going on,
> Be kind to one's old friends, and seem to care,
> While no one (O God) through the years will say
> The simplest, common word in just your way.

People expected Jack to find consolation in his faith, but he couldn't: "Talk to me about the truth of religion and I'll listen gladly. Talk to me about the duty of religion and I'll listen submissively. But don't come talking to me about the consolations of religion or I shall suspect that you don't understand." Time and again he constructed complex arguments of faith only to find them demolished by his grief as if they were no more than a house of cards.

A door had been slammed shut, locked, barred, and double-bolted (or so it seemed) from the inside. No amount of knocking brought a reply. Jack found that he did not even have a good photograph of Joy by which to remember her, and while the face of a stranger passed in the street would return suddenly and vividly to his mind, he could not properly recall the face of the woman he loved. His attempts to pray to God about Joy were like "speaking into a vacuum about a nonentity." It was a vacuum sucked out by Jack's anger and bitterness towards God:

"What chokes every prayer and every hope is the memory of all the prayers we offered and all the false hopes we had. Not hopes raised merely by our own wishful thinking; hopes encouraged, even forced upon us, by false diagnoses, by x-ray photographs, by strange remissions, by one temporary recovery that might have ranked as a miracle. Step by step we were 'led up the garden path.' Time after time, when He seemed most gracious He was really preparing the next torture."

Jack had arrived, more by anguish than by logic, at an extraordinary theory: supposing God were bad? Supposing men were nothing more than rats trapped in the laboratory of a mad celestial vivisectionist?

The idea was conceived in the passion of pain—it was, said Jack, "a yell rather than a thought"—but it had to be argued through nevertheless. "Is it rational," he asked, "to believe in a bad God? Anyway, in a God so bad as all that? The Cosmic Sadist, the spiteful imbecile?" No, he decided, it was not. To do so would be to wipe God off the slate, and there would then be "no motive for obeying Him. Not even fear. If cruelty is from this point of view 'good.' . . . what He calls 'Heaven' might well be what we should call Hell, and vice-versa."

Many of Jack's admirers would have been deeply shocked if they had known that he had even entertained such doubts, or admitted such fears. In a sense, it shocked Jack himself—"Why do I make room in my mind for such filth and nonsense?"—but it was only by confronting his worst imaginings that he could overcome them.

Day by day, as he wrote about his grief, his conception of God began to change. There was nothing in the nature of God's dealing with him that was experimental: "God has not been trying an experiment on my faith or love, in order to find out their quality. He knew it already. It was I who didn't. In this trial He makes us occupy the dock, the witness box, and the bench all at once. He always knew my temple was a house of cards. His only way of making me realize the fact was to knock it down."

A note of peace began to enter the writings with which he had now filled three exercise books: "I have gradually been coming to feel that the door is no longer shut and bolted. Was it my own frantic need that slammed it in my face? The time when there is nothing at all in your soul except a cry for help may be just the time when God can't give it: you are like a drowning man who can't be helped because he clutches and grabs. Perhaps your own reiterated cries deafen you to the voice you hoped to hear."

Two months after Joy's death, he wrote to his American lady correspondent who had asked how he took his sorrow: "the answer is 'In nearly all possible ways.' Because, as you probably know, it isn't a state but a process. It keeps on changing—like a winding road with quite a new landscape at each bend."

He had made, however, two important discoveries in traveling this road: one was his realization that the times when he most loudly called to God for help were when he never received it; the other was that "the moments at which I feel nearest to Joy are precisely those when I mourn her least." It was as if "clamorous need seems to shut one off from the thing needed. It is almost like 'Don't knock and it shall be opened to you'. . . ."

In the fourth and last exercise book he wrote: "These notes have been about myself, and about Joy, and about God. In that order. The order and the proportions exactly what they ought not to have been."

Once he had come to this conclusion, he suddenly found the door no longer locked. If God didn't answer his unanswerable human questions about suffering and grief it was, at least, "a rather special sort of 'No answer' . . . more like a silent, certainly not uncompassionate, gaze. As though He shook His head not in refusal but waiving the question. Like, 'Peace, child; you don't understand.'"

As Orual says at the end of *Till We Have Faces:* "I know now, Lord, why you utter no answer. Before your face questions die away. What other answer would suffice? Only words, words, words; to be led out to battle against other words. . . ."

Jack's expressions of raw emotion gave place to a logically argued, and poetically described, analysis of the nature of bereavement. When a loved one dies, he wrote, "we think of this as love cut short; like a dance stopped in mid career or flower with its head unluckily snapped off—something truncated and therefore, lacking its due shape," whereas it is really "a universal and integral part of our experience of love. It follows marriage as normally as marriage follows courtship or as autumn follows summer. It is not a truncation of the process but one of its phases; not the interruption of the dance but the next figure."

Bereavement, Jack decided, was a potentially dangerous state in which the bereaved can so easily "fall back to loving our past, or our memory, or our sorrow, or our relief from sorrow, or our own love."

With the restoration of his faith, Jack looked for a new way to describe Joy. He eventually adopted a much-loved simile; Joy he wrote was "like a garden. Like a nest of gardens, wall within wall, hedge within hedge, more secret, more full of fragrant and fertile life the further you entered. . . . In some way, in its unique way, like Him who made it." Then, at last, he was able to turn his gaze "from the garden to the Gardener. . . . To the life-giving Life and the Beauty that makes beautiful."

Jack began to rediscover a greater truth still, a truth of which he had written—twenty years before—in the mystical conclusion to *Perelandra:* "All that is made seems planless to the darkened mind, because there are more plans than it looked for. . . .So with the Great Dance. . . . plans without number interlock, and each movement becomes in its season the breaking flower of the whole design. . . . Set your eyes on one movement and it will lead you through all patterns and it will seem to you the master movement. But the seeming will be true. There seems no plan because it is all the plan: there seems no center because it is all center."

In September, Jack felt able to talk over some of his recent experiences with his friend Roger Lancelyn Green. He even told Roger that he had been writing about his feelings of grief, adding—under pledge of secrecy—that he might possibly publish what he had written, in the hope that it might help others in bereavement. This he did, in 1961, under the title *A Grief Observed;* Joy's identity was disguised by the initial H. (Joy's first name was Helen).

Jack had enjoyed a harmony with Joy: "The most precious gift that marriage gave me was this constant impact of something very close and intimate yet all the time unmistakably other, resilient—in a word, real. . . . No cranny of heart or body remained unsatisfied." They had been, as the Bible calls it, one flesh—or, as Jack described it, one ship.

The ship of their love had had a rough passage through cruel seas. The storms were over, but they had taken their toll: "The starboard engine has gone. I, the port engine, must chug along somehow till we make harbour. . . ."

***

It was the Unicorn who summed up what everyone was feeling. He stamped his right fore-hoof on the ground and neighed and then cried: "'I have come home at last! This is my real country! I belong here. This is the land I have been looking for all my life, though I never knew it till now. . . . Come further up, come further in!'"

It was five years since Jack had written *The Last Battle* and sent the characters of Narnia across the frontier into Aslan's country. In those five years, he had fallen in love with, married, and lost the woman whom he described as: "my daughter, my mother, my pupil and my teacher, my subject and my sovereign . . . my trusty comrade, friend, shipmate, fellow-soldier."

Like Jewel the Unicorn, Joy had now found her way to the land where she belonged. Jack, however, had been left in the shadowlands. He was sixty-three years old and had lived nine-tenths of his life without even knowing this woman who had turned his world upside down. Yet he could never now completely return to the life he had lived before. He wrote: "Did you ever know, dear, how much you took away with you when you left? You have stripped me even of my past, even of the things we never shared."

THE PATCH ON THE QUILT

SAPPER

FROM THE DINNER CLUB BY H. C. MCNEILE

"The trouble in my game," began the Actor, "is that the greatest plays can never be staged. There would be no money in them. The public demands a plot—a climax; after that the puppets cease strutting, the curtain rings down. But in life—in real life—there's no plot. It's just a series of anticlimaxes strung together like a patchwork quilt, until there comes the greatest anticlimax of all and the quilt is finished."

He passed his hand through his fast-graying hair, and stared for a moment or two at the fire. The Soldier was filling his pipe; the Writer, his legs stretched out in front of him, had his hands thrust deep in his trouser pockets.

"It's one of the patches in one of the quilts that my story is about," continued the Actor thoughtfully. "Just an episode in the life of a woman—or shall I say, just the life of a woman in an episode.

"You remember that play of mine—John Pendlesham's Wife?" He returned to the Barrister, who nodded.

"Very well," he answered. "Molly Travers was your leading lady."

"I was out of England," said the Soldier. "Never saw it."

"It's immaterial. The play itself has nothing to do with my story, except indirectly. But as you didn't see it, I will just explain this much. I, of course, was John Pendlesham—Molly was my wife, and the third act constituted what, in my opinion, was the finest piece of emotional acting that consummate actress has ever done in her career."

The Writer nodded. "I agree. She was superb."

"Night after night the fall of the curtain found her nearly fainting; night after night there was that breathless moment of utter silence followed by a perfect crash of applause. I am mentioning these old facts because her marvelous performance does concern my story directly—even though the play does not.

"We had been running about a month, I suppose, when my story begins. I had just come off the third act and was going to my dressing-room. For some reason, instead of going by the direct door that led into it from the stage, I went outside into the passage. There were some hands moving furniture or something.

"I think you've been behind at my theater. First you come to the swing doors out of the street, inside which the watch-dog sits demanding callers' business. Then there is another door, and beyond that there are three steps down to my room. And it was just as I was opening my door on that night that I happened to look round.

"Standing at the top of the three stairs was a woman who was staring at me. I only saw her for a moment; then the watch-dog intervened, and I went into my room. But I had seen her for a moment; I had seen her for long enough to get the look in her eyes.

"We get all sorts and conditions of people behind, as you'd expect—stage-struck girls, actors out of a shop, autograph hunters, beggars. And the watch-dog knew my invariable rule: only personal friends and people who had made an appointment by letter were allowed inside the second door. But a rule can not legislate for every case.

"Gad! you fellows, it's many years now since that night, but I can still feel, as clearly as if it were yesterday, the message in that girl's eyes. There had been hope and fear and pitiful entreaty: the look of one who had staked everything on a last desperate throw; the look of a mother who is fighting for her child. It was amazing; I couldn't understand it. As I stood just inside my door I couldn't have told you whether she was old or young, plain or pretty. And yet in that one fleeting second this vivid jumbled message had reached me.

"For a moment I hesitated, then I rang the bell for the watch-dog.

"'Who is that lady I saw outside there?' I asked, as he came in.

"'Won't give no name, sir,' he answered. 'Wants to see you, but I told her the rules.'

"Once again I hesitated; probably I'd exaggerated—put a totally false construction on her expression, probably she was looking for a job like the rest of them. And then I knew that I'd got to see that woman, and that I should have no peace of mind until I'd heard what she had to say. The watch-dog was regarding me curiously; plainly he could see no reason whatever for my hesitation. He was a matter-of-fact fellow, was the guardian of the door.

"'Show her in, I'll see her now.' I had my back to him, but I could feel his virtuous indignation. After all, rules are rules.

"'Now, sir?' he echoed.

"'Now; at once.'

"He went out, and I heard him go up the steps.

"'Mr. Trayne will see you. Come this way.'

"And then the door opened again, and I turned to face the woman. She was young—very young, dressed in a kind of cheap suburban frock. Her shoes had been good ones—once, now—well, however skillfully a patch is put on, it is still a patch. Her gloves showed traces of much needle and cotton; the little bag she carried was rubbed and frayed. And over the cheap suburban frock she had on a coat which was worn and threadbare.

"'It was good of you to see me, Mr. Trayne.'

"She was nervous and her voice shook a little, but she faced me quite steadily.

"'It's a very unusual thing for me to do,' I said. 'But I saw you at the top of the stairs, and . . .'

"'I know it's unusual,' she interrupted. 'The man outside there told me your rule. But believe me'—she was talking with more assurance now—'my reason for coming to see you is very unusual also.'

"I pulled up a chair for her. 'What is your reason?' I asked.

"She took a deep breath and began fumbling with her handkerchief.

"'I know you will think me mad,' she began, 'but I don't want to tell you my reason now. I want to wait until after the play is over, and I know you go on at once in the fourth act.'

"'You've seen the play, then?' I remarked.

"'I've seen the play,' was her somewhat astonishing answer, 'every night since the first.'

"'Every night!' I stared at her in surprise. "But . . .'

"I must have glanced at her clothes or something and she saw what was in my mind.

"'I suppose you think that I hardly look as if I could afford such luxuries.' She smiled faintly. 'I've only seen it from the gallery and pit, you know. And even that has meant that I've had to go without lunch. But—you see—it was necessary for me to see it: I had to. It was part of my plan—a necessary part.'

"'I don't want to seem dense,' I said gently, 'but I'm afraid I don't quite follow. How can seeing my play thirty-odd times be a necessary part of your plan?'

"'That's what I don't want to tell you now,' she repeated, and once more her hands began twisting nervously. 'I want to wait till afterward, when perhaps you'll—of your kindness—do as I ask you. Oh! Mr. Trayne—for God's sake, don't fail me!' She leaned forward beseechingly in her chair.

"'My dear child,' I answered quietly—I don't think she can have been much more than twenty, 'you haven't told me yet what you want me to do.'

"'I want you to come to a house in Kensington with me.'"

Once again the Actor paused and stared at the fire. Then he gave a short laugh.

"When she said that, I looked at her pretty sharply. Without appearing conceited or anything of that sort, one has occasionally in the course of one's career, received certain flattering attentions from charming women—

attentions which—er—one is tempted to conceal from one's wife."

"And for a moment, I must confess that the thought passed through my mind that this was one of those occasions. And it wasn't until the color rose to her face and stained it scarlet, that I realized that not only had I made a mistake, but that I had been foolish enough to let her see that I had.

"'My God!' she whispered, 'you don't think—you couldn't think—that I meant . . .'

"She rose and almost cowered away from me. 'Why, I'm married.'

"I refrained from remarking that the fact was hardly such a conclusive proof of the absurdity of my unspoken thought as she seemed to imagine. I merely bowed, and said a little formally: 'Please don't jump to conclusions. May I ask why you wish me to come to a house in Kensington with you?'

"The color ebbed away from her cheeks, and she sat down again.

"'That's the very thing I don't want to tell you, until you come,' she answered very low. 'I know it sounds absurd—it must sound so—it seems as if I were being unnecessarily mysterious. But I can't tell you, Mr. Trayne, I can't tell you . . . not yet. . . .'

"And then the call boy knocked, and I had to go on for the last act. In a way I suppose it was absurd of me—but life is made up of impulses. I confess that the whole thing intrigued me. When a woman comes and tells you that she has seen your play every night since it started; that she's had to go without her lunch to do so; that it was a necessary part of some wonderful plan and that she wants you to go to a house in Kensington, the least curious man would be attracted. And from my earliest infancy I've always been engrossed in other people's business.

"'All right,' I said briefly. 'I'll come with you.'

"And then I had to put out my hand to steady her, I thought she was going to faint. *Reaction*, I thought at the time; later, it struck me that the reason was much more prosaic—lack of food. I stopped for a moment till she seemed herself again; then I told her to wait outside.

"'I shall be about half an hour,' I said, 'and then we'll take a taxi, and go down to Kensington. Tell them to give you a chair. . . .'

"And my last impression as I went on to the stage was of a white-faced girl clutching the table, staring at me with great brown eyes that held in them a dawning triumph.

"I think," went on the Actor thoughtfully, "that that is where the tragedy of it all really lay. Afterward she told me that the part of her plan that had seemed most difficult to her was getting my consent to go with her to Kensington. Once that was done, she knew all would be well, she was absolutely and supremely confident. And when I went on to the stage for the fourth act, she felt that success had crowned her efforts, that what was to come after was nothing compared with that which she had already done. The inaccessible stronghold had been stormed, the ogre had proved to be a lamb.

"Well, we went to Kensington. I sent my own car home, and we took a taxi. During the drive she was very silent, and I didn't try to make her talk. Evidently no inkling of the mysterious plan was to be revealed until we arrived at the address she had given the driver. It was some obscure street that I had never heard of and the name of which I have completely forgotten. I know it was somewhere not far from Baker's.

"The door was opened by a repulsive-looking woman who peered at me suspiciously. And then the girl took her on one side and whispered something in her ear. Apparently it had the desired effect, as the gorgon retired, grumbling, to an odoriferous basement, leaving us alone in the hall.

"When she had shut the door the girl turned to me.

"'Will you come up-stairs, Mr. Trayne? I want you to meet my husband.'

"I bowed. 'Certainly,' I said, and she led the way.

"'So the husband is in the plan,' I reflected as I followed her. Was he a genius with a play that he proposed to read to me? I had suffered from the plays of genius before. Or was he some actor down on his luck? If so, why all the mystery? And then, when I'd made up my mind that it was a mere begging case, we arrived at the room. Just before she turned the handle of the door she again looked at me.

"'My husband is ill, Mr. Trayne. You'll excuse his being in bed.'

"Then we went in. Good Lord! you fellows," the Actor leaned forward in his chair. "I've been pretty hard up in the old days, but as I stood inside that door I realized for the first time what poverty—real poverty—meant. Mark you, the girl was a lady; the weak, cadaverous-looking fellow propped up in bed with a tattered shawl round his shoulders was a gentleman. And beyond the bed, and one chair, and a rickety old chest of drawers there wasn't a stick of furniture in the room. There was a curtain in the corner with what looked like a washstand behind it, and a shelf by the bed with two cups and some plates on it. And nothing else except an appalling oleograph of Queen Victoria on the wall.

"'This is Mr. Trayne, dear.' She was bending over her husband, and after a moment he looked up at me.

"'It was good of you to come, sir,' he said. 'Very good.' And then he turned to his wife and I heard him say: 'Have you told him yet, Kitty?'

"She shook her head. 'Not yet, darling, I will now.' She left his side and came over to me.

"'Mr. Trayne, I know you thought me very peculiar at the theater. But I was afraid that if I told you what I really wanted you'd have refused to come. You get hundreds and hundreds of people coming to see you who think they can act. Asking you to help them get a job and that sort of thing. Well, I was afraid that if I told you that that was what I wanted, you'd have told me to go away. Perhaps you'd have given me a straw of comfort—taken my address— said you'd let me know if anything turned up. But nothing would have turned up. . . . And you see, I was rather desperate.'

"The big brown eyes were fixed on me pleadingly, and somehow I didn't feel quite as annoyed as I should have done at what was nothing more nor less than a blatant trick to appeal to my sympathy.

"'Perhaps nothing would have turned up,' I said gently, 'but you must remember that to-day the stage is a hopelessly overstocked profession. There are hundreds of trained actors and actresses unable to obtain a job.'

"'I know that,' she cried eagerly, 'and that's why I—why I thought out this plan. I thought that if I could really convince you that I could act above the average . . .'

"'And she can, Mr. Trayne,' broke in her husband. 'She's good, I know it.'

"'We must leave Mr. Trayne to be the judge of that, Harry,' she smiled. 'You see,' she went on to me, 'what I felt was that there is an opening for real talent. There is, isn't there?

"'Yes,' I agreed slowly. 'There is an opening for real talent. But even that is a small one. Have you ever acted before?'

"'A little. In amateur theatricals!'

"I turned away. Amateur theatricals! More heartburning and disappointment has been caused by those abominable entertainments than their misguided originators will ever realize.

"'But don't think I'm relying on that.' The girl was speaking again, and I almost laughed. 'I want you to judge me to-night.'

"I swung around and looked at her. So this was the mysterious plan: I was to witness an impromptu performance, which was to convince me that the second Sarah Bernhardt had been discovered.

"'I couldn't have shown you, you see, in your dressing room. I shouldn't have had time. That's why I asked you to come here.'

"'You have the courage of your convictions anyway,' I said quietly. 'I am perfectly ready to be convinced.'

"'Then will you sit there.'

"She took off her hat and coat as I sat down on the only available chair, and from underneath his pillow the man produced a paper-covered book.

"'You'll forgive me if I read my lines, Mr. Trayne,' he said. 'I find I can't learn them—I can't concentrate.' He passed a thin emaciated hand over his forehead. 'And it's her you want to see.'

"He turned over the pages weakly; then he began to read. And I—I sat up as if I'd been stung. At last everything was clear: the continual visits to the theater—everything. The part of all other which they had selected to prove her ability, was the love-scene between Molly Travers and myself in the third act of *John Pendlesham's Wife*.

For a while there was silence.

"This unknown child," he went on after a moment, "who had acted a little in amateur theatricals, had deliberately challenged London's greatest emotional actress in her most marvelous success before, heaven help us, me—of all people. I suppose if I was writing a story I should say that she triumphed; that as I sat in that bare and hideous room I realized that before me was a genius—a second and greater Molly; that from that moment her foot was set on the ladder of fame, and there was no looking back."

The Actor laughed a little sadly. "Unfortunately, I'm not writing a story, I'm telling the truth. I don't know how I sat through the next twenty minutes. It was the most ghastly caricature of Molly that I have ever thought of; the more ghastly because it was so intensely unintentional. Every little gesture was faithfully copied; every little trick and mannerism had been carefully learned by heart. And this, as I say, to me who acted with that divine genius every night. God! it was awful. That marvelous line of Molly's, when, standing in the center of the stage facing me across the table, she said: 'Then you don't want me back?' that line which was made marvelous merely through the consummate restraint with which she said it, sounded from this poor child like a parlor-maid giving notice.

"And then, at last it was over, and I realized I had to say something. They were both staring at me, hope shining clear in the girl's eyes and pride in the man's.

"'She's great, isn't she, Mr. Trayne?' he said. 'I've not had the privilege of seeing you and Miss Travers in the part—but I feel that now—why,' he gave a little shaky laugh, 'that it's hardly necessary.'

"You see," said the Actor slowly, "that was the devil of it all. They were both so utterly certain, especially the man. The difficulty had been to get me there; after that it had been easy. I glanced at the poor fellow in the bed, and his thoughts were plain to read. No more grinding poverty, no more unfurnished bed-sitting rooms, and—fame for the woman he loved. And then he spoke again.

"'I'm such a hopeless crock, Mr. Trayne, and she'—he took one of her hands in both his own—'she's had to do all the work. Beastly grinding work in an office, when she was capable of this.'

"The girl bent over him, and I looked away. It seemed to me that the ground on which I stood was holy."

The Actor gave a short laugh which deceived no one. "I suppose I was an ass," he went on, "but I'd do it again to-day. 'It was wonderful,' I said, 'quite wonderful.' And because I'm an actor they believe me. Not that he, at any rate, required much convincing—he only wanted his knowledge confirmed. Of course, when I spoke I didn't realize what I was letting myself in for. I should have done, I suppose, but—I wasn't left long in doubt. If she was wonderful—and had not I, Herbert Trayne, said so?—what about a job? At once. . . . With my backing it was easy. . . . Which was all very true except for the one vital fact of my having lied. But, hang it, you fellows!" he exploded, "Could you have told 'em it was the most appalling exhibition of utter futility you'd ever witnessed?"

"No, I couldn't," said the Soldier. "What happened?"

"I can see them now," continued the Actor. "He was holding her hand and looking up into her face—as a dog looks at the being it adores. And she was smiling a little, and crying a little—tears of pure joy. The strain was over, the lunches had not been missed in vain. And I stood there like a dumb idiot racking my brains for something to say. They thought I was wondering what job to offer her; they were right, I was." The Actor laughed shortly.

"But I'd gone into the morass, and there was nothing for it but to blunder in deeper. The one vital essential was that in no circumstances the poor child ever be allowed to act. The other was money—and at once. So I offered her then and there the job as Molly Travers' understudy at five pounds a week."

"Great Scott!" The Doctor sat up with a jerk. "Understudy Molly?"

"I explained, of course," went on the Actor, "that there was an understudy already, and that to save unpleasantness it would be better if she didn't come to the theater, unless I sent for her. That, of course, it was more than likely that Miss Travers wouldn't be ill during the run of the play, and that in those circumstances I didn't want to offend the present understudy. And when another play came along, we must see what we could do. That, thank heaven, I knew was some way off yet! It gave me breathing space.

"I gave her a week's salary in advance, and I got away—somehow. I think they were both a little dazed with the wonder of it, and they wanted to be alone. I heard his voice—weak and quavering—as I shut the door.

"'Oh! my very dear girl,' he was whispering—and she was on her knees beside the bed. And I blundered my way down-stairs, cursing myself for a sentimental fool. There's whisky on the table, you fellows. Help yourselves."

But no one moved.

"I saw her occasionally during the next two or three months," he continued, "though I never went to their rooms again. They had moved—I knew that—because I used to post the check every week. But the few times I did see her, I gathered that her husband was not getting any better. And one day I insisted on Lawrence, the specialist, going to see him. I couldn't have one of my company being worried, I told her, over things of that sort. I can see her face now as I said 'one of my company.' I don't know what Lawrence said to her, but he rang me up at the theater that night, and he did not mince his words to me.

"'I give him a month,' he said. 'It's galloping consumption.'

"It was just about a month later that the thing happened which I had been dreading. Molly went down with the flu. Her understudy—the real one—was Violet Dorman, who was unknown then. And of course it was her chance."

"One moment," interrupted the Barrister. "Did any one at the theater know about this girl?"

"Good God! no," cried the Actor. "Not a soul. In this censorious world actions such as mine in that case are apt to be misconstrued, which alone was sufficient to make me keep it dark. No one knew.

"The first night—all was well. Molly went down in the afternoon, and it didn't come out in any of the evening papers. Violet acted magnificently. She wasn't Molly, of course—she isn't now. But it was her chance and she took it—and took it well. Next morning the papers, naturally, had it in. 'Temporary indisposition of Miss Molly Travers. Part filled at a moment's notice with great credit by Miss Violet Dorman.' She had a press agent and he boomed her for all he was worth. And I read the papers and cursed. Not that I grudged her her success in the slightest, but I was thinking of the afternoon. It was matinée day and the girl must read it in the papers.

"There was only one thing for it—to go round and see her. Whatever happened I had to prevent her coming to the theater. How I was going to do it without giving the show away I hadn't an idea, but somehow or other it had got to be done. My blundering foolishness—even though it had been for the best—had caused the trouble; it was up to me to try to right it. So I went round and found her with a doctor in the sitting-room. He was just going as I came in, and his face was grave.

"'Harry's dying,' she said to me quite simply, and I glanced at the doctor who nodded.

"Poor child! I crossed over to her side, and though it seems an awful thing to say, my only feeling was one of relief. After what Lawrence had said I knew it was hopeless, and since the poor devil had to go he couldn't have chosen a more opportune moment from my point of view. It solved the difficulty. If he was dying she couldn't come to the theater, and by the time the funeral was over Molly would be back. I didn't realize that one doesn't get out of things as easily as that.

"'I've only just realized how bad he was,' she went on in a flat dead voice.

"'Does he know?' I asked.

"'No. He thinks he's going to get better. Why didn't you send for me last night, Mr. Trayne?'

"It was so unexpected that I hesitated and stammered.

"'I couldn't get word to you in time,' I said finally. 'Miss Travers only became ill late in the afternoon.'

"'It says here,' she went on slowly, 'that she was confined to her bed all yesterday. Oh! It doesn't matter much, does it?' She put the paper down wearily, and gave the most heartrending little sobbing laugh I've ever heard.

"I was fingering a book on the table and for the life of me I couldn't think of anything to say. 'He doesn't know,' she went on. 'He still thinks I'm a God-sent genius. And he mustn't know.'

"'Why should he?' I said. And then I put my hand on her arm. 'Tell me, how did you find out?'

"'You admit it then?'

"'Yes,' I said quietly, 'I admit that I lied. I was so desperately sorry for you.'

"'I mentioned it to some one—a man who knew the stage—about a week ago. He looked at me in blank amazement, and then he laughed. I suppose he couldn't help it; it was so ridiculous. I was furious—furious. But afterward I began to think, and I asked other people one or two questions—and then that came,' she pointed to the paper, 'and I knew. And now—oh! He's dying. He mustn't know, Mr. Trayne, he mustn't.'

"And at that moment he came into the room—tottered in is a better word.

"'Boy,' she cried in an agony, 'what are you doing?'

"'I thought I heard Mr. Trayne's voice,' he whispered, collapsing in the chair. 'I'm much better to-day, much. Bit weak still—'

"And then he saw the paper, and he leaned forward eagerly.

"'Ill,' he cried. 'Molly Travers ill. Why, my dear—but it's your chance.'

He read on a bit, and she looked at me desperately. 'But why weren't you there last night? Who is this woman, Violet Dorman?'

"'You see, Tracy,' I said, picking up the paper and putting it out of his reach, "it was so sudden, Miss Travers' illness, that I couldn't get word to your wife in time.'

"'Quite,' he whispered. 'Of course. But there's a matinée this afternoon, isn't there? Oh! I wonder if I'm well enough to go. I'm so much better today.' And then he looked at his wife. 'My dear! My dear—at last!'

"I don't think I've ever seen such pathetic pride and love shining in a man's face before or since.

"'I'm afraid you won't be well enough to go,' I muttered.

"'Perhaps it would be wiser not to,' he whispered. 'But to think I shall miss her first appearance. Have you come to fetch her now, Mr. Trayne?'

"'Yes, darling,' the girl replied, and her voice sounded as steady as a rock. 'Mr. Trayne has come to fetch me. But it's early yet, and I want you to go back to bed now.'

"Without a glance at me, she helped him from the room and left me standing there. I heard their voices—hers clear and strong, his barely audible. And not for the first time in my life I marveled at the wonder of a woman who loves. I was to marvel more in a moment or two.

"She came back and shut the door. Then she stood facing me.

"'There's only one way, Mr. Trayne, though I think it's going to break my heart. I must go to the theater.'

"'But—your husband,' I stammered.

"'Oh! I'm not really going. I shall be here—at hand—the whole time. Because if the end did come—why then—I must be with him. But he's got to think I've gone; I've got to hide from him until after the matinée is over. And then I must tell him'—she faltered a little—'of my success. I'll keep the papers away from him—if it's necessary.' She turned away and I heard her falter: 'Three hours away from him—when he's dying. Oh, my God!'"

The Actor paused, and the Soldier stirred restlessly in his chair.

"I left shortly after," he went on at length; "I saw she wanted me to.

"All through the play that afternoon it haunted me—the pathos of it— aye, the horror of it. I pictured that girl hiding somewhere, while in the room above the sands were running out. Longing with all the power of her being to go to him—to snatch every fleeting minute with him—and yet condemned by my stupidity to forfeit her right. And then at last the show was over, and I went to her room again.

"She was by his side, kneeling on the floor, as I came in. As he saw me he struggled up on his elbow, and one could see it was the end.

"'Dear fellow,' I said, 'she was wonderful—just wonderful!'

"And the girl looked up at me through her blinding tears.

"'Just wonderful,' I said again. Five minutes later he died."

The Actor fell silent.

"Did you ever see her again?" asked the Soldier thoughtfully.

"Never; she disappeared. Just a patch on the quilt as I said. But there was one thread missing. Three years later I received a registered envelope. There was no letter inside, nor word of any sort. Just these." He fumbled in his pocket. "There are twenty of them."

He held out his hand, and the Soldier leaning forward saw that it contained a little bundle of five-pound notes.

THE MELANCHOLY HUSSAR OF THE GERMAN LEGION

THOMAS HARDY

Here stretch the downs, high and breezy and green, absolutely unchanged since those eventful days. A plough has never disturbed the turf, and the sod that was uppermost then is uppermost now. Here stood the camp; here are distinct traces of the banks thrown up for the horses of the cavalry, and spots where the midden-heaps lay are still to be observed. At night, when I walk across the lonely place, it is impossible to avoid hearing, amid the scourings of the wind over the grass-bents and thistles, the old trumpet and bugle calls, the rattle of the halters; to help seeing rows of spectral tents and the impedimenta of the soldiery. From within the canvases come guttural syllables of foreign tongues, and broken songs of the fatherland; for they were mainly regiments of the King's German Legion that slept round the tent-poles hereabout at that time.

It was nearly ninety years ago. The British uniform of the period, with its immense epaulettes, queer cocked-hat, breeches, gaiters, ponderous cartridge-box, buckled shoes, and what not, would look strange and barbarous now. Ideas have changed; invention has followed invention. Soldiers were monumental objects then. A divinity still hedged kings here and there; and war was considered a glorious thing.

Secluded old manor-houses and hamlets lie in the ravines and hollows among these hills, where a stranger had hardly ever been seen till the King chose to take the baths yearly at the sea-side watering-place a few miles to the south; as a consequence of which battalions descended in a cloud upon the open country around. Is it necessary to add that the echoes of many characteristic tales, dating from that picturesque time, still linger about here in more or less fragmentary form, to be caught by the attentive ear? Some of them I have repeated; most of them I have forgotten; one I have never repeated, and assuredly can never forget.

Phyllis told me the story with her own lips. She was then an old lady of seventy-five, and her auditor a lad of fifteen. She enjoined silence as to her share in the incident, till she should be "dead, buried, and forgotten." Her life was prolonged twelve years after the day of her narration, and she has now been dead nearly twenty. The oblivion which in her modesty and humility she courted for herself has only partially fallen on her, with the unfortunate result of inflicting an injustice upon her memory; since such fragments of her story as got abroad at the time, and have been kept alive ever since, are precisely those which are most unfavorable to her character.

It all began with the arrival of the York Hussars, one of the foreign regiments above alluded to. Before that day scarcely a soul had been seen near her father's house for weeks. When a noise like the brushing skirt of a visitor was heard on the doorstep, it proved to be a scudding leaf; when a carriage seemed to be nearing the door, it was her father grinding his sickle on the stone in the garden for his favorite relaxation of trimming the box-tree borders to the plots. A sound like luggage thrown down from the coach was a gun far away at sea; and what looked like a tall man by the gate at dusk was a yew bush cut into a quaint and attenuated shape. There is no such solitude in country places now as there was in those old days.

Yet all the while King George and his court were at his favorite sea-side resort, not more than five miles off.

The daughter's seclusion was great, but beyond the seclusion of the girl lay the seclusion of the father. If her social condition was twilight, his was darkness. Yet he enjoyed his darkness, while her twilight oppressed her. Dr. Grove had been a professional man whose taste for lonely meditation over metaphysical questions had diminished his practice till it no longer paid him to keep it going; after which he had relinquished it and hired at a nominal rent the small, dilapidated, half farm half manor-house of this obscure inland nook, to make a sufficiency of an income which in a town would have been inadequate for their maintenance. He stayed in his garden the greater part of the day, growing more and more irritable with the lapse of time, and the increasing perception that he had wasted his life in the pursuit of illusions. He saw his friends less and less frequently. Phyllis became so shy that if she met a stranger anywhere in her short rambles she felt ashamed at his gaze, walked awkwardly, and blushed to her shoulders.

Yet Phyllis was discovered even here by an admirer, and her hand most unexpectedly asked in marriage.

The King, as aforesaid, was at the neighboring town, where he had taken up his abode at Gloucester Lodge; and his presence in the town naturally brought many county people thither. Among these idlers—many of whom professed to have connections and interests with the Court—was one Humphrey Gould, a bachelor; a personage neither young nor old; neither good-looking nor positively plain. Too steady-going to be "a buck" (as fast and unmarried men were then called), he was an approximately fashionable man of a mild type. This bachelor of thirty found his way to the village on the down, beheld Phyllis, made her father's acquaintance in order to make hers, and by some means or other she sufficiently inflamed his heart to lead him in that direction almost daily, till he became engaged to marry her.

As he was of an old local family, some of whose members were held in respect in the county, Phyllis, in bringing him to her feet, had accomplished what was considered a brilliant move for one in her constrained position. How she had done it was not quite known to Phyllis herself. In those days unequal marriages were regarded rather as a violation of the laws of nature than as a mere infringement of convention, the more modern view, and hence when Phyllis, of the watering-place *bourgeoisie,* was chosen by such a gentlemanly fellow, it was as if she were going to be taken to heaven, though perhaps the uninformed would have seen no great difference in the respective positions of the pair, the said Gould being as poor as a crow.

This pecuniary condition was his excuse—probably a true one—for postponing their union, and as the winter drew nearer, and the King departed for the season, Mr. Humphrey Gould set out for Bath, promising to return to Phyllis in a few weeks. The winter arrived, the date of his promise passed, yet Gould postponed his coming, on the ground that he could not very easily leave his father in the city of their sojourn, the elder having no other relative near him. Phyllis, though lonely in the extreme, was content. The man who had asked her in marriage was a desirable husband for her in many ways; her father highly approved of his suit; but this neglect of her was awkward, if not painful, for Phyllis. Love him in the true sense of the word she assured me she never did, but she had a genuine regard for him; admired a certain methodical and dogged way in which he sometimes took his pleasure; valued his knowledge of what the Court was doing, had done, or was about to do; and she was not without a feeling of pride that he had chosen her when he might have exercised a more ambitious choice.

But he did not come; and the spring developed. His letters were regular though formal; and it is not to be wondered that the uncertainty of her position, linked with the fact that there was not much passion in her thoughts of Humphrey, bred an indescribable dreariness in the heart of Phyllis Grove. The spring was soon summer, and the summer brought the King; but still no Humphrey Gould. All this while the engagement by letter was maintained intact.

At this point of time a golden radiance flashed in upon the lives of people here, and charged all youthful thought with emotional interest. This radiance was the aforesaid York Hussars.

***

The present generation has probably but a very dim notion of the celebrated York Hussars of ninety years ago. They were one of the regiments of the King's German Legion, and (though they somewhat degenerated later on) their brilliant uniform, their splendid horses, and above all, their foreign air and mustachios (rare appendages then), drew crowds of admirers of both sexes wherever they went. These with other regiments had come to encamp on the downs and pastures, because of the presence of the King in the neighboring town.

The spot was high and airy, and the view extensive, commanding the Isle of Portland in front, and reaching to St. Aldhelm's Head eastward, and almost to the Start on the west.

Phyllis, though not precisely a girl of the village, was as interested as any of them in this military investment. Her father's home stood somewhat apart, and on the highest point of ground to which the lane ascended, so that it was almost level with the top of the church tower in the lower part of the parish. Immediately from the outside of the garden-wall the grass spread away to a great distance, and it was crossed by a path that came close to the wall. Ever since her childhood, it had been Phyllis's pleasure to clamber up this fence and sit on the top—a feat not so difficult as it may seem, the walls in this district being built of rubble, without mortar, so that there were plenty of crevices for small toes.

She was sitting up here one day, listlessly surveying the pasture without, when her attention was arrested by a solitary figure walking along the path. It was one of the renowned German Hussars, and he moved onward with his eyes on the ground, and with the manner of one who wished to escape company. His head would probably have been bent like his eyes but for his stiff neck-gear. On nearer view she perceived that his face was marked with deep sadness. Without observing her, he advanced by the footpath till it brought him almost immediately under the wall.

Phyllis was much surprised to see a fine, tall soldier in such a mood as this. Her theory of the military, and of the York Hussars in particular (derived entirely from hearsay, for she had never talked to a soldier in her life), was that their hearts were as gay as their accoutrements.

At this moment the Hussar lifted his eyes and noticed her on her perch, the white muslin neckerchief which covered her shoulders and neck were left bare by her low gown and her white raiment in general, showing conspicuously in the bright sunlight of this summer day. He blushed a little at the suddenness of the encounter, and without halting a moment from his pace, passed on.

All that day the foreigner's face haunted Phyllis; its aspect was so striking, so handsome, and his eyes were so blue, and sad, and abstracted. It was perhaps only natural that on some following day at the same hour she should look over that wall again and wait till he had passed a second time. On this occasion he was reading a letter, and at the sight of her his manner was that of one who had half expected or hoped to discover her. He almost stopped, smiled, and made a courteous salute. The end of the meeting was that they exchanged a few words. She asked him what he was reading, and he readily informed her that he was perusing letters from his mother in Germany; he did not get them often, he said, and was forced to read the old ones a great many times. This was all that passed at the present interview, but others of the same kind followed.

Phyllis used to say that his English, though not good, was quite intelligible to her, so that their acquaintance was never hindered by difficulties of speech. Whenever the subject became too delicate, subtle, or tender, for such words of English as were at his command, the eyes no doubt helped out the tongue, and—though this was later on—the lips helped out the eyes. In short this acquaintance, unguardedly made, and rash enough on her part, developed and ripened. Like Desdemona, she pitied him, and learnt his history.

His name was Matthäus Tina, and Saarbrück his native town, where his mother was still living. His age was twenty-two, and he had already risen to the grade of corporal, though he had not long been in the army. Phyllis used to assert that no such refined or well-educated young man could have been found in the ranks of the purely English regiments, some of these foreign soldiers having rather the graceful manner and presence of our native officers than of our rank and file.

She by degrees learned from her foreign friend a circumstance about himself and his comrades that Phyllis would least have expected of the York Hussars. So far from being as gay as its uniform, the regiment was pervaded by a dreadful melancholy, a chronic homesickness, which depressed many of the men to such an extent that they could hardly attend to their drill. The worst sufferers were the younger soldiers who had not been over here long. They hated England and English life; they took no interest whatever in King George and his island kingdom, and they only wished to be out of it and never to see it any more. Their bodies were here, but their hearts and minds were always far away in their dear fatherland, of which—brave men and stoical as they were in many ways—they would speak with tears in their eyes. One of the worst of the sufferers from this home-woe, as he called it in his own tongue, was Matthäus Tina, whose dreamy musing nature felt the gloom of exile still more intensely from the fact that he had left a lonely mother at home with nobody to cheer her.

Though Phyllis, touched by all this and interested in his history, did not disdain her soldier's acquaintance, she declined (according to her own account, at least) to permit the young man to overstep the line of mere friend-ship for a long while—as long, indeed, as she considered herself likely to become the possession of another; though it is probable that she had lost her heart to Matthäus before she was herself aware. The stone wall of necessity made anything like intimacy difficult; and he had never ventured to come, or to ask to come, inside the garden, so that all their conversation had been overtly conducted across this boundary.

***

News reached the village from a friend of Phyllis's father concerning Mr. Humphrey Gould, her remarkably cool and patient betrothed. This gentleman had been heard to say in Bath that he considered his overtures to

Miss Phyllis Grove to have reached only the stage of a half-understanding; and in view of his enforced absence on his father's account, who was too great an invalid now to attend to his affairs, he thought it best that there should be no definite promise as yet on either side. He was not sure, indeed, that he might not cast his eyes elsewhere.

This account—though only a piece of hearsay and as such entitled to no absolute credit—tallied so well with the infrequency of his letters and their lack of warmth, that Phyllis did not doubt its truth for one moment; and from that hour she felt herself free to bestow her heart as she should choose. Not so her father; he declared the whole story to be a fabrication. He had known Mr. Gould's family from his boyhood; and if there was one proverb that expressed the matrimonial aspect of that family well, it was "Love me little, love me long." Humphrey was an honorable man, who would not think of treating his engagement so lightly. "Do you wait in patience," he said; "all will be right enough in time."

From these words Phyllis at first imagined that her father was in correspondence with Mr. Gould, and her heart sank within her; for in spite of her original intentions she had been relieved to hear that her engagement had come to nothing. But she presently learned that her father had heard no more of Humphrey Gould than she herself had done; while he would not write and address her affianced directly on the subject, lest it should be deemed an imputation on that bachelor's honor.

"You want an excuse for encouraging one or other of those foreign fellows to flatter you with his unmeaning attentions," her father exclaimed, his mood having of late been a very unkind one toward her. "I see more than I say. Don't you ever set foot outside that garden-fence without my permission. If you want to see the camp, I'll take you myself some Sunday afternoon."

Phyllis had not the smallest intention of disobeying him in her actions, but she assumed herself to be independent with respect to her feelings. She no longer checked her fancy for the Hussar, though she was far from regarding him as her lover in the serious sense in which an Englishman might have been regarded as such. The young foreign soldier was almost an ideal being to her, with none of the appurtenances of an ordinary house-dweller; one who had descended she knew not whence, and would disappear she knew not whither; the subject of a fascinating dream—no more.

They met continually now—mostly at dusk—during the brief interval between the going down of the sun and the minute at which the last trumpet-call summoned him to his tent. Perhaps her manner had become less restrained latterly; at any rate that of the Hussar was so; he had grown more tender every day, and at parting after these hurried interviews she reached down her hand from the top of the wall that he might press it. One evening he held it so long that she exclaimed, "The wall is white, and somebody in the field may see your shape against it!"

He lingered so long that night that it was with the greatest difficulty that he could run across the intervening stretch of ground and enter the camp in time. On the next occasion of his awaiting her, she did not appear in her usual place at the usual hour. His disappointment was unspeakably keen; he remained staring blankly at the spot, like a man in a trance. The trumpets and tattoo sounded, and still he did not go.

She had been delayed purely by an accident. When she arrived she was anxious because of the lateness of the hour, having heard as well as he the sounds denoting the closing of the camp. She implored him to leave immediately.

"No," he said gloomily. "I shall not go in yet—the moment you come—I have thought of your coming all day."

"But you may be disgraced at being after time."

"I don't mind that. I should have disappeared from the world some time ago if it had not been for two persons—my beloved, here, and my mother in Saarbrück. I hate the army. I care more for a minute of your company than for all the promotion in the world."

Thus he stayed and talked to her, and told her interesting details of his native place, and incidents of his childhood, till she was in a simmer of distress at his recklessness in remaining. It was only because she insisted on bidding him good-night and leaving the wall that he returned to his quarters.

The next time she saw him he was without the stripes that had adorned his sleeve. He had been broken to the level of private for his lateness that night; and as Phyllis considered herself to be the cause of his disgrace, her sorrow was great. But the position was now reversed; it was his turn to cheer her.

"Don't grieve, meine Liebliche!' he said. "I have got a remedy for whatever comes. First, even supposing I regain my stripes, would your father allow you to marry a non-commissioned officer in the York Hussars?"

She flushed. This practical step had not been in her mind in relation to such an unrealistic person as he was, and a moment's reflection was enough for it. "My father would not—certainly would not," she answered unflinchingly. "It cannot be thought of! My dear friend, please do forget me—I fear I am ruining you and your prospects!"

"Not at all!" said he. "You are giving this country of yours just sufficient interest to me to make me care to keep alive in it. If my dear land were here also, and my old parent, I could be happy as I am with you, and would do my best as a soldier. But it is not so. And now listen. This is my plan. Go with me to my own country, be my wife, and live there with my mother and me. I am not a Hanoverian, as you know, though I entered the army as such; my country is by the Saar and is at peace with France, and if I were once in it I should be free."

"But how do you plan to get there?" she asked. Phyllis had been rather more amazed than shocked at his proposition. Her position in her father's house was growing irksome and painful in the extreme; his parental affection seemed to be quite dried up. She was not a native of the village, like all the joyous girls around her; and in some way Matthäus Tina had infected her with his own passionate longing for his country, his mother, and his home.

"But how?" she repeated, finding that he did not answer. "Will you buy your discharge?"

"Ah, no," he said. "That's impossible in these times. No, I came here against my will; why should I not escape? Now is the time, as we shall soon be striking camp, and I might see you no more. This is my scheme. I will ask you to meet me on the highway two miles off on some calm night next week that may be appointed. There will be nothing unbecoming in it or to cause you shame. You will not fly alone with me, for I will bring with me my devoted young friend Christoph, an Alsatian, who has lately joined the regiment, and who has agreed to assist in this enterprise. We shall have come from yonder harbor, where we shall have examined the boats and found one suited to our purpose. Christoph has already a chart of the Channel, and we will then go to the harbor, and at midnight cut the boat from her moorings, and row away round the point out of sight. By the next morning, we will be on the coast of France, near Cherbourg. The rest is easy, for I have saved money for the land journey, and can get a change of clothes. I will write to my mother, who will meet us on the way."

He added details in reply to her inquiries, which left no doubt in Phyllis's mind of the feasibility of the undertaking. But its magnitude almost appalled her; and it is questionable if she would ever have gone further in the wild adventure if, on entering the house that night, her father had not accosted her in the most significant terms.

"How about the York Hussars?" he said.

"They are still at the camp; but they are soon going away, I believe."

"It is useless for you to attempt to cloak your actions in that way. You have been meeting one of those fellows; you have been seen walking with him—foreign barbarians, not much better than the French themselves! I have made up my mind—don't speak a word till I have done, please—I have made up my mind that you shall stay here no longer while they are on the spot. You shall go to your aunt's."

It was useless for her to protest that she had never taken a walk with any soldier or man under the sun except himself. Her protestations were feeble, too, for though he was not literally correct in his assertion, he was virtually only half in error.

The house of her father's sister was a prison to Phyllis. She had quite recently undergone experience of its gloom; and when her father went on to direct her to pack what would be necessary for her to take, her heart died within her. In after years she never attempted to excuse her conduct during this week of agitation; but the result of her self-communing was that she decided to join in the scheme of her lover and his friend and fly to the country that he had colored with such lovely hues in her imagination. She always said that the one feature in his proposal that overcame her hesitation was the obvious purity and straightforwardness of his intentions. He showed himself to be so virtuous and kind, he treated her with a respect to which she had never before been accustomed; and she was braced to the obvious risks of the voyage by her confidence in him.

***

It was on a soft, dark evening of the following week that they engaged in the adventure. Tina was to meet her at a point in the highway at which the lane to the village branched off. Christoph was to go ahead of them to the harbor where the boat lay, row it round the Nothe—or Lookout as it was called in those days—and pick them up on the other side of the promontory, which they were to reach by crossing the harbor bridge on foot and climbing over the Lookout hill.

As soon as her father had ascended to his room she left the house, and, bundle in hand, proceeded at a trot along the lane. At such an hour not a soul was afoot anywhere in the village, and she reached the junction of the lane with the highway unobserved. Here she took up her position in the obscurity formed by the angle of a fence, from whence she could discern every one who approached along the turnpike-road without being seen herself.

She had not remained thus waiting for her lover longer than a minute—though from the tension of her nerves the lapse of even that short time was trying—when, instead of the expected footsteps, the stage-coach could be heard descending the hill. She knew that Tina would not show himself till the road was clear and waited impatiently for the coach to pass. Nearing the corner where she was, it slackened speed, and, instead of going by as usual, drew up within a few yards of her. A passenger alighted, and she heard his voice. It was Humphrey Gould's.

He had brought a friend with him and luggage. The luggage was deposited on the grass, and the coach went on its route to the royal watering-place.

"I wonder where that young man is with the horse and trap?" said her former admirer to his companion. "I hope we shan't have to wait here long. I told him ten o'clock precisely."

"Have you got her present safe?"

"Phyllis's? O, yes. It is in this trunk. I hope it will please her."

"Of course it will. What woman would not be pleased with such a handsome peace-offering?"

"Well—she deserves it. I've treated her rather badly. But she has been in my mind these last two days much more than I should care to confess to everybody. Ah, well; I'll say no more about that. It cannot be that she is so bad as they make out. I am quite sure that a girl of her good wit would know better than to get entangled with any of those Hanoverian soldiers. I won't believe it of her, and there's an end on't."

More words in the same strain were casually dropped as the two men waited; words that revealed to her, as by a sudden illumination, the enormity of her conduct. The conversation was at length cut off by the arrival of the man with the vehicle. The luggage was placed in it, they mounted and were driven on in the direction from which she had just come.

Phyllis was so conscience-stricken that she was at first inclined to follow them; but a moment's reflection led her to feel that it would only be bare justice to Matthäus to wait till he arrived and explain candidly that she had changed her mind—difficult as the struggle would be when she stood face to face with him. She bitterly reproached herself for having believed reports that represented Humphrey Gould as false to his engagement, when, from what she now heard from his own lips, she gathered that he had been living full of trust in her. But she knew well enough who had won her love. Without him her life seemed a dreary prospect, yet the more she looked at his proposal the more she feared to accept it—so wild as it was, so vague, so venturesome. She had promised Humphrey Gould, and it was only his assumed faithlessness that had led her to treat that promise as nothing. His solicitude in bringing her these gifts touched her; her promise must be kept, and esteem must take the place of love. She would preserve her self-respect. She would stay at home, and marry him, and suffer.

Phyllis had thus braced herself to an exceptional fortitude when, a few minutes later, the outline of Matthäus Tina appeared behind a field-gate, over which he lightly leaped as she stepped forward. There was no evading it; he pressed her to his breast.

It is the first and last time! she wildly thought as she stood encircled by his arms.

How Phyllis got through the terrible ordeal of that night she could never clearly recollect. She always attributed her success in carrying out her resolve to her lover's honor, for as soon as she declared to him in feeble words that she had changed her mind and felt that she could not, dared not, fly with him, he forbore to urge her, grieved as he was at her decision. Unscrupulous pressure on his part, seeing how romantically she had become attached to him, would no doubt have turned the balance in his favor. But he did nothing to tempt her unduly or unfairly.

On her side, fearing for his safety, she begged him to remain. This, he declared, could not be. "I cannot break faith with my friend," said he. Had he stood alone he would have abandoned his plan. But Christoph, with the boat and compass and chart, was waiting on the shore; the tide would soon turn; his mother had been warned of his coming; go he must.

Many precious minutes were lost while he tarried, unable to tear himself away. Phyllis held to her resolve, though it cost her many a bitter pang. At last they parted, and he went down the hill. Before his footsteps had quite died away, she felt a desire to behold at least his outline once more and running noiselessly after him regained view of his diminishing figure. For one moment she was sufficiently excited to be on the point of rushing forward and linking her fate with his. But she could not. The courage which at the critical instant failed Cleopatra of Egypt could scarcely be expected of Phyllis Grove.

A dark shape, similar to his own, joined him in the highway. It was Christoph, his friend. She could see no more; they had hastened on in the direction of the town and harbor, four miles ahead. With a feeling akin to despair, she turned and slowly pursued her way homeward.

Tattoo sounded in the camp; but there was no camp for her now. It was as dead as the camp of the Assyrians after the passage of the Destroying Angel.

She noiselessly entered the house, seeing nobody, and went to bed. Grief, which kept her awake at first, ultimately wrapped her in a heavy sleep. The next morning her father met her at the foot of the stairs.

"Mr. Gould is come!" he said triumphantly.

Humphrey was staying at the inn, and had already called to inquire for her. He had brought her a present of a very handsome looking-glass in a frame of repoussé silverwork, which her father held in his hand. He had promised to call again in the course of an hour to ask Phyllis to walk with him.

Pretty mirrors were rarer in country-houses at that day than they are now, and the one before her won Phyllis's admiration. She looked into it, saw how heavy her eyes were, and endeavored to brighten them. She was in that wretched state of mind that leads a woman to move mechanically onward in what she conceives to be her allotted path. Mr. Humphrey had, in his undemonstrative way, been adhering all along to the old understanding; it was for her to do the same, and to say not a word of her own lapse. She put on her bonnet and tippet, and when he arrived at the hour named she was at the door awaiting him.

***

Phyllis thanked him for his beautiful gift; but the talking was soon entirely on Humphrey's side as they walked along. He told her of the latest movements of the world of fashion—a subject she willingly discussed to the exclusion of anything more personal—and his measured language helped to still her disquieted heart and brain. Had not her own sadness been what it was, she would have observed his embarrassment. At last he abruptly changed the subject.

"I am glad you are pleased with my little present," he said. "The truth is that I brought it to propitiate 'ee, and to get you to help me out of a mighty difficulty."

It was inconceivable to Phyllis that this independent bachelor, whom she admired in some respects, could have a difficulty.

"Phyllis—I'll tell you my secret at once; for I have a monstrous secret to confide before I can ask your counsel. The case is, then, that I am married: yes, I have privately married a dear young belle; and if you knew her, and I hope you will, you would say everything in her praise. But she is not quite the one that my father would have chose for me—you know the paternal idea as well as I—and I have kept it secret. There will be a terrible noise, no doubt; but I think that with your help I may get over it. If you would only do me this good turn—when I have told my father, I mean—say that you never could have married me, you know, or something of that sort—upon my life it will help to smooth the way vastly. I am so anxious to win him round to my point of view and not to cause any estrangement."

What Phyllis replied she scarcely knew, or how she counseled him as to his unexpected situation. Yet the relief that his announcement brought her was perceptible. To have confided her trouble in return was what her aching heart longed to do; and had Humphrey been a woman, she would instantly have poured out her tale. But to him she feared to confess; and there was a real reason for silence till a sufficient time had elapsed to allow her lover and his comrade to get out of harm's way.

As soon as she reached home again, she sought a solitary place and spent the time in half regretting that she had not gone away and in dreaming over the meetings with Matthäus Tina from their beginning to their end. In his own country, amongst his own countrywomen, he would possibly soon forget her, even to her very name.

Her listlessness was such that she did not go out of the house for several days. There came a morning that broke in fog and mist, behind which the dawn could be discerned in greenish grey; and the outlines of the tents, and the rows of horses at the ropes. The smoke from the canteen fires drooped heavily.

The spot at the bottom of the garden where she had been accustomed to climb the wall to meet Matthäus was the only inch of English ground in which she took any interest; and in spite of the disagreeable haze prevailing, she walked out there till she reached the well-known corner. Every blade of grass was weighted with little liquid globes, and slugs and snails had crept out upon the plots. She could hear the usual faint noises from the camp, and in the other direction the trot of farmers on the road to the town, for it was market-day. She observed that her frequent visits to this corner had quite trodden down the grass in the angle of the wall and left marks of garden soil on the stepping-stones by which she had mounted to look over the top. Seldom having gone there till dusk, she had not considered that her traces might be visible by day. Perhaps it was these which had revealed her trysts to her father.

While she paused in melancholy regard, she fancied that the customary sounds from the tents were changing their character. Indifferent as Phyllis was to camp doings now, she mounted by the steps to the old place. What she beheld at first awed and perplexed her; then she stood rigid, her fingers hooked to the wall, her eyes staring out of her head, and her face as if hardened to stone.

On the open green stretching before her all the regiments in the camp were drawn up in line, in the mid-front of which two empty coffins lay on the ground. The unwonted sounds she had noticed came from an advancing procession. It consisted of the band of the York Hussars playing a dead march; next two soldiers of that regiment in a mourning coach, guarded on each side, and accompanied by two priests. Behind came a crowd of rustics who had been attracted by the event. The melancholy procession marched along the front of the line, returned to the centre, and halted beside the coffins, where the two condemned men were blindfolded, and each placed kneeling on his coffin; a few minutes pause was now given, while they prayed.

A firing party of twenty-four men stood ready with leveled carbines. The commanding officer, who had his sword drawn, waved it through some cuts of the sword-exercise till he reached the downward stroke, whereat the firing party discharged their volley. The two victims fell, one upon his face across his coffin, the other backward.

As the volley resounded, there arose a shriek from the wall of Dr. Grove's garden, and some one fell down inside; but nobody among the spectators without noticed it at the time. The two executed Hussars were Matthäus Tina and his friend Christoph. The soldiers on guard placed the bodies in the coffins almost instantly; but the colonel of the regiment, an Englishman, rode up and exclaimed in a stern voice, "Turn them out—as an example to the men!"

The coffins were lifted endwise, and the dead Germans flung out upon their faces on the grass. Then all the regiments wheeled in sections, and marched past the spot in slow time. When the survey was over, the corpses were again coffined and borne away.

Meanwhile Dr. Grove, attracted by the noise of the volley, had rushed out into his garden, where he saw his wretched daughter lying motionless against the wall. She was taken indoors, but it was long before she recovered consciousness; and for weeks they despaired of her reason.

It transpired that the luckless deserters from the York Hussars had cut the boat from her moorings in the adjacent harbor, according to their plan, and, with two other comrades who were smarting under ill-treatment from their colonel, had sailed in safety across the Channel; but mistaking their bearings they steered into Jersey, thinking that island the French coast. Here they were perceived to be deserters and delivered up to the authorities. Matthäus and Christoph interceded for the other two at the court-martial, saying that it was entirely by the former's representations that these were induced to go. Their sentence was accordingly commuted to flogging, the death punishment being reserved for their leaders.

The visitor to the old Georgian watering-place who may care to ramble to the neighboring village under the hills and examine the register of burials, will there find two entries in these words:

"Matth: Tina (Corpl.) in His Majesty's Regmt. of York Hussars, and Shot for Desertion, was Buried June 30th, 1801, aged 22 years. Born in the town of Sarrbruk, Germany.

"Christoph Bless, belonging to His Majesty's Regmt. of York Hussars, who was Shot for Desertion, was Buried June 30th, 1801, aged 22 years. Born at Lothaargen, Alsatia."

Their graves were dug at the back of the little church, near the wall. There is no memorial to mark the spot, but Phyllis pointed it out to me. While she lived she used to keep their mounds neat; but now they are overgrown with nettles and sunk nearly flat. The older villagers, however, who know of the episode from their parents, still recollect the place where the soldiers lie. Phyllis lies near.

JUST AS I AM:
The Autobiography of Billy Graham

THE COURTSHIP OF BILLY AND RUTH BELL GRAHAM

AN EXCERPT

"Saturday nights I dedicate to prayer and study in preparation for the Lord's day."

What kind of a romance could a college man have with a woman who said a thing like that? Dating Ruth Bell had to be creative. And I did my best. For example, on one occasion we took a long walk in the countryside surrounding Wheaton to a graveyard where we read tombstone epitaphs! It was a far cry from careening through Charlotte in a jalopy.

Ruth, born in China, had spent her first seventeen years in Asia. Her father, Dr. L. Nelson Bell, was a medical missionary in the eastern Chinese province of Northern Kiangsu, and her family lived in the hospital compound. Theirs was a hard existence and certainly not a sheltered one. She remembers it as a happy, interesting childhood with strict but loving parents, among happy Christians, both fellow missionaries and Christian Chinese friends and helpers. But they were all exposed to everything from monsoons, sandstorms, and epidemics to bandit attacks and civil war. For high school, Ruth went to the Foreign School in Pyongyang, Korea (now North Korea).

In more ways than one, she was one of the belles of Wheaton campus. This I learned during my first term from a fellow I met at the Lane home—Johnny Streater. To pay his way through college, Johnny ran his own trucking service. For a price, he would haul anything in his little yellow pickup. I gladly accepted his offer of work at 50 cents an hour and spent many afternoons at hard labor, moving furniture and other items around the western Chicago suburbs.

Johnny was a little older than I and had been in the Navy before coming
to Wheaton. He had a vision for the mission field and felt that God had called
him to serve in China, where he intended to go as soon as he graduated.
He told me about a girl in the junior class—one of the most beautiful and
dedicated Christian girls he had ever met. Sounded like my type. I paid
attention.

One day we were hanging around in our sweaty work clothes in front of
Williston Hall—the girls' dorm—getting ready to haul some furniture for a
lady in Glen Ellyn, the next town over, when Johnny let out a whoop. "Billy,
here's the girl I was telling you about," he said. "It's Ruth Bell."

I straightened up, and there she was. Standing there, looking right at
me, was a slender, hazel-eyed movie starlet! I said something polite, but I was
flustered and embarrassed. It took me a month to muster the courage to ask
her out for a date.

The Christmas holidays were fast approaching, and the combined glee
clubs were presenting Handel's Messiah. One day in the library in Blanchard
Hall, I saw Ruth studying at one of the long tables. Johnny Streater and Howard
Van Buren urged me to make my pitch to her right there. The expression of
the librarian at the desk turned to a frown as we whispered among ourselves.
Undaunted, I sauntered nonchalantly across to Ruth and scribbled my proposal
for a date to the concert. To my surprise and delight, she agreed to go.

That Sunday afternoon was cold and snowy. With Ruth Bell sitting
beside me in Pierce Chapel, I did not pay much attention to the music.
Afterward we walked over to the Lane house for a cup of tea, and we had a
chance to talk. I just could not believe that anyone could be so spiritual and so
beautiful at one and the same time.

Ruth went back to her room (she told me later), got on her knees, and
told the Lord that if she could spend the rest of her life serving Him with me,
she would consider it the greatest privilege imaginable. So why did she make
it so hard for me to get her to say yes out loud?

If I had not been smitten with love at the first sight of Ruth Bell, I would certainly have been the exception. Many of the men at Wheaton thought she was stunning. Petite, vivacious, smart, talented, witty, stylish, amiable, and unattached. What more could a fellow ask for?

Add to that the fact that her Virginia-based parents and their missionary companions were all in China under the auspices of the Southern Presbyterian denomination. Not the Associated Reformed Presbyterian Church I had grown up in, but close enough.

"Billy, hold your horses!" I fell so head-over-heels in love with her that Johnny had to caution me. "You're going too fast."

And there was one minor problem that kept coming up. She wanted me to go with her as a missionary to Tibet! My mind was not closed to such a possibility. Not completely. After all, I had chosen to major in anthropology with just such a contingency in mind. But missionary work was a lot more comfortable to consider in the global abstract than in the Tibetan concrete.

In that list of good adjectives I just assigned to Ruth, I omitted one: *determined.*

She felt that God had called her to be a missionary to the remote borders of Tibet just as strongly as I felt that He had called me to preach the Gospel. In my case, though, there was not a geographical stipulation.

Ruth was deeply impressed by the life of Amy Carmichael, that single—and indeed singular—woman whom God had called to devote herself utterly to the children of Dohnavur, in southern India.

She reinforced her case by telling me about Mildred Cable, who had rejected the young man she loved because marriage to him would have cut across her call from God to do pioneer work in China.

Two things I felt sure of: first, that Ruth was bound to get married someday; and second, that I was the man she would marry. Beyond that, I did not try to pressure her or persuade her—that is to say, not *overly* much. I let God do my courting for me.

But as the months went by, I asked her to at least consider me. It would not have been right to let her assume that what seemed to be my heroic understanding of her concerns was a lack of interest or expectation on my part. We had lots of discussions about our relationship. I wouldn't call them arguments exactly, but we certainly did not see eye to eye.

In the meantime, Ruth enjoyed the social life at Wheaton, as I did, with many friends. One day she went canoeing on the Fox River in St. Charles—about ten miles west of Wheaton—with classmates Harold Lindsell, Carl Henry, and Carl's fiancée, Helga. Somehow the canoe capsized, and Ruth went under. Since both men were staunch Baptists, I suspected them of wanting to immerse the pretty Presbyterian missionary kid from China!

Because I was already an ordained Baptist minister, our divided denominational allegiance was another topic of conversation between us. Ruth stuck to her convictions.

"We've both got such strong wills or minds or something, I almost despaired of ever having things go peacefully between us," she wrote to her parents, "but I wouldn't want him any other way, and I can't be any other way. But you know, it's remarkable how two strong minds (or wills) like that can gradually begin to sort of fuse together. Or maybe we're learning to give in and don't realize it."

I was making some adjustments, certainly. At the Lane house one evening, I was so busy talking at the supper table that I ate three helpings of macaroni and cheese before I woke up to the fact that I had told Ruth I hated macaroni and cheese. That incident encouraged her to hope she could feed me anything and get away with it!

One Sunday evening after church, I walked into the parlor of the Gerstung home, where I was rooming and collapsed into a chair. That dear professor of German and his wife, with three young boys of their own, were getting accustomed to my moods and always listened patiently. This time I bemoaned the fact that I did not stand a chance with Ruth. She was so superior to me in culture and poise. She did not talk as much as I did, so she seemed superior in her intelligence too. "The reason I like Ruth so much," I wrote home to Mother, "is that she looks and reminds me of you."

By now I had directly proposed marriage to Ruth, and she was struggling with her decision. At the same time, she encouraged me to keep an open mind about the alternative of my going to the mission field. She was coming to realize, though, that the Lord was not calling me in that direction.

One day I posed a question to Ruth point-blank: "Do you believe that God brought us together?"

She thought so, without question.

"In that case," I said, "God will lead me, and you'll do the following."

She did not say yes to my proposal right then and there, but I knew she was thinking it over.

A test of our bond came when her sister Rosa was diagnosed as having tuberculosis. Ruth dropped out of school in the middle of my second semester to care for her. Rosa was placed in a hospital in New Mexico, and Ruth stayed with her the next fall too.

That summer I returned home and preached in several churches in the South. Ruth's parents had returned from China on a furlough—actually, the Japanese had invaded the mainland, so the Bells were not sure if they could ever return—and had settled temporarily in Virginia, their home state.

While I was in Florida, preaching in Dr. Minder's church, I got a thick letter from Ruth postmarked July 6, 1941. One of the first sentences made me ecstatic, and I took off running. "I'll marry you," she wrote.

When I went back to my room, I read that letter over and over until church time. On page after page, Ruth explained how the Lord had worked in her heart and said she felt He wanted her to marry me. That night I got up to the pulpit and preached. When I finished and sat down, the pastor turned to me.

"Do you know what you just said?" he asked.

"No," I confessed.

"I'm not sure the people did either!"

After I went to bed, I switched my little lamp on and off all night, rereading that letter probably another dozen times.

At the close of a preaching series just after that at Sharon Presbyterian Church in Charlotte, those dear people gave me, as I recall, an offering of $165. I raced right out and spent almost all of it on an engagement ring with a diamond so big you could almost see it with a magnifying glass! I showed it off at home, announcing that I planned to present it to Ruth over in Montreat in the middle of the day. But daytime was not romantic enough, I was told.

Ruth was staying part of that summer at the cottage of Buck Currie and his wife, whom she called uncle and aunt, and their niece Gay. Buck was the brother of Ed Currie, one of Ruth's father's fellow missionaries in China. Their house on Craigmont Road in Black Mountain was built near a stream and had swings that went out over the water.

As I turned off the main road and drove toward the house, which was some distance off, I saw a strange creature walking down the road. She had long, straight hair sticking out all over, an awful-looking faded dress, bare feet, and what looked to be very few teeth. I passed her by, but when I suddenly realized it was Ruth playing a trick on me—her teeth blacked out so that she looked toothless—I slammed on the brakes. She got in and we went on to the Currie house deep in the woods.

I had the ring with me.

We went up to what is now the Blue Ridge Parkway. The sun was sinking on one side of us and the moon rising on the other. I kissed Ruth on the lips for the first time. I thought it was romantic, but she thought, or so she told me later, that I was going to swallow her.

"I can't wear the ring until I get permission from my parents," she said apologetically.

They were away, so she sent them a telegram: "Bill has offered me a ring. May I wear it?"

"Yes," they wired back, "if it fits."

Later in that summer of 1941, Ruth decided to visit her parents. She took a train to Waynesboro, Virginia, where I was to join her. I had to go, of course, to meet them. No, to do more than that—to pass inspection. I drove my Plymouth from Charlotte through North Carolina, stopping on the way to give a brief message on a Christian radio station. About five miles out of Waynesboro, I stopped and changed into a suit and tie. I finally found the small brick house; and when I pulled up, Ruth rushed out to greet me. She had expected me to hug and kiss her, but I was so nervous about meeting her parents that I froze.

Dr. and Mrs. Bell came out right behind her. That night we all had dinner together with Dr. Bell's mother. I enjoyed it, though I was still tense. Dr. Bell had booked a room for me at the General Wayne Hotel, and I was surprised (and relieved) in the morning to find that the $3 room charge had been paid.

When I went to visit Ruth later in the morning, Dr. Bell asked if we would like to follow him and Mrs. Bell to Washington, D.C., where he had several appointments. We did, and enjoyed a memorable walk down by the Potomac River. Only later did I learn that he had gone to warn the State Department about the danger of the Japanese and their increasing military power. Dr. Bell said he could not get anyone in Washington to take him seriously, though—except Congressman Walter Judd, who himself had been a missionary to China.

Ruth was the woman of my dreams, but the delightful in-laws I would gain in the process would make our eventual marriage all the better.

Our relationship deepened in the next year. I was studying, working on the truck with Johnny Streater, and preaching regularly at the Tab. I began to listen to Torrey Johnson's *Midwest Bible Hour* on Sunday afternoons at five o'clock, and to *Songs in the Night*, a forty-five-minute program on WCFL,

Chicago's most powerful radio station, on Sunday nights.

During this time, after Rosa got better and Ruth returned to Wheaton, there came into Ruth's mind a serious doubt about me centered on my uncertainty about my calling (if any) to the mission field. She even reached the point of feeling that we ought to quit dating and not see each other for a while. I said I would appreciate having the ring back, in that case. She could not accept that, though. She was emotional about the ring and would not give it back to me. And that was the end of her doubt.

But we did not move ahead with any haste. Although we were engaged, we felt that it was right for us not to get married until after our graduation.

During the next academic year, 1941–42, I changed where I lived, now rooming with Ken Hansen and Lloyd Fesmire. Ruth roomed with Helen Stam. Lloyd and I both admired the other's girl greatly, and Helen would later become Lloyd's wife.

The early months of 1943 found Ruth making trips to Oak Park or to the downtown Chicago Loop to shop for her trousseau. I could not get all that excited about the shopping, but when her folks offered to give us silver tableware as a wedding gift, I decided to go along with her to Peacock's Jewelry. And it was a good thing too. The pattern she chose had knives and forks in two sizes, and I talked her into getting one of each in the super size for me to use; they cost 20 cents extra.

In addition to Ruth's shopping and finishing up her senior year at college (with an earnest plea to her parents to pray that she would pass the comprehensive exams in the spring), she joined me on Sunday mornings, first at the Lane home for a Plymouth Brethren meeting, then later at the Tab, where I preached.

But I too had schoolwork to finish, and I think she was exasperated by the fact that I was on the road so often. After telling her folks about my coming itinerary in Flint, Michigan; Rockford, Illinois; and then "Wisconsin or Pennsylvania or somewhere," she wrote, "I can't keep control of him much less keep track of him."

Already she sensed what kind of future we faced together. "I'm a rotten sport when it comes to his leaving. It's no fun. I never thought about this side of it. What is it going to be like after we're married? I probably won't see as much of him then as I do *now*."

Something loomed immediately ahead, though, that made Ruth and me both expect me to stay put a little more.

One day a big Lincoln Continental pulled up in front of the house where I was rooming. Out of it popped a young man who bounded up the steps and asked to see me. He turned out to be president of Hitchcock Publishing Company in Chicago and treasurer of the National Gideon Association, the group that distributed Bibles to hotels.

His name was Bob Van Kampen, and he wanted to sound me out about becoming pastor of the church where he was a deacon, Western Springs Baptist Church, about twenty miles southeast of Wheaton. Since my work at the Tab had been an extracurricular, part-time thing, I felt ready to consider a change.

In January 1943, midway through my senior year, I began to feel the responsibility of supporting a wife. I was also attracted by the proximity of the University of Chicago, with its strong anthropology department offering advance-study opportunities. Hence, I accepted the call to Western Springs; I had already preached there as a student, and I could begin work there after college commencement. In my enthusiasm, however, I forgot to consult my bride-to-be! She let me know in no uncertain terms that she did not appreciate such insensitivity. And I could not blame her.

Both Ruth and I felt sure the pastorate would be a temporary thing. For me, it was a possible stepping-stone to qualifying for the Army chaplaincy. I made this priority clear to the church in Western Springs, and they accepted the condition. They even gave me the freedom to travel occasionally to evangelistic meetings. In the next months, I preached there several times, and Ruth was introduced to people as "our pastor's future wife." She had her own reasons for viewing the placement as temporary—"since we're planning on going to the mission field as soon as we can," she wrote home. For that reason, we asked the church to find us a furnished apartment so that we would not get encumbered with a lot of possessions.

In June 1943, Ruth and I graduated from Wheaton College in the same class. (Although she was a junior when I entered as a second-semester freshmen, we ended up graduating in the same class. She fell behind because of the time she took out for Rosa's illness, while I advanced because the school later transferred some additional credits from Florida Bible Institute.) During the ceremony, she sat in front of me. When she received her diploma, I laughingly whispered, "At long last!" She turned around, and I could see that she was not amused. Even so, she made a cute little face at me.

Ruth's parents had moved from Virginia to a house on the Presbyterian conference grounds at Montreat, North Carolina, just east of Asheville. We were married there in August, on the night of Friday the thirteenth, with a full moon in the sky. In Gaither Chapel at eight-thirty in the evening, amid candles and clematis, my beloved Florida mentor, Dr. John Minder, pronounced us husband and wife. Dr. Kerr Taylor, close friend of the Bells and former missionary to China, assisted him in the ceremony. Sophie Graham (No relation), a missionary from Haichow, China, played the piano and accompanied Roy Gustafson in two solos before the ceremony. Andrew Yang from Chinkiang, China, sang two solos during the service. All the details took up two columns on the social-news page of the Asheville paper; that was because Dr. Bell was well known in the area. It was the most memorable day of my life.

For a wedding present, my father had already given me $50. I had $25 of my own saved up. That meant I had $75 to pay for a honeymoon and get us back to Chicago.

The first night we went to the Battery Park Hotel in Asheville; that cost us $5 for the night. I had wanted Ruth to have the best, but the Grove Park Inn would have cost $20. I couldn't sleep in the bed, so after Ruth fell asleep, I got up quietly, lay down on the floor, and dropped right off. (I had suffered from insomnia all through school, and Chief Whitefeather, who had come through town once and given his Christian testimony, had suggested that I sleep on the floor. He promised that though it would take a couple of weeks to get used to, it would help my problem, and he was right.) The next morning, when Ruth woke up, I was gone . . . or at least appeared to be gone. It took a few minutes for her to find me on the floor, sleeping like a baby.

We then drove to Boone, where we went to a private home that let out rooms; ours cost $1. To get to the bathroom at night, we had to go through two other rooms where people were sleeping. At the end of our stay, Ruth confided in the lady of the house that we were on our honeymoon.

"Yes, I know," she said. "I've been sweeping up the rice every day."

We ate out at little sandwich places and played golf. Ruth knew nothing about the game, and I knew little more, in spite of the caddying I had done in Florida. There were many people behind us on the course each time, and we did not know we were supposed to let them play through.

One time we decided to splurge. We ate a meal at Mayview Manor, the place to eat in town. Lunch was $3. My money was going fast. But we decided, just for one night, to spend $2 at the Boone Hotel.

Then we went back to my family's home in Charlotte, but there was no room for us. My sister Catherine was getting married; Jean had a room, and so did Melvin. So we slept on the floor in what my mother called her sunroom.

Our trip back to Chicago, after our brief honeymoon in the Blue Ridge Mountains near home, was uneventful. "Hit two starlings, that was all," Ruth recorded. "Everything else we ran over had already been run over before." Like most travelers in those days, we had along a trusty thermos bottle filled with Dr. Pepper and crushed ice, plus a supply of cheese and crackers and raisin wafers.

We stopped at a hotel in Indianapolis and got a small, dirty room. After the maid changed the soiled bed linens, we still had to scrub the ring out of the tub ourselves. Then, in the dimly lighted and thickly carpeted restaurant downstairs, the host would not admit me without my jacket (packed in the car) or Ruth with her pigtails. We were as disgusted as could be at the management, and as happy as could be with each other!

When we arrived at 214 South Clay Street, Hinsdale, Illinois—the furnished apartment found for us by someone at Western Springs—our landlady, Mrs. Pantke, had our four upstairs rooms tidy, with a welcoming bouquet of flowers from her own garden. We unloaded the car and stowed everything away in less than an hour, including more than two bushels of canned goods that the church people had brought in. Ruth served us supper using all her lace, china, crystal, and silver. Then I did dishes while she rushed through a bath and pressed her travel suit so that we could get to the church in time for our reception.

The small group in the Western Springs church—fewer than a hundred members—had been able to construct only the basement of what they hoped someday would become a church building. It was not a very impressive place to meet. Ruth thought of it, in those war days, as an air-raid shelter. But the congregation really put themselves out to make us feel welcome. After hearing various speeches, we were handed an envelope with a gift of $48 in it. In addition, Ruth received two dozen red roses, and I was presented with a huge bouquet made out of fresh vegetables. They even had a wedding cake for us to cut.

The aftermath was anything but romantic. Soon Ruth came down with a sore throat and a 101-degree fever. I nursed her as well as I could, cooking my own meals and eating them on the floor in the bedroom so I could be near her. Her temperature was higher the next day. I put her in the Seventh Day Adventist hospital because I had to go out of town for the week; it was for a speaking engagement in Ohio substituting for Dr. Edman that I felt I had to take. She recovered quickly and was discharged. By the time I got home at seven on Friday morning, she had the apartment straightened up from my mess.

As newlyweds in a first pastorate, Ruth and I were pretty typical lovebirds, I guess. We took hikes in the sunshine and in the rain, especially enjoying the arboretum nearby. On rare occasions, I went golfing and Ruth caddied for me. It was a major excursion to go into Chicago to see movies at Telenews, an all-newsreel theater on North State Street.

On the spur of the moment late one Monday, which was my day off, I took Ruth out for supper at a restaurant in La Grange. I was wearing my battered Li'l Abner brogans, and Ruth was in her loafers and sport coat. While we waited for an empty table, a lot of people pouring in—and quite a crowd it was—stopped and shook hands with us, saying how glad they were to see us there. Then it dawned on me that there was a youth banquet upstairs at which I had been invited to speak—an invitation that I had declined. We ducked out in a hurry.

Our old car was in bad shape and needed about $100 worth of repairs. But I got a good trade-in allowance from a local dealer on a 1942 maroon Pontiac. Our budget was given a big break by the fact that the church paid the $55 in monthly rent directly to the Pantkes. That meant that by law our dwelling was considered a church parsonage; therefore, the money paid toward rent wasn't chargeable to us for income tax purposes. That kept our total income so low that we did not even have to file a return. Ruth thought that put us in a class with tramps, but we were the happier for it.

We lived in downtown Hinsdale, a block or two from the Burlington railroad tracks. We enjoyed hamburgers and Cokes when we stepped out for a newspaper, and hot gingerbread and Postum when we stayed in. Sometimes we listened to a murder mystery or *Henry Aldrich* or *Truth or Consequences* on the radio while we ate supper by candlelight. While I studied, Ruth looked up sermon illustrations for me in old *Reader's Digest* magazines.

I needed to do a lot of studying, as well as work on my sermons. I was still blithely mixing my metaphors, as in this letter I once wrote to Ruth's parents after we returned from vacationing down South: "Things were so piled up here in my absence that I have had quite a time catching up, but at last I can see daylight. It was hard to come back from a month of do-nothing and get down to brass tacks, but I am again in the rut."

I had addressed them fondly for the first time as Mother and Dad in that letter; for the rest of his life, though, I generally referred to my father-in-law as Dr. Bell.

Occasionally Ruth's sense of humor landed us in hot water, even with her parents. One day she sent one of her regular postcards home to her folks in North Carolina, keeping them informed on developments with the newlyweds. It was postmarked October 26, 1943, about ten weeks into our marriage. At the very bottom and squeezed up along the left side, she penned an apparent afterthought: "Guess what? Bill and I are going to have an addition to our family. He's not so enthusiastic. Says it will be too much trouble, but I think it will be fun. More later. Adoringly, Ruth."

The rejoicing in the Bell household down South immediately prompted her doctor father to send us by return mail a glowing letter of congratulations—a classic of paternal pride, love, and fatherly advice. What second thoughts they might have had about their son-in-law, I could not imagine, but Dr. Bell assured us of their prayers.

For the *three* of us. For Ruth. For me. And for "Junior," the name Ruth gave the alley cat we had just adopted!

Instantly remorseful over her little joke, Ruth followed up the postcard the next day with a letter of explanation. It crossed her father's in the mail. The damage was done.

I did not let her off easily. "Now they will never believe you," I scolded her. "You've forfeited the privilege of ever getting another letter like that from your father when the real thing comes!"

She promised her folks that the next time she announced an addition to the family, it would not have whiskers and a long tail.

I rubbed it in. "Just think of your mother and daddy praying for a cat!"

Things could only get better after that.

In spite of my rough edges, the church people could not have been nicer to us. Attendance began to grow steadily, getting into the 90s by October and passing 100 two months later—about double the previous average.

It was still a basement church with high windows that we could not see out of. In the winter, visibility was obscured because of snow; in the summer, the weeds interfered. The "sort of junky" building, as Ruth described it, was redecorated free of charge by a member who was in the business, and the building committee met constantly to discuss completion plans. I preached twice on Sundays and attended youth meetings in members' homes after the evening service. In addition to a midweek prayer meeting, Ruth and I both taught Child Evangelism classes on Wednesday afternoons. She went with me on many pastoral calls.

NOW LOVE HAS A NAME:
Isaac and Rebekah

GENESIS 24

RETOLD BY VICKI J. KUYPER

The color of the clouds was what first drew Isaac's eye. The sky was ablaze with puffs of crimson, looking like a harvest of ripe pomegranates low on the horizon. "Thank you, Lord," Isaac whispered, awed once more by the God who had filled his life with moments of wonder. The God who stayed the blade of his father Abraham's knife—a knife that was ready to offer the ultimate sacrifice, as it hung over Isaac's head as a young boy. The God who opened his mother Sarah's womb so Isaac's life could begin, long after Sarah's time for bringing a child into the world should have passed.

Even after three years, Sarah's death remained fresh in Isaac's mind. He pictured his mother bent over the cooking pot stirring the evening's stew, the sound of her gentle humming rising with the smoke as the burning twigs crackled below. He could hear the timbre of her laugh, the laughter God heard the day Isaac's birth was foretold. The laughter he and his mother shared still echoed whenever someone called his name: Isaac . . . he who laughs.

But Isaac no longer searched in the distance for his mother's familiar robed figure calling him home for supper. Today he scanned the horizon for another woman. Every evening for the last few weeks he'd wandered the fields, talking to God, searching for a first glimpse of his answer to prayer. Searching for the woman God would send to be his bride.

***

Rebekah raised her hand above her eyes and scanned the rock-strewn landscape. The color of the quickly disappearing sun seemed to be setting the fields on fire with its light.

"We are close," Eliezar said with a smile.

Not so long ago—another evening, another sunset—Eliezar had simply been a stranger by the well, an aged traveler asking for a drink of water. Rebekah was happy to share a cool draught from her jar. When Rebekah had first approached the well, the elderly man smiled so deeply at her that for a moment Rebekah thought perhaps they'd met before. But as she drew closer, lowering the clay jug from her shoulder to offer the man a drink, Rebekah noticed the man's clothing differed from that of those in Haran. His clothes were coarser, well-worn, and covered with a layer of dust as thick as that on the camels that knelt beside him.

Rebekah thought, *Perhaps it's just the kindness in his voice that makes him feel so familiar. Undoubtedly he's far from home.* As the stranger withdrew the jar from his visibly parched lips, Rebekah had quickly added, "I'll draw water for your camels too, until they've finished drinking." She then emptied her jar into a nearby trough.

The camels instinctively rose to their feet, noisily crowding around the stone trough. Their long tongues anxiously lapped up every drop. It took Rebekah several trips to and from the well to satiate the camels' thirst. Meanwhile, the stranger simply sat there, a warm smile on his face and childlike joy in his eyes as he watched Rebekah's every move.

Since it was the end of the day, a number of women from town were also gathered at the well, drawing water for their families. The old man in the tattered robe, stray curls of gray hair forming a silvery crown around his balding head, was the focus of more than a few hushed whispers. But it wasn't the stranger's appearance that had the women gossiping amongst themselves. It was the way the man looked at Rebekah. Surely it was innocent enough. It wasn't the look of an old man trying to relive the lost vigor of his youth by following the willowy movements of a beautiful young girl. It was more like that of a proud father watching a beloved daughter, finding delight in simply spending time in her presence.

When the camels finally ceased drinking from the trough, Rebekah turned to bid the stranger farewell. When the man reached out his brown, wrinkled hand, Rebekah assumed it was to offer a simple gesture of thanks. But instead the stranger placed two thick gold bracelets on Rebekah's wrist and held high a gold ring for her nose. Rebekah gave the man a questioning glance and then turned to meet the eyes of the other women, who were by this time all looking her way.

Rebekah knew the nose ring could mean only one thing—a promise of marriage. But to who?

"Whose daughter are you?" the old man asked Rebekah. "Please tell me, is there room in your father's house for my traveling party to spend the night?"

Rebekah's mind was racing so fast she could hardly form an answer in reply . . . "I'm the daughter of Bethuel, the son that Milcah bore to Mahor." *Why would a stranger offer me a nose ring without even knowing who I am?* "We have plenty of food and shelter for your camels, as well as a room where you and your men can spend the night." *What will my father think when I return home bearing gifts of gold along with my jug of water?*

The aged stranger crumpled to his knees. A single tear cut a crooked path through the dust on the man's face. As he raised his hands toward the last streaks of scarlet in the early evening sky the old man cried out, "Praise be to the Lord, the God of my master Abraham who has not abandoned his kindness and faithfulness to my master! The Lord has answered our prayers. He's led me to the house of my master's relatives, to the granddaughter of my master's brother!"

Rebekah's eyes grew wide as she began to see her "chance" meeting at the well was nothing of the kind. This man, this moment, was a gift sent straight from God! Like a child half her age, Rebekah lifted her skirts above the dusty trail and began to run toward home. "Follow me!" she called to the stranger, the herald of her good fortune, the messenger of God's plan for her future.

As dusk signaled the close of another day, Laban, Rebekah's brother, was herding the sheep toward home. He stopped and listened. Was that his name? Or was it just the wind? He strained to listen above the bleating of the sheep. It was clearer now, his sister's voice calling out to him. Her voice was coming from the direction of the well.

Laban's heart raced as he ran toward his sister's cries. *Maybe there's been an accident. Perhaps she's hurt or frightened or . . .* Laban's mind filled with images of the young men of Haran. Men he'd heard joke about the beauty and innocence of his little sister. His feet felt as swift as an eagle's wings as he made his way over the fields toward the dark silhouette that called his name.

"Laban! Laban!" Rebekah cried as she fell into her brother's arms. As she lifted her head to look into Laban's troubled eyes, her brother saw the gold ring in his sister's nose. Laban's questions flowed together with Rebekah's story like water tumbling over smooth stones in a stream. As Laban's fears turned to wonder, he sent Rebekah on toward home to prepare a place for their honored guest. Then Laban continued on toward the edge of town to escort the man sent by God back to their home.

As Eliezar, the man who was no longer considered a stranger, entered the home of Bethuel and his family, the story of God's provision was told and retold. The faithful servant shared how his master Abraham longed for his son Isaac to marry a woman who shared Abraham's own family line and faith in God. Sixty-five years earlier, at God's bidding, Abraham had left his home in Haran. He traveled hundreds of miles to the south to the land of Canaan. Here God fulfilled many miraculous promises to him, one of which was the birth of a son to Sarah, aged 90, and Abraham, 100.

But God's promise did not end with Isaac's birth. For the Lord told Abraham that his descendents would outnumber the sand on the shore of the sea. And Abraham wanted every grain of that generational sand to follow the God who had been so faithful to him. He couldn't allow Isaac, his son of promise, to marry any of the Canaanite women in Hebron. So he sent Eliezar, the chief servant of his household, back to his home in Haran, back to the land of his relatives, to bring a wife back to Canaan. But Eliezar didn't go alone.

Abraham told Eliezar that an angel would accompany the servant and his men on their arduous journey. More than once Eliezar felt the presence of an unseen hand keeping them safe as they traveled over 700 miles to the north. And when they finally arrived at Haran, Eliezar's adventure was still not complete. He settled his men and their camels by the well drawn from the spring on the outskirts of town. It was here he would wait for God's sign, for a woman who would not only give Eliezar a drink, but who would offer to water his camels. Then Eliezar would know God's woman of choice for Abraham's son of promise.

"Rebekah is that woman," Eliezar said to Bethuel. "Rebekah is God's answer to that prayer."

Bethuel looked at his daughter with new eyes. The light-hearted, giggling child he had known, the girl with hair that fell in ebony ringlets down to the small of her back had a destiny that would take her far away from all she had ever known. Far away from him and the home she loved.

"This is from the Lord," Bethuel said with a waver in his voice that only his wife knew meant he was holding back tears. "You have my blessing to take my daughter back to Canaan to become the wife of your master's son, just as the Lord has directed."

Eliezar bowed before the Lord, praising Him for His faithfulness. Then the servant directed his men to bring in the sacks from the camels. Sack after sack was filled with wedding gifts, offerings that Abraham had prepared in faith months before. There were rings, bangles, and bracelets of gold and silver, clothes of fine linen, and a wedding veil the color of the setting sun, a fiery red, delicately edged in gold.

The memory of that night seemed so far away to Rebekah, as distant as her parents' home was from her now. The journey has been long, but she knew it was now near an end. She scanned the horizon anxiously, not even sure what she was looking for. Rebekah's camel came to an abrupt halt in a shallow gulley, as though it sensed something she did not. Rebekah glanced up toward the path of the setting sun. That's when she saw him, a lone figure silhouetted against the backdrop of the dying embers of day.

Rebekah turned to Eliezar. "Who's that man coming to greet us?" she asked.

"My master's son," Eliezar said with a smile as wide as the one Rebekah first saw at the well.

Rebekah climbed down from her camel and reached into the leather sack tied securely to its side. Her hand touched the cool silk of her gilt-edged veil. With a gentle tug, she pulled it free from the rest of her belongings. The silk danced in the evening breeze like a floating flame. She wrapped the veil around herself, carefully hiding her face from the one she longed to see.

Rebekah watched Isaac draw near through the weave of a silken cloud. She could make out the gentle curve of his shoulders and the confident gait with which he walked. She watched Isaac greet Eliezar with a warm embrace.

"So my friend," Isaac said to the servant, "I trust God gave you success on your long journey." Isaac's voice sounded smooth and strong, like a piece of tanned leather that had faithfully helped pull a plow over many a field.

"Oh yes, master," Eliezar replied. "This is Rebekah, the daughter of Bethuel."

As Isaac approached Rebekah she could hear the sound of her breath beneath the silk coming faster than it had just a moment before. She strained to see Isaac's face more clearly . . . the cut of his nose, the curl of his hair, the kindness in his eyes.

As Isaac touched the edge of the blowing silk with his outstretched hand, Rebekah felt herself blush the same color as the veil she wore. They were not strangers, although they'd just met. Rebekah was certain of this. She felt God had created them both for this time, for this moment, for this love.

"Rebekah . . ." Isaac said in a whisper meant only for her. "God's answer to prayer finally has a name."

THE IMPORTANCE OF BEING EARNEST

OSCAR WILDE

AN EXCERPT

This engaging and humorous morality play is actually an ongoing debate about the nature of marriage, each character taking differing views. Algernon's opinions are all quite cynical—until he falls in love with Cecily. When he attempts to propose to her, he is surprised to learn that Cecily already considers them engaged, and charmed when she reveals that her fascination with her Uncle Jack's brother Earnest—a character who does not actually exist—has led her to invent an elaborate romance between them.

The story is part intrigue and part tongue-in-check word play. Puns abound!

❖

ALGERNON: I hope, Cecily, I shall not offend you if I state quite frankly and openly that you seem to me to be in every way the visible personification of absolute perfection.

CECILY: I think your frankness does you great credit, Ernest. If you will allow me, I will copy your remarks into my diary. (Goes over to table and begins writing in diary.)

ALGERNON: Do you really keep a diary? I'd give anything to look at it. May I?

CECILY: Oh no. (Puts her hand over it.) You see, it is simply a very young girl's record of her own thoughts and impressions, and consequently meant for publication. When it appears in volume form I hope you will order a copy. But pray, Ernest, don't stop. I delight in taking down from dictation. I have reached "absolute perfection." You can go on. I am quite ready for more.

ALGERNON: (Somewhat taken aback.) Ahem! Ahem!

CECILY: Oh, don't cough, Ernest. When one is dictating one should speak fluently and not cough. Besides, I don't know how to spell a cough. (Writes as ALGERNON speaks.)

ALGERNON: (Speaking very rapidly.) Cecily, ever since I first looked upon your wonderful and incomparable beauty, I have dared to love you wildly, passionately, devotedly, hopelessly.

CECILY: I don't think that you should tell me that you love me wildly, passionately, devotedly, hopelessly. Hopelessly doesn't seem to make much sense, does it?

ALGERNON: Cecily!

(Enter MERRIMAN.)

MERRIMAN: The dog-cart is waiting, sir.

ALGERNON: Tell it to come round next week, at the same hour.

MERRIMAN: (Looks at CECILY, who makes no sign.) Yes, sir.

(MERRIMAN retires.)

CECILY: Uncle Jack would be very much annoyed if he knew you were staying on till next week, at the same hour.

ALGERNON: Oh, I don't care about Jack. I don't care for anybody in the whole world but you. I love you, Cecily. You will marry me, won't you?

CECILY: You silly boy! Of course. Why, we have been engaged for the last three months.

ALGERNON: For the last three months?

CECILY: Yes, it will be exactly three months on Thursday.

ALGERNON: But how did we become engaged?

CECILY: Well, ever since dear Uncle Jack first confessed to us that he had a younger brother who was very wicked and bad, you of course have formed the chief topic of conversation between myself and Miss Prism. And of course a man who is much talked about is always very attractive. One feels there must be something in him, after all. I daresay it was foolish of me, but I fell in love with you, Ernest.

ALGERNON: Darling! And when was the engagement actually settled?

CECILY: On the 14th of February last. Worn out by your entire ignorance of my existence, I determined to end the matter one way or the other, and after a long struggle with myself I accepted you under this dear old tree here. The next day I bought this little ring in your name, and this is the little bangle with the true lover's knot I promised you always to wear.

ALGERNON: Did I give you this? It's very pretty, isn't it?

CECILY: Yes, you've wonderfully good taste, Ernest. It's the excuse I've always given for your leading such a bad life. And this is the box in which I keep all your dear letters. (Kneels at table, opens box, and produces letters tied up with blue ribbon.)

ALGERNON: My letters! But, my own sweet Cecily, I have never written you any letters.

CECILY: You need hardly remind me of that, Ernest. I remember only too well that I was forced to write your letters for you. I wrote always three times a week, and sometimes oftener.

ALGERNON: Oh, do let me read them, Cecily.

CECILY: Oh, I couldn't possibly. They would make you far too conceited. (Replaces box.) The three you wrote me after I had broken off the engagement are so beautiful, and so badly spelled, that even now I can hardly read them without crying a little.

ALGERNON: But was our engagement ever broken off?

CECILY: Of course it was. On the 22nd of last March. You can see the entry if you like. (Shows diary.) "To-day I broke off my engagement with Ernest. I feel it is better to do so. The weather still continues charming."

ALGERNON: But why on earth did you break it off? What had I done? I had done nothing at all. Cecily, I am very much hurt indeed to hear you broke it off. Particularly when the weather was so charming.

CECILY: It would hardly have been a really serious engagement if it hadn't been broken off at least once. But I forgave you before the week was out.

AGERNON: (Crossing to her, and kneeling.) What a perfect angel you are, Cecily.

CECILY: You dear romantic boy. (He kisses her, she puts her fingers through his hair.) I hope your hair curls naturally, does it?

ALGERNON: Yes, darling, with a little help from others.

CECILY: I am so glad.

ALGERNON: You'll never break off our engagement again, Cecily?

CECILY: I don't think I could break it off now that I have actually met you. Besides, of course, there is the question of your name.

ALGERNON: Yes, of course. (Nervously.)

CECILY: You must not laugh at me, darling, but it had always been a girlish dream of mine to love some one whose name was Ernest. (ALGERNON rises, CECILY also.) There is something in that name that seems to inspire absolute confidence. I pity any poor married woman whose husband is not called Ernest.

ALGERNON: But, my dear child, do you mean to say you could not love me if I had some other name?

CECILY: But what name?

ALGERNON: Oh, any name you like—Algernon, for instance . . .

CECILY: But I don't like the name Algernon.

ALGERNON: Well, my own dear, sweet, loving little darling, I really can't see why you should object to the name of Algernon. It is not at all a bad name. In fact, it is rather an aristocratic name. Half of the chaps who get into the Bankruptcy Court are called Algernon. But seriously, Cecily . . . (Moving to her) . . . if my name was Algy, couldn't you love me?

CECILY: (Rising.) I might respect you, Ernest, I might admire your character, but I fear that I should not be able to give you my undivided attention.

ALGERNON: Ahem! Cecily! (Picking up hat.) Your Rector here is, I suppose, thoroughly experienced in the practice of all the rites and ceremonials of the Church?

CECILY: Oh, yes. Dr. Chasuble is a most learned man. He has never written a single book, so you can imagine how much he knows.

ALGERNON: I must see him at once on a most important christening—I mean on most important business.

CECILY: Oh!

ALGERNON: I sha'n't be away more than half an hour.

CECILY: Considering that we have been engaged since February the 14th, and that I only met you today for the first time, I think it is rather hard that you should leave me for so long a period as half an hour. Couldn't you make it twenty minutes?

ALGERNON: I'll be back in no time.

(Kisses her and rushes down the garden.)

CECILY: What an impetuous boy he is! I like his hair so much. I must enter his proposal in my diary.

BEAUTY AND THE BEAST

MADAME DE VILLENEUVE

Once upon a time, in a far-off country, there lived a merchant who was enormously rich. As he had six sons and six daughters, however, who were accustomed to have everything they fancied, he did not find he had a penny too much. But misfortunes befell them. One day their house caught fire and was speedily burned to the ground, along with all the splendid furniture, books, pictures, gold, silver and precious goods it contained. The father suddenly lost every ship he had upon the sea, either by dint of pirates, shipwreck or fire. Then he heard that his clerks in distant countries, whom he trusted entirely, had proved unfaithful. And at last from great wealth, he fell into the direst poverty.

All that he had left was a little house in a desolate place at least a hundred leagues from the town. The daughters at first hoped their friends, who had been so numerous while they were rich, would insist on their staying in their houses, but they soon found that they were left alone. Their former friends even attributed their misfortunes to their own extravagance and showed no intention of offering them any help.

So nothing was left for them but to take their departure to the cottage, which stood in the midst of a dark forest. As they were too poor to have any servants, the girls had to work hard, and the sons, for their part, cultivated the fields to earn their living. Roughly clothed, and living in the simplest way, the girls regretted unceasingly the luxuries and amusements of their former life. Only the youngest daughter tried to be brave and cheerful.

She had been as sad as anyone when misfortune first overtook her father, but soon recovering her natural gaiety, she set to work to make the best of things, to amuse her father and brothers as well as she could and persuade her sisters to join her in dancing and singing. But they would do nothing of the sort, and because she was not as doleful as they, her siblings declared this miserable life was all she was fit for. But she was really far prettier and cleverer than they were. Indeed, she was so lovely that she was always called Beauty.

After two years, their father received the news of one of his ships, which he had believed lost, had come safely into port with a rich cargo. All the sons and daughters at once thought that their poverty was at an end and wanted to set out directly for the town; but their father, who was more prudent, begged them to wait a little, and though it was harvest time, and he could ill be spared, determined to go himself first to make inquiries.

Only the youngest daughter had any doubt but that they would soon again be as rich as they were before. They all loaded their father with commissions for jewels and dresses which it would have taken a fortune to buy; only Beauty did not ask for anything. Her father, noticing her silence, said:

"And what shall I bring for you, Beauty?"

"The only thing I wish for is to see you come home safely," she answered.

But this reply vexed her sisters, who fancied she was blaming them for having asked for such costly things. Her father, however, was pleased, but as he thought she certainly ought to like pretty presents, he told her to choose something.

"Well, dear father," she said, "as you insist upon it, I beg that you will bring me a rose. I have not seen one since we came here, and I love them so much."

So the merchant set out, only to find that his former companions, believing him to be dead, had divided his cargo between them. After six months of trouble and expense he found himself as poor as when he started on his journey. To make matters worse, he was obliged to return in the most terrible weather. By the time he was within a few leagues of his home, he was almost exhausted with cold and fatigue. Though he knew it would take some hours to get through the forest, he resolved to go on. But night overtook him, and the deep snow and bitter frost made it impossible for his horse to carry him any farther.

The only shelter he could get was the hollow trunk of a great tree, and there he crouched all the night, which seemed to him the longest he had ever known. The howling of the wolves kept him awake, and when at last the day broke the falling snow had covered up every path, and he did not know which way to turn.

At length he made out some sort of path, but it was so rough and slippery that he fell down more than once. Presently it led him into an avenue of trees that ended in a splendid castle. It seemed to the merchant very strange that no snow had fallen in the avenue of orange trees covered with flowers and fruit. When he reached the first court of the castle, he saw before him a flight of agate steps. He went up them and passed through several splendidly furnished rooms.

The pleasant warmth of the air revived him, and he felt very hungry; but there seemed to be nobody in all this vast and splendid palace. Deep silence reigned everywhere, and at last, tired of roaming through empty rooms and galleries, he stopped in a room smaller than the rest, where a clear fire was burning and a couch was drawn up cozily before it. Thinking this must be prepared for someone who was expected, he sat down to wait till he should come, and very soon fell into a sweet sleep.

When his extreme hunger wakened him after several hours, he was still alone; but a little table, with a good dinner on it, had been drawn up close to him. He lost no time in beginning his meal, hoping he might soon thank his considerate host, whoever it might be. But no one appeared, and even after another long sleep, from which he awoke completely refreshed, there was no sign of anybody, though a fresh meal of dainty cakes and fruit was prepared upon the little table at his elbow.

Being naturally timid, the silence began to terrify him, and he resolved to search once more through all the rooms; but it was of no use, there was no sign of life in the palace! Then he went down into the garden, and though it was winter everywhere else, here the sun shone, and the birds sang, and the flowers bloomed, and the air was soft and sweet. The merchant, in ecstasies with all he saw and heard, said to himself:

All this must be meant for me. I will go this minute and bring my children to share all these delights.

In spite of being so cold and weary when he reached the castle, he had taken his horse to the stable and fed it. Now he thought he would saddle it for his homeward journey, and he turned down the path that led to the stable. This path had a hedge of roses on each side of it, and the merchant thought he had never seen or smelt such exquisite flowers. They reminded him of his promise to Beauty, and he stopped and had just gathered one to take to her when he was startled by a strange noise behind him. Turning round, he saw a frightful Beast, which seemed to be very angry and said, in a terrible voice:

"Who told you that you might gather my roses? Was it not enough that I allowed you to be in my palace and was kind to you? This is the way you show your gratitude, by stealing my flowers! But your insolence shall not go unpunished."

The merchant, terrified by these furious words, dropped the fatal rose, and, throwing himself on his knees, cried, "Pardon me, noble sir. I am truly grateful for your hospitality, which was so magnificent I could not imagine that you would be offended by my taking such a little thing as a rose."

But the Beast's anger was not lessened by this speech.

"You are very ready with excuses and flattery," he cried. "But that will not save you from the death you deserve."

Alas, thought the merchant, if my daughter could only know what danger her rose has brought me! And in despair he began to tell the Beast all his misfortunes and the reason of his journey, not forgetting to mention Beauty's request.

"A king's ransom would hardly have procured all that my other daughters asked for," he said. "But I thought that I might at least take Beauty her rose. I beg you to forgive me, for you see I meant no harm."

The Beast said, in a less furious tone, "I will forgive you on one condition—that you will give me one of your daughters."

"Ah!" cried the merchant, "if I were cruel enough to buy my own life at the expense of one of my children's, what excuse could I invent to bring her here?"

"None," answered the Beast. "If she comes at all she must come willingly. On no other condition will I have her. See if any one of them is courageous enough, and loves you enough, to come and save your life. You seem to be an honest man, so I will trust you to go home. I give you a month to see if any of your daughters will come back with you and stay here, to let you go free. If none of them is willing, you must come alone, after bidding them good-bye forever, for then you will belong to me. And do not imagine that you can hide from me, for if you fail to keep your word, I will come and fetch you!" added the Beast grimly.

The merchant accepted this proposal. He promised to return at the time appointed, and then, anxious to escape from the presence of the Beast, he asked permission to set off at once. But the Beast answered that he could not go until next day.

"Then you will find a horse ready for you," he said. "Now go and eat your supper and await my orders."

The poor merchant, more dead than alive, went back to his room, where the most delicious supper was already served on the little table drawn up before a blazing fire. But he was too terrified to eat and only tasted a few of the dishes for fear the Beast should be angry if he did not obey his orders. When he had finished, the Beast warned him to remember their agreement and prepare his daughter exactly for what she had to expect.

"Do not get up tomorrow," he added, "until you see the sun and hear a golden bell ring. Then you will find your breakfast waiting for you, and the horse you are to ride will be ready in the courtyard. He will also bring you back again when you come with your daughter a month hence. Farewell. Take a rose to Beauty, and remember your promise!"

The merchant lay down until the sun rose. Then, after breakfast, he went to gather Beauty's rose, and mounted his horse, which carried him off so swiftly that in an instant he had lost sight of the palace, and he was still wrapped in gloomy thoughts when it stopped before the door of the cottage.

His sons and daughters, who had been very uneasy at his long absence, rushed to meet him, eager to know the result of his journey which, seeing him mounted upon a splendid horse and wrapped in a rich mantle, they supposed to be favorable. But he hid the truth from them at first, only saying sadly to Beauty as he gave her the rose:

"Here is what you asked me to bring you. Little you know what it has cost."

Presently he told them his adventures from beginning to end, and then they were all very unhappy. The girls lamented loudly over their lost hopes, and the sons declared their father should not return to the terrible castle. But he reminded them he had promised to go back. Then the girls were very angry with Beauty and said it was all her fault. If she had asked for something sensible, this would never have happened.

Poor Beauty, much distressed, said to them, "I have, indeed, caused this misfortune, but who could have guessed that to ask for a rose in the middle of summer would cause so much misery? But as I did the mischief it is only just that I should suffer for it. I will therefore go back with my father to keep his promise."

At first nobody would hear of it. Her father and brothers, who loved her dearly, declared that nothing should make them let her go. But Beauty was firm. As the time drew near, she divided her little possessions between her sisters, and said good-bye to everything she loved. When the fatal day came, she encouraged and cheered her father as they mounted together the horse that had brought him back. It seemed to fly rather than gallop, but so smoothly that Beauty was not frightened. Indeed, she would have enjoyed the journey if she had not feared what might happen to her at the end of it. Her father still tried to persuade her to go back—but in vain.

While they were talking, the night fell. Then, to their great surprise, wonderful colored lights began to shine in all directions, and splendid fireworks blazed out before them; all the forest was illuminated. They even felt pleasantly warm, though it had been bitterly cold before. They reached the avenue of orange trees and saw that the palace was brilliantly lighted from roof to ground, and music sounded softly from the courtyard.

"The Beast must be very hungry," said Beauty, trying to laugh, "if he makes all this rejoicing over the arrival of his prey." But, in spite of her anxiety, she could not help admiring all the wonderful things she saw.

When they had dismounted, her father led her to the little room. Here they found a splendid fire burning, and the table daintily spread with a delicious supper.

Beauty, who was rather less frightened now that she had passed through so many rooms and seen nothing of the Beast, was quite willing to begin, for her long ride had made her very hungry. But they had hardly finished their meal when the noise of the Beast's footsteps was heard approaching, and Beauty clung to her father in terror, which became all the greater when she saw how frightened he was. But when the Beast really appeared, though she trembled at the sight of him, she made a great effort to hide her terror, and saluted him respectfully.

This evidently pleased the Beast. After looking at her, he said, in a tone that might have struck terror into the boldest heart, though he did not seem to be angry:

"Good-evening, old man. Good-evening, Beauty."

The merchant was too terrified to reply, but Beauty answered sweetly, "Good-evening, Beast."

"Have you come willingly?" asked the Beast. "Will you be content to stay here when your father goes away?"

Beauty answered bravely that she was quite prepared to stay.

"I am pleased with you," said the Beast. "As you have come of your own accord, you may stay. As for you, old man," he added, turning to the merchant, "at sunrise tomorrow take your departure. When the bell rings, get up quickly and eat your breakfast, and you will find the same horse waiting to take you home."

Then turning to Beauty, he said, "Take your father into the next room, and help him choose gifts for your brothers and sisters. You will find two traveling trunks there; fill them as full as you can. It is only just that you should send them something very precious as a remembrance."

Then he went away, after saying, "Good-bye, Beauty; good-bye, old man." Beauty was beginning to think with great dismay of her father's departure, but they went into the next room, which had shelves and cupboards all round it. They were greatly surprised at the riches it contained. There were splendid dresses fit for a queen, with all the ornaments to be worn with them, and when Beauty opened the cupboards she was quite dazzled by the gorgeous jewels that lay in heaps upon every shelf. After choosing a vast quantity, which she divided between her sisters—for she had made a heap of the wonderful dresses for each of them—she opened the last chest, which was full of gold.

"I think, father," she said, "that, as the gold will be more useful to you, we had better take out the other things again, and fill the trunks with it."

So they did this, but the more they put in, the more room there seemed to be, and at last they put back all the jewels and dresses they had taken out, and Beauty even added as many more of the jewels as she could carry at once. Even then the trunks were not too full, but they were so heavy that an elephant could not have carried them!

"The Beast was mocking us!" cried the merchant. "He pretended to give us all these things, knowing that I could not carry them away."

"Let us wait and see," answered Beauty. "I cannot believe that he meant to deceive us. All we can do is to fasten them up and leave them ready."

So they did this and returned to the little room, where they found breakfast ready. The merchant ate his with a good appetite, as the Beast's generosity made him believe he might perhaps venture to come back soon and see Beauty. But she felt sure that her father was leaving her forever, so she was very sad when the bell rang sharply.

They went down into the courtyard, where two horses were waiting, one loaded with the two trunks, the other for him to ride. They were pawing the ground in their impatience to start, and the merchant was forced to bid Beauty a hasty farewell. As soon as he was mounted, he went off at such a pace that she lost sight of him in an instant. Then Beauty began to cry and wandered sadly back to her own room. But she soon found she was very sleepy, and as she had nothing better to do, she lay down and instantly fell asleep. And then she dreamed that she was walking by a brook bordered with trees, and lamenting her sad fate, when a young prince, handsomer than anyone she had ever seen, and with a voice that went straight to her heart, came and said to her:

"Ah, Beauty! you are not so unfortunate as you suppose. Here you will be rewarded for all you have suffered elsewhere. Your every wish shall be gratified. Only try to find me out, no matter how I may be disguised, as I love you dearly, and in making me happy you will find your own happiness. Be as true-hearted as you are beautiful, and we shall have nothing left to wish for."

"What can I do, Prince, to make you happy?" said Beauty.

"Only be grateful," he answered, "and do not trust too much to your eyes. Above all, do not desert me until you have saved me from my cruel misery."

After this she thought she found herself in a room with a stately and beautiful lady, who said to her. "Dear Beauty, try not to regret all you have left behind you; you are destined to a better fate. Only do not let yourself be deceived by appearances."

Beauty found her dreams so interesting that she was in no hurry to awake, but presently the clock roused her by calling her name softly twelve times. Then she rose and found her dressing-table set out with everything she could possibly want, and when her toilet was finished she found dinner was waiting in the room next to hers. But dinner does not take very long when you are all by yourself, and very soon she sat down cozily in the corner of a sofa, and began to think about the charming Prince she had seen in her dream.

"He said I could make him happy," said Beauty to herself. "It seems, then, that this horrible Beast keeps him a prisoner. How can I set him free? I wonder why they both told me not to trust in appearances? But, after all, it was only a dream, so why should I trouble myself about it? I had better go and find something to do to amuse myself."

So she got up and began to explore some of the many rooms of the palace. The first she entered was lined with mirrors. Beauty saw herself reflected on every side, and thought she had never seen such a charming room. Then a bracelet hanging from a chandelier caught her eye, and on taking it down, she was greatly surprised to find that it held a portrait of her unknown admirer, just as she had seen him in her dream. With great delight she slipped the bracelet on her arm, and went on into a gallery of pictures, where she soon found a portrait of the same handsome Prince, as large as life, and so well painted that as she studied it, he seemed to smile kindly at her.

Tearing herself away from the portrait at last, she passed through into a room that contained every musical instrument under the sun, and here she amused herself for a long while in trying them and singing. The next room was a library, and she saw everything she had ever wanted to read, as well as everything she had read. By this time it was growing dusk, and wax candles in diamond and ruby candlesticks lit themselves in every room.

Beauty found her supper served just at the time she preferred to have

it, but she did not see anyone or hear a sound, and though her father had
warned her that she would be alone, she began to find it rather dull.

But presently she heard the Beast coming, and wondered tremblingly if
he meant to eat her up now. However, he did not seem at all ferocious, and
only said gruffly:

"Good-evening, Beauty."

She answered cheerfully and managed to conceal her terror. Then the
Beast asked her how she had been amusing herself, and she told him all the
rooms she had seen. Then he asked if she thought she could be happy in his
palace; and Beauty answered that everything was so beautiful that she would
be very hard to please if she could not be happy. And after about an hour's
talk, Beauty began to think that the Beast was not nearly so terrible as she had
supposed at first. Then he got up to leave her, and said in his gruff voice:

"Do you love me, Beauty? Will you marry me?"

"Oh! what shall I say?" cried Beauty, for she was afraid to make the Beast
angry by refusing.

"Say 'yes' or 'no' without fear," he replied.

"Oh, no, Beast," said Beauty hastily.

"Since you will not, good-night, Beauty," he said.

And she answered, "Good-night, Beast," very glad to find that her refusal
had not provoked him. After he was gone, she was very soon in bed and
asleep, and dreaming of her unknown Prince.

She thought he came and said to her, "Ah, Beauty! Why are you so
unkind to me? I fear I am fated to be unhappy for many a long day still."

And then her dreams changed, but the charming Prince figured in them
all. When morning came her first thought was to look at the portrait and see
if it was really like him, and she found that it certainly was.

She decided to amuse herself in the garden, for the sun shone, and all
the fountains were playing. She was astonished to find that every place was
familiar to her, and presently she came to the very brook and the myrtle trees

where she had first met the Prince in her dream. That made her think more than ever that he must be kept a prisoner by the Beast.

When she was tired, she went back to the palace and found a new room full of materials for every kind of work—ribbons to make into bows and silks to work into flowers. Then there was an aviary full of rare birds, which were so tame that they flew to Beauty as soon as they saw her and perched upon her shoulders and her head.

"Pretty little creatures," she said, "how I wish that your cage were nearer my room that I might often hear you sing!" So saying she opened a door and found to her delight that it led into her own room, though she had thought it was quite the other side of the palace.

There were more birds in a room farther on, parrots and cockatoos that could talk, and they greeted Beauty by name. Indeed, she found them so entertaining that she took one or two back to her room, and they talked to her while she was at supper. The Beast paid her his usual visit and asked her the same questions as before, and then with a gruff good night he took his departure, and Beauty went to bed to dream of her mysterious prince.

The days passed swiftly in different amusements, and after a while Beauty found another strange thing in the palace, which often pleased her when she was tired of being alone. There was one room that she had not noticed particularly; it was empty, except that under each of the windows stood a very comfortable chair. The first time she had looked out of the window it seemed a black curtain prevented her from seeing anything outside. But the second time she went into the room, happening to be tired, she sat down in one of the chairs. Instantly, the curtain was rolled aside and a most amusing pantomime was acted before her. There were dances and colored lights, and music and pretty dresses, and it was all so gay that Beauty was in ecstasies. After that she tried the other seven windows in turn, and there was some new and surprising entertainment to be seen from each of them, so Beauty never could feel lonely any more. Every evening after supper, the Beast came to see her, and always before saying good night asked her in his terrible voice:

"Beauty, will you marry me?"

And it seemed to Beauty, now she understood him better, that when she said, "No, Beast," he went away quite sad. Her happy dreams of the handsome young prince soon made her forget the poor Beast, and the only thing that disturbed her was being told to distrust appearances, to let her heart guide her, and not her eyes. Consider as she would, she could not understand.

So everything went on for a long time, until at last, happy as she was, Beauty began to long for the sight of her father and her brothers and sisters. One night, seeing her look very sad, the Beast asked her what was the matter. Beauty had quite ceased to be afraid of him. Now she knew that he was really gentle in spite of his ferocious looks and dreadful voice. So she answered that she was longing to see her home once more. Upon hearing this, the Beast seemed sadly distressed, and cried miserably:

"Ah! Beauty, have you the heart to desert an unhappy Beast like this? What more do you want to make you happy? Is it because you hate me that you want to escape?"

"No, dear Beast," answered Beauty softly, "I do not hate you, and I should be very sorry never to see you any more, but I long to see my father again. Only let me go for two months, and I promise to come back to you and stay for the rest of my life."

The Beast, who had been sighing dolefully while she spoke, now replied, "I cannot refuse you anything you ask, even though it should cost me my life. Take the four boxes you will find in the room next to your own and fill them with everything you wish to take with you. But remember your promise and come back when the two months are over, or you may have cause to repent it, for if you do not come in good time, you will find your faithful Beast dead. You will not need any chariot to bring you back. Only say good-bye to all your brothers and sisters the night before you come away and, when you have gone to bed, turn this ring round upon your finger and say firmly, 'I wish to go back to my palace and see my Beast again.' Good-night, Beauty. Fear nothing, sleep peacefully, and before long you shall see your father once more."

As soon as Beauty was alone, she hastened to fill the boxes with all the rare and precious things she saw about her, and only when she was tired of heaping things into them did they seem to be full. Then she went to bed, but could hardly sleep for joy. When at last she did begin to dream of her beloved prince, she was grieved to see him stretched upon a grassy bank, sad and weary, and hardly like himself.

"What is the matter?" she cried.

He looked at her reproachfully, and said, "How can you ask me, cruel one? Are you not leaving me to my death perhaps?"

"Ah, don't be so sorrowful," cried Beauty. "I am only going to assure my father that I am safe and happy. I have promised the Beast faithfully that I will come back, and he would die of grief if I did not keep my word!"

"What would that matter to you?" said the Prince "Surely you would not care?"

"Indeed I should be ungrateful if I did not care for such a kind Beast," cried Beauty indignantly. "I would die to save him from pain. I assure you it is not his fault that he is so ugly."

Just then a strange sound woke her—someone was speaking not very far away; and opening her eyes she found herself in a room she had never seen before, which was certainly not as splendid as those she was used to in the Beast's palace. Where could she be? She got up and dressed hastily and then saw that the boxes she had packed the night before were all in the room. She suddenly heard her father's voice and rushed out to greet him joyfully. Her brothers and sisters were all astonished at her appearance, for they had never expected to see her again. Beauty asked her father what he thought strange dreams meant and why the Prince constantly begged her not to trust to appearances. After much consideration he answered:

"You tell me yourself that the Beast, frightful as he is, loves you dearly, and deserves your love and gratitude for his gentleness and kindness. I think the Prince must mean you to understand you ought to reward him by doing as he wishes, in spite of his ugliness."

Beauty could not help seeing that this seemed very probable; still, when she thought of her dear Prince who was so handsome, she did not feel at all inclined to marry the Beast. At any rate, for two months she need not decide but could enjoy herself with her sisters. But though they were rich now, and lived in a town again and had plenty of acquaintances, Beauty found that nothing amused her very much. She often thought of the palace, where she was so happy, especially as at home she never once dreamed of her dear Prince, and she felt quite sad without him.

Then her sisters seemed quite used to being without her, and even found her rather in the way, so she would not have been sorry when the two months were over but for her father and brothers. She had not the courage to say good-bye to them. Every day when she rose, she meant to say it at night, and when night came, she put it off again, until at last she had a dismal dream that helped her to make up her mind.

She thought she was wandering in a lonely path in the palace gardens, when she heard groans. Running quickly to see what could be the matter, she found the Beast stretched out upon his side, apparently dying. He reproached her faintly with being the cause of his distress, and at the same moment a stately lady appeared, and said very gravely:

"Ah, Beauty, you are only just in time to save his life. If you had delayed one day more, you would have found him dead."

Beauty was so terrified by this dream that the very next evening she said good-bye to her father and all her brothers and sisters, and as soon as she was in bed, she turned her ring round upon her finger, and said firmly:

"I wish to go back to my palace and see my Beast again."

Then she fell asleep instantly, and only woke up to hear the clock saying,

"Beauty, Beauty" twelve times in its musical voice, which told her at once that she was really in the palace once more. Everything was just as before, and her birds were so glad to see her, but Beauty thought she had never known such a long day. She was so anxious to see the Beast again that she felt as if supper-time would never come.

But when it came, no Beast appeared. After listening and waiting for a long time, she ran down into the garden to search for him. Up and down the paths and avenues ran poor Beauty, calling him. No one answered, and not a trace of him could she find. At last, she saw that she was standing opposite the shady path she had seen in her dream. She rushed down it and, sure enough, there was the cave, and in it lay the Beast—asleep, so Beauty thought. Quite glad to have found him, she ran up and stroked his head, but, to her horror, he did not move or open his eyes.

"Oh, he is dead; and it is all my fault!" moaned Beauty, crying bitterly.

But then, looking at him again, she fancied he still breathed. Hastily fetching some water from the nearest fountain, she sprinkled it over his face, and, to her great delight, he began to revive.

"Oh! Beast, how you frightened me!" she cried. "I never knew how much I loved you until just now, when I feared I was too late to save your life."

"Can you really love such an ugly creature as I am?" said the Beast faintly. "Ah, Beauty, you came only just in time. I was dying because I thought you had forgotten your promise. But go back now and rest, I shall see you again by-and-by."

Beauty, who had half expected that he would be angry with her, was reassured by his gentle voice and went back to the palace, where supper was awaiting her. And afterward the Beast came in as usual and talked about the time she had spent with her father, asking if she had enjoyed herself and if they had all been very glad to see her.

Beauty quite enjoyed telling him all that had happened to her. And when at last the time came for him to go, he asked, as he had so often asked before:

"Beauty, will you marry me?"

She answered softly, "Yes, dear Beast."

As she spoke a blaze of light sprang up before the windows of the palace; fireworks crackled and guns banged, and across the avenue of orange trees, in letters all made of fireflies, was written: Long live the Prince and his Bride.

Turning to ask the Beast what it could all mean, Beauty found that he had disappeared, and in his place stood her long-loved Prince! At the same moment the wheels of a chariot were heard upon the terrace, and two ladies entered the room. One of them Beauty recognized as the stately lady she had seen in her dreams; the other was so queenly that Beauty hardly knew which to greet first. But the one she already knew said to her companion:

"Well, Queen, this is Beauty, who has had the courage to rescue your son from the terrible enchantment. They love one another, and only your consent to their marriage is wanting to make them perfectly happy."

"I consent with all my heart," cried the Queen. "How can I ever thank you enough, charming girl, for having restored my dear son to his natural form?" And then she tenderly embraced Beauty and the Prince.

Then the stately woman said to Beauty, "I suppose you would like me to send for all your brothers and sisters to dance at your wedding?"

And so she did, and the marriage was celebrated the very next day with the utmost splendor, and Beauty and the Prince lived happily ever after.

PRIDE AND PREJUDICE

JANE AUSTEN

AN EXCERPT

Marriage and manners—two topics that draw much attention in rural nineteenth-century England. Mr. and Mrs. Bennet have five daughters in all, but the plot swirls around the intelligent second daughter—Elizabeth.

When the Bingleys move into a nearby estate, the Bennets are delighted. Mr. Bingley is rich and single. Mrs. Bennet is sure that a match can be made with one of her daughters.

Elizabeth first meets Mr. Darcy, Bingley's handsome and well-to-do friend, shortly after the Bingleys arrive, but she is put off by his lack of manners when she hears him make an unflattering comment about dancing with her.

In the time the Bingleys live at Netherfield, many romances bloom, some lasting, some short-lived between the Bennet girls and Bingley's friends and acquaintances. Elizabeth does not again encounter Mr. Darcy until the Bingleys move back to London. It is on a visit to London to visit mutual friends that Mr. Darcy declares his love for her and proposes marriage. Once again, his lack of manners is obvious. In the very verbiage of the proposal, he manages to insult Elizabeth and her family's social standing again—she flatly refuses him.

It isn't until Bennet sister number five (Lydia) runs away to Scotland with a military officer that Mr. Darcy is able to right his previous blunders by finding the couple and convincing them to return home and be properly married. As Elizabeth considers his actions on Lydia's behalf, her prejudice toward him and her misplaced pride begin to melt. The two become friends and often walk and talk together. As their love grows stronger, Mr. Darcy repeats his proposal and Elizabeth happily accepts.

Elizabeth's spirits soon rising to playfulness again, she wanted Mr. Darcy to account for his having ever fallen in love with her. "How could you begin?" said she. "I can comprehend your going on charmingly, when you had once made a beginning; but what could set you off in the first place?"

"I cannot fix on the hour, or the spot, or the look, or the words, which laid the foundation. It is too long ago. I was in the middle before I knew that I had begun."

"My beauty you had early withstood, and as for my manners—my behavior to you was at least always bordering on the uncivil, and I never spoke to you without rather wishing to give you pain than not. Now be sincere; did you admire me for my impertinence?"

"For the liveliness of your mind, I did."

"You may as well call it impertinence at once. It was very little less. The fact is that you were sick of civility, of deference, of officious attention. You were disgusted with the women who were always speaking, and looking, and thinking for your approbation alone. I roused and interested you, because I was so unlike them. Had you not been really amiable, you would have hated me for it; but in spite of the pains you took to disguise yourself, your feelings were always noble and just; and in your heart, you thoroughly despised the persons who so assiduously courted you. There—I have saved you the trouble of accounting for it; and really, all things considered, I begin to think it perfectly reasonable. To be sure, you knew no actual good of me—but nobody thinks of that when they fall in love."

"Was there no good in your affectionate behavior to Jane while she was ill at Netherfield?"

"Dearest Jane! Who could have done less for her? But make a virtue of it by all means. My good qualities are under your protection, and you are to exaggerate them as much as possible; and, in return, it belongs to me to find occasions for teasing and quarrelling with you as often as may be; and I shall begin directly, by asking you what made you so unwilling to come to the point at last? What made you so shy of me when you first called, and afterward dined here? Why, especially, when you called, did you look as if you did not care about me?"

"Because you were grave and silent, and gave me no encouragement."

"But I was embarrassed."

"And so was I."

"You might have talked to me more when you came to dinner."

"A man who had felt less, might."

"How unlucky that you should have a reasonable answer to give and that I should be so reasonable as to admit. But I wonder how long you would have gone on if you had been left to yourself! I wonder when you would have spoken, if I had not asked you! My resolution of thanking you for your kindness to Lydia had certainly great effect—too much, I am afraid; for what becomes of the moral, if our comfort springs from a breach of promise? For I ought not to have mentioned the subject. This will never do."

"You need not distress yourself. The moral will be perfectly fair. Lady Catherine's unjustifiable endeavors to separate us were the means of removing all my doubts. I am not indebted for my present happiness to your eager desire of expressing your gratitude. I was not in a humor to wait for any opening of yours. My aunt's intelligence had given me hope, and I was determined at once to know every thing."

"Lady Catherine has been of infinite use, which ought to make her happy, for she loves to be of use. But tell me, what did you come down to Netherfield for? Was it merely to ride to Longbourn and be embarrassed? or had you intended any more serious consequence?"

"My real purpose was to see you, and to judge, if I could, whether I might ever hope to make you love me. My avowed one, or what I avowed to myself, was to see whether your sister were still partial to Bingley, and, if she were, to make the confession to him which I have since made."

"Shall you ever have courage to announce to Lady Catherine what is to befall her?"

"I am more likely to want time than courage, Elizabeth. But it ought to be done, and if you will give me a sheet of paper, it shall be done directly."

"And if I had not a letter to write myself, I might sit by you and admire the evenness of your writing, as another young lady once did. But I have an aunt, too, who must not be longer neglected."

From an unwillingness to confess how much her intimacy with Mr. Darcy had been over-rated, Elizabeth had never yet answered Mrs. Gardiner's long letter; but now, having that to communicate which she knew would be most welcome, she was almost ashamed to find that her uncle and aunt had already lost three days of happiness, and immediately wrote as follows:

"I would have thanked you before, my dear aunt, as I ought to have done, for your long, kind, satisfactory, detail of particulars; but to say the truth, I was too cross to write. You supposed more than really existed. But now suppose as much as you choose; give a loose to your fancy, indulge your imagination in every possible flight which the subject will afford, and unless you believe me actually married, you cannot greatly err. You must write again very soon, and praise him a great deal more than you did in your last. I thank you, again and again, for not going to the Lakes. How could I be so silly as to wish it! Your idea of the ponies is delightful. We will go round the Park every day. I am the happiest creature in the world. Perhaps other people have said so before, but no one with such justice. I am happier even than Jane; she only smiles. I laugh. Mr. Darcy sends you all the love in the world that can be spared from me. You are all to come to Pemberley at Christmas.—Yours, etc."

Mr. Darcy's letter to Lady Catherine was in a different style, and still different from either was what Mr. Bennet sent to Mr. Collins, in reply to his last.

"DEAR SIR,

"I must trouble you once more for congratulations. Elizabeth will soon be the wife of Mr. Darcy. Console Lady Catherine as well as you can. But, if I were you, I would stand by the nephew. He has more to give."—Yours sincerely, etc."

Happy for all her maternal feelings was the day on which Mrs. Bennet got rid of her two most deserving daughters. With what delighted pride she afterwards visited Mrs. Bingley, and talked of Mrs. Darcy, may be guessed. I wish I could say, for the sake of her family, that the accomplishment of her earnest desire in the establishment of so many of her children produced so happy an effect as to make her a sensible, amiable, well-informed woman for the rest of her life; though, perhaps it was lucky for her husband, who might not have relished domestic felicity in so unusual a form, that she still was occasionally nervous and invariably silly.

Mr. Bennet missed his second daughter exceedingly; his affection for her drew him oftener from home than any thing else could do. He delighted in going to Pemberley, especially when he was least expected.

THE QUAKERESS

CHARLES HEBER CLARK (MAX ADELER)

AN EXCERPT

Young Abigail is content in the community of Friends (Quakers) in which she has grown up. Her faith is strong and pure, and it was expected that she would one day become the bride of George Sotherby, a fellow member of her Friends congregation, who though much older, courted her tenderly and loved her deeply.

Abby felt good about becoming George's wife, she held him in high esteem and great affection, but she wondered—as any beautiful young woman would—if she would ever know what true love is?

Mrs. Ponder another member of the congregation introduces Abby to her niece, Dolly, and eventually to her nephew, Clayton. The young man is grown and unlearned in the ways of the Quakers, but he takes both an interest in Abby and her faith.

Clayton struggles with his love for Abby and his deep emotions about the issues rising to fever pitch in the country. Civil war seems unavoidable, and he finds himself torn between his sense of duty and the pacifist views of the woman he has come to love.

When Clayton left the picnic ground with Abby, they strolled through the wood to the place where a great rock overhanging the pathway and upheld by the stony earth on either side made a kind of cave that the people of the countryside named the Indian Cave. A rustic seat had been made there and Abby and Clayton tarried to look at the cave, which was blackened by the smoke of fires kindled by sojourners in the forest. Then they turned and sat to face the view to the north. The brown, dead leaves, gathered for a century, made a cushion for their feet, and over them and around them the foliage of the great trees shaded them and framed the picture of the valley below them. A thread of a stream dashed vehemently down the narrow gorge a dozen feet from them and plunged into the river far down the hillside. Over and beyond the river, softened by the faint haze that filled the air, lay Connock and behind it the sweet Plymouth valley with tilled fields and low farm houses and clumps of woodland, and here and there the white gash of a quarry. There was no sound but of the rushing water of the brook and of the fluttering leaves, excepting when from the riverside came the roar of a swift flying train or the shrill scream of a steam whistle.

They sat in silence for a while and upon Abby's spirit came a feeling of solemnity that was almost oppressive. She felt that serious things were to be said today, and that she should not go home with her love still voiceless.

"It is more beautiful than my own country," at last said Clayton, making with his right hand a quick gesture toward the distant scene, "although I think that very beautiful. But perhaps it is not just the loveliness of the landscape that makes it so charming for me. The mind gives its own coloring to the picture always, does it not?"

"I think so," answered Abby.

"Beautiful as it is, however," said Clayton with mournfulness, "I shall see it no more," and he thrust out his hand again as if to wave farewell to the valley, the river, and the trees.

A little shiver ran through Abby's frame and she clinched her hands closer as she held them in her lap.

"Is thee going away? Must thee go home again?" she asked in a low voice.

"Today," he answered, still looking at the far scene, as if he dared not turn his eyes to her, "I must go today."

"I am sorry," she said quietly.

He seemed not to hear her, and then he said: "I have no summons to go. There is no business to call me. My father has not said he needed me. Perhaps I may not go to my home. Perhaps—"

"Thee will not become a soldier, will thee? O do not do that." Abby's cheeks were white and her eyes were moist with the coming tears.

"I do not know," said Clayton, still not turning his face to hers. "I am in a strange tangle of perplexity. The South seems sometimes to call me to come to help her in her cause; but—but there is something else—there is something mightier than the home tie or the love of country; something that— Do you know why these woods and waters and all these rolling hills and green valleys are lovely to me? Do you know?" he asked almost fiercely, and then, turning his face full to hers and dropping his voice to tones of tenderness, he answered his own question. "It is because you are here."

Abby did not speak. She clenched her hands tighter and the flush rose upon her cheek and spread to her forehead.

"Yes," said Clayton, passion beginning to color his voice. "I came to Connock reluctantly, because I ought; because my mother wished me to be considerate of my aunt. I thought to be wearied of it in a day or two and go back, leaving my sister here. But when I saw you sitting on the porch with your mother, I knew that I should stay. I knew that the crisis of my life had come. You will not believe me that I passed a sleepless night that first night of my arrival here. You will not believe that I have been in half delirium since that time; exaltation sometimes so that it seemed as if I could not bear such joy, and then despair that would fill all my soul with pain."

He saw that the tears were trickling down Abby's cheeks as he spoke.

"For, while it was plain to me that there could be no peace for me again, no peace unless you were mine, I said to myself. *How shall such an one as I with his life all stained and sinful, dare to ask that girl to join her pure and holy life to his?* You seemed beyond me, far, far beyond me, and you seem so now; and yet you have been very gracious to me and have not disdained me and have put your hand sometimes in mine. So I could not help loving you, and then the hope would come that perhaps despite my unworthiness—despite— despite—(I cannot say it) you might stoop to return that love."

Abby arose and walked to the brink of the little stream and put her hands over her face. Clayton, surprised at the movement, sat still for a moment, and then, rising, he went toward her.

"It is over then?" he said, standing close behind her. "I should not have spoken. I knew that I ought not to speak. But I am going away. I shall be gone at once. But oh! That I may see your face once more and hear you say that you forgive me!"

She turned and a swift glance showed him that he had misjudged her. He flung his arms passionately about her, and with her arms clasping his neck, she hid her face upon his breast half crying. He lifted her head gently and kissed her fondly and with misty eyes she looked into his eyes.

'You love me my dearest, you do love me then?"

"Yes!" she whispered, and once more he held her to him and kissed her again and again. He led her to the rustic bench.

"Thee will not go now?" she asked with a tremulous voice.

"No, I will not go today. I cannot bear to leave you, my darling, my love, my Abby! I must have time to think, time to tell you things you must know."

"What things?" asked Abby. There was in his voice and manner that which gave her foreboding of evil, even in this very ecstasy of her joy.

"Not now," he said, waving his hand as though to dispel a vision that was hateful. "Not now, when this splendor of happiness, this miracle of peace has come to us. Let me look into your eyes and see there your love for me! Let me hold you fast and kiss you, my sweet, dear love. God gave you to me from the very beginning. You were always mine, my precious wife."

"I thank Him for it. It is His gift to us both."

"Did you love me from the first, dear Abby?"

" O yes!" she said, dropping her eyes.

"When you first saw me?" demanded this lover with eager curiosity.

"Yes, and before. When Mrs. Ponder told me thee was coming; then—I do not know why; I did not understand, but I felt sure thee was coming to claim me; sure of it."

"It was from eternity! I will be forever," said Clayton with solemn fervor.

"Forever!" repeated Abby. "I will never change."

"Not if sorrow comes and separation? Not if bitter fortune says disown him? Not if I go away to the Southland and to the wild chance of war."

"Not that, dear Clayton! O not that! I cannot bear that you should fight. We are peace people. But to fight against my country! I pray, pray that you will not do that."

"I feel sometimes like a coward that I stay at home when all my people are in arms, but it is my strong love for you that holds me. I may not go if you will weep for me, but O my love! There may be other things to thrust us apart and give us heartache. Though your father and your mother should frown upon us and your Friends in the meeting should disapprove, you will love me still, will you not?"

"I cannot help it," answered Abby, with a shadow of dread in her heart. "I have lost the power to control my feelings. Father and mother will be most sorrowful and Friends will cast me out, but if I must die for thee I will."

Again he kissed her passionately.

"I asked too much of you when I asked you to be mine," he said. "I am not worthy any sacrifice and yet I summon you to it. I summon myself to it. I am ready for it. I cannot help loving you until love seems to me the whole of life, but, rather than you should suffer, I will give it all up. I will go away and never see your face again. Shall I go?"

She put her hand in his and looked gravely in his face: "No; anything but that; anything. I cannot give thee up."

"I have asked myself a thousand times," he said, "the source of this strange and wonderful passion that impelled you to me and me to you. We did not create it; we are not responsible for it; we dare not defy it. The impulse is divine. The creator of all things created us for each other; and no human authority can put us asunder."

"Let us wait patiently," she said with a tranquil voice. "The same Spirit that led you to me and gave you to me, will show us the right way if we trust ourselves wholly to Him."

Clayton looked troubled and he made as if he would speak to her; but he held his peace, and at last he said: "If we are helped in that way, it will be your fellowship with Him that helps us. I dare not ask for a blessing for myself."

He took her hand, and slowly they walked along—Abby loyal in her love for Clayton and without a doubt of him. "And now," she said, "shall we not return to the company? It is growing dark."

***

It would seem that Clayton and Abby had each found the one they would love forever, but all was not as it seemed. One of them had a terrible secret.

Clayton Harley had already married when he declared his love for Abby and asked her to be his wife. The marriage was hidden from the members of his family and his friends, and his wife was far away from him in another country. He bore the burden of his secret lightly while he cared no more for any woman than he cared for his wife; but it had become heavy since he began to love Abby, and all but intolerable since she had plighted her troth to him.

He had come home from the picnic and from that entrancing love passage with her to a night of misery and self reproach. In the sleepless hours he thought of a hundred plans for extricating himself from the dishonor in which he was involved; but every one of these was shattered against the hard facts that his marriage with Abby was barred by another marriage and that, even if he could free himself from the wife he scorned, the pure and gentle Quaker girl would be unlikely to marry a man in such a situation. Another thing was clear to him: he could not give her up. He had gone too far for that; too far for him and for her. He truly loved her and he was not capable of such a sacrifice. He knew that she loved him truly and he feared both the effect upon her of revelation of the truth, and that she would despise him if she did not hate him.

But out of bewilderment and conflicting emotion, out of struggle between inclination and positive obligation there came at last conviction that he must find courage to tell the truth to Abby, and to accept the consequences. This he resolved to do, dreadful as the task was for him and repulsive as the revelation must be for her.

***

Clayton came and sat in the pew with the girl in the gloomy corner almost behind one of the great pillars that upheld the yellow timbers. She was glad to have him there. He took her hand in his. She felt entirely happy, and she had no impulse to speak. The sacredness of the place seemed to give a kind of consecration to her affection. She began to perceive in what manner the colors, the atmosphere, the trappings of the sanctuary warm the emotions of the worshipers. It would have given her contentment to sit there for hours, in silence, holding the hand of her beloved. Her home, and all Connock seemed far away, as if she were in a strange distant country, filled with the glory of a new and higher and holier life.

"Abby," Clayton said in a voice that was not quite his own, and that seemed to him to come from a throat all the muscles of which were tense. "I wish to tell you a story."

"Very well," she said, but the strangeness of his voice and his manner gave her a feeling of dread.

" I knew a boy once who when he had quitted college went upon an errand to Mexico. Some of his people had property there, mines and other things, and he was sent thither partly that he might look into the business and report upon it, but chiefly, I suppose, that he might see a bit of the world and learn to take care of himself. He was gone for a year, and so little did he learn about taking care of himself that he became the victim of a sharp woman and a mercenary father and like a fool married the woman."

"Why do you tell me this?" asked Abby, into whose mind a faint gleam of fear had come.

Clayton did not heed her inquiry.

"This stupid boy persuaded himself that he was in love, and the woman and the father so entangled him that, when he found he had deluded himself, he could not retreat. He married her and then, his eyes wide opened by the ghastly consequences of his folly, he left her forever. This boy afterward met a lovely girl to whom he was drawn by the force of a passion high and holy and it became his duty to tell her the truth."

Abby was weeping and her face was white.

"I am that boy," continued Clayton. "I have sinned against you, and I have brought you here that I might make confession to you and ask your forgiveness."

Abby made no answer. In a moment all her joy had shriveled up and vanished and she found herself enveloped in misery which almost paralyzed her faculties. Clayton leaned toward her and waited for her to speak; but she looked out through her tears into what seemed thick darkness beyond her and still held her peace.

He could say nothing. Then turning to him she said: "Will thee not go back to her and be faithful to her? Then I can take up my heavy burden and bear it and thee can bear thine as thee ought to do. This is what people have meant when they spoke of enduring pain and sorrow. It is hard, but it is better than disgrace."

"I cannot give you up," he said passionately, and seized her hand and kissed it. She looked down at him as she caught her hand away.

"I pray that you will understand," he said, "that I never for a single moment loved any woman but you. I am actually not responsible for the marriage I told you of. That I was not much more than a child when it occurred is not excuse enough. I was ensnared, cajoled, and intimidated.

The woman is coarse, illiterate, and much older than I am. She never really attracted me for a moment, but in an instant of blind and reckless folly I was made to seem to ask her to marry me. I was surrounded by men of violence, in a lawless mining settlement, and partly to save my life, partly from a false sense of humor, to make good what in my childish ignorance seemed to me my word, I consented to have a ceremony performed. The next day I fled and I have never seen the woman since. She may be dead for aught I know."

Abby looked at his handsome face, pale with the violence of his emotion, and she felt her resolution becoming weaker.

"I have no right," he continued, "to involve you in the consequences of my weakness and my misfortune. But you have moved me and I know you can pity me and withhold your scorn. I should have fled away as soon as I saw you. The first word I spoke to you was fatal to me. I forgot everything but the longing of my soul for you. Even now I would rather part with my life than give you up; life will have nothing for me when I am forced to do that. But I will do it if you wish. Yes, I will do it."

"What else is there to do?" asked Abby with a tremulous voice.

"Nothing else, if that woman lives; I know it. But can we not, when we part, have some communication with one another, so that if she shall die—?"

"To wish for the death of another person is murder!" said Abby.

"Not to wish for it," he said piteously, "but to wait for it. It may have come already. I will make inquiry. I will at once try to discover the truth. May I not remain in touch with you until then?"

Abby did not answer.

Clayton lifted his head and standing up with his face pallid and his eyes filled with tears, said: "I will go, then!"

Abby sat long in the church, how long she did not know, and while her pulse grew quieter and the flush passed from her face, her mind lost none of its disquiet. Upon arrive home, she hid herself in her room; and with her was one thought: *Clayton had gone!* She felt half glad and half sorry. It was brave and right for him to go away and yet she had a rebellious feeling that he was deserting her in the bitterest hour of her trouble. When a note was slipped under the door, she read it eagerly.

My Dear Abby,

It is better that I leave you for the present. I cannot help loving you dearly wherever I am and I do not fear you will cease to love me until I shall be free and shall have a right to claim you for my own. We shall wait; if not with patience, then with hopefulness. Every moment I shall have you in my mind and sometimes I will write to you, if I may. Will you give me permission to do so?"

Abby kissed the letter and thrust it into the bosom of her dress. She said to herself that she would consider the request that he might write to her, but way down in her inner self she knew that she would permit him to write and would find happiness in reading his letters.

Clayton and Abby never married, though they did see each other again many times. He thought her resolve would be tempered over time and she would agree that they should be together, but she did not give in.

Clayton joined the Confederate Army and ironically, he died in battle a short distance from where she was teaching school. Abby knew he was there for he had paid her a very short visit the night before as Lee's and McClellan's armies were gathering.

When the battle ended, 20,000 men lay dead, but Abby was determined to find and recover Clayton's body. With her discovery made, she sat long with him on the battlefield, his head in her lap. She then had his body returned to his mother. Some time later, she married George, but she never fully recovered from the loss of her greatest earthly love, and legend has it that she died of a broken heart.

LOVE AT FIRST SIGHT:
Jacob and Rachel

GENESIS 29:1-30

RETOLD BY VICKI J. KUYPER

It was an impulsive kiss. Tender, yet timid. Driven by passion, yet tempered with the fear of rejection. As Rachel pulled back from Jacob's unexpected embrace, Jacob slowly opened his eyes, drinking in every detail of the mysteriously alluring woman who stood before him. The curl of auburn hair peeking out of her scarf. The glittering olive-green eyes. The delicately curved fingers. The shy smile that made Jacob believe in love at first sight. The captivating beauty of the woman he longed to call his bride.

Rachel's eyes met Jacob's for just a moment, then darted self-consciously toward the ground. Jacob wanted to say something, anything, to reassure Rachel that his intentions were honorable. But from the moment he laid eyes on Laban's daughter, words had fled like frightened sheep. Now all that remained were tears of thanks to the God who had led him here.

A group of shepherds who had gathered nearby watched the encounter with curiosity. Every day at this same time they came together to talk as they watered their sheep. But today this stranger from Canaan had arrived from the south. The traveler had been inquiring about the health of his relative, Laban, when suddenly the young man's attention turned to the western fields, where he saw a shepherdess herding her flock toward the well.

"That's Laban's daughter, Rachel . . ." one of the shepherds began. But the stranger seemed caught up in a dream. He'd left the shepherd in mid-sentence and hurried to the young woman's side.

The band of men had watched in amazement as Jacob pushed aside the large stone that covered the mouth of the well, the stone they had planned on moving once all of the local shepherds arrived. It took at least five of them, working together, to shift the awkwardly heavy slab of rock each day. But this stranger, who in appearance certainly seemed to be a mere man, moved it as though it were made of reeds. Then came the stolen kiss.

Now that same stranger sat on the ground, his head in hands, weeping, as Rachel stood nearby. She seemed pale, almost breathless as she tried to attend to watering her sheep. She paused for a moment, gently placing her hand on the man's shoulder and whispering something in his ear. Perhaps the kiss wasn't stolen after all.

The local shepherds shook their heads, muttering a few words to each other under their breath, and then got back to work caring for their sheep. The next day when the shepherds gathered at the well, Rachel never arrived. But the news already had. Laban had promised Rachel's hand in marriage to the smitten stranger. Since Jacob had no money to pay the customary bride price, he'd agreed to work in Laban's fields for seven years.

As the years passed, Jacob told his friends—the shepherds he first met at the well—over and over about the blessing God brought his way that day. How he'd traveled from Canaan to find a bride, a daughter from the family of his mother's brother, Laban. He repeated how his love story was so much like that of his father Isaac, who also married a woman from Haran. For Isaac and Rebekah it was a tale of love at first sight, just like it had been for himself and Rachel. But Jacob never shared the other side of the story. The real reason he'd left Canaan. How he deceived his father to steal his older brother's birthright. That part of his past remained a secret. That part of the past he tried to forget.

For seven years Jacob continued to tell his friends how working Laban's land was a small price to pay for a treasure like Rachel. "When you're in love," he always said with a grin, "years fly by like days."

The time finally came when Jacob was counting down minutes instead of days, months, or years. The wedding feast had begun! Laban's home was filled with friends and relatives, music, food, and wine. Jacob's hearty laugh could be heard above the hubbub of song and celebration. Laban's sons gathered around Jacob offering blessing after blessing for a home filled with children, heirs to carry on the family name. As Jacob reveled in his newfound family, he noticed that Rachel's older sister, Leah, was nowhere to be seen. Quiet and rather awkward, Leah always had been nervous around crowds.

She's probably sitting alone in a corner somewhere . . . Jacob's thoughts were interrupted by the hush of voices as the bride entered the room, escorted by her father. She was wrapped in red, her features hidden behind the intricately decorated wedding veil that covered her from head to toe. But Jacob could picture his bride as clearly as if the billowing veil were made of air. He could see the stray curl of red hair that refused to be tamed dancing on her forehead. The warmth of her smile, so timid when she was with others, but always in full bloom whenever he was by her side. The willowy curve of her neck. The emerald fire that lit her eyes.

Laban put the bride's hand into Jacob's. The father of the bride offered a blessing and then guided the couple into the room where they would spend their first night together. Not a single candle burned inside. Like another veil separating him from his bride, the darkness closed around Jacob as Laban shut the door. With the noise of the feast still continuing down the hall, the room seemed strangely quiet and still. Not a word passed between Jacob and his long-awaited bride. As Jacob's hands pulled the veil aside in the dark, and his lips searched the night for the one he loved, it seemed words were unnecessary.

But as the morning light lifted the veil of night, plenty of words rolled off Jacob's tongue. Angry words. Tear-filled words. Words filled with venom and accusation. They began the moment the groom awakened to find his bride already alert, her eyes downcast, ashamed to meet his. They were chestnut eyes, rimmed with dark lashes. It was Leah, not Rachel, who had shared his bed.

Jacob ran out in the courtyard to find Laban, who greeted Jacob's tirade with an air of indifference. "It's not the custom in our land to marry the younger daughter before the eldest is wed," Jacob's uncle said, his lips twisted into a confident smirk.

Jacob knew deceit when he saw it. The truth was, he knew it all too well. His own trickery was what had made him flee Canaan in the first place. His own shame overshadowed his anger. As the color rose in his cheeks Jacob became silent. But within him a cry echoed loud and clear: The deceiver has become the deceived.

Laban's voice broke the silence. "I have an idea," Laban said, his calculated smile growing even wider. "Finish out your bridal week with my eldest daughter. Then you can marry Rachel. The bride price remains the same. Seven years."0

Jacob looked up to see Rachel standing in the arch of the doorway, her eyes rimmed with tears. Almost hidden in her shadow stood Leah, her eyes on the ground, her hands hidden in the folds of her robe. Jacob stared at the two women, there lives bound together with the cords of love and deceit, passion and indifference.

"I'll work," Jacob replied. "I'll work for what's mine."

MIDDLEMARCH

GEORGE ELIOT

AN EXCERPT

"And now good-morrow to our waking souls
Which watch not one another out of fear;
For love all love of other sights controls,
And makes one little room, an everywhere."

—DR. DONNE

Young Dorothea Brooke has a thirst for learning and, for that reason, when she reaches the age to marry, she chooses Casaubon—an older clergyman—hoping to join him in his service to others. Though her friends and family caution her against it, she is determined, confident that her husband-to-be will one day include her in his work. Of course, Casaubon does not love Dorothea and does not allow her to take part in his ministry. He is looking only for a woman who will care for his needs in his old age. Lonely and disappointed, Dorothea remains faithful to her husband and humbly cares for him.

Soon after their marriage, Dorothea meets her husband's younger cousin, Will Ladislaw. The attraction is strong, but she dismisses it, honoring her vows. Still her husband notices, and puts a clause in his will stating that should Dorothea marry Will after his death, she would forfeit all her estate except a small stipend of seven hundred pounds a year.

Nicholas Bulstrode is a wealthy Middlemarch banker. He professes to be a deeply religious Evangelical Protestant, but he has a dark past: he made his fortune as a pawnbroker selling stolen goods. He married Will's grandmother after her first husband died. Her daughter had run away years before, and she insisted that Bulstrode find her before she re-married, because she wanted to leave her wealth to her only surviving child. Bulstrode located the daughter and her child, Will

Ladislaw, but he kept her existence a secret and bribed the man he hired to find her.

After the death of Dorothea's husband, Will declares his love for her, but he is now deeply in debt and has no family wealth to fall back on. Bulstrode offers him money to atone for keeping his existence from his grandmother. But Will refuses the money as it was earned illegally.

When Will learns of the clause in Casaubon's will, he feels he cannot ask Dorothea to give up her property and live in poverty with him. He leaves for London, but his love for Dorothea causes him to return, with the purpose of speaking to her one last time.

On the second morning after Dorothea's visit to Rosamond, she had had two nights of sound sleep, and had not only lost all trace of fatigue, but felt as if she had a great deal of superfluous strength—that is to say, more strength than she could manage to concentrate on any occupation. The day before, she had taken long walks outside the grounds, and had paid two visits to the Parsonage; but she never in her life told any one the reason why she spent her time in that fruitless manner, and this morning she was rather angry with herself for her childish restlessness. Today was to be spent quite differently. What was there to be done in the village? Oh dear! nothing. Everybody was well and had flannel; nobody's pig had died; and it was Saturday morning, when there was a general scrubbing of floors and door-stones, and when it was useless to go into the school. But there were various subjects that Dorothea was trying to get clear upon, and she resolved to throw herself energetically into the gravest of all.

She sat down in the library before her particular little heap of books on political economy and kindred matters, out of which she was trying to get light as to the best way of spending money so as not to injure one's neighbors, or—what comes to the same thing—so as to do them the most good. Here was a weighty subject which, if she could but lay hold of it, would certainly keep her mind steady. Unhappily her mind slipped off it for a whole hour;

and at the end she found herself reading sentences twice over with an intense consciousness of many things, but not of any one thing contained in the text.

This was hopeless. Should she order the carriage and drive to Tipton? No; for some reason or other she preferred staying at Lowick. But her vagrant mind must be reduced to order: there was an art in self-discipline; and she walked round and round the brown library considering by what sort of maneuver she could arrest her wandering thoughts. Perhaps a mere task was the best means—something to which she must go doggedly. Was there not the geography of Asia Minor, in which her slackness had often been rebuked by Mr. Casaubon? She went to the cabinet of maps and unrolled one: this morning she might make herself finally sure that Paphlagonia was not on the Levantine coast, and fix her total darkness about the Chalybes firmly on the shores of the Euxine. A map was a fine thing to study when you were disposed to think of something else, being made up of names that would turn into a chime if you went back upon them. Dorothea set earnestly to work, bending close to her map, and uttering the names in an audible, subdued tone, which often got into a chime. She looked amusingly girlish after all her deep experience—nodding her head and marking the names off on her fingers, with a little pursing of her lip, and now and then breaking off to put her hands on each side of her face and say, "Oh dear! oh dear!"

There was no reason why this should end any more than a merry-go-round; but it was at last interrupted by the opening of the door and the announcement of Miss Noble.

The little old lady, whose bonnet hardly reached Dorothea's shoulder, was warmly welcomed, but while her hand was being pressed, she made many of her beaver-like noises, as if she had something difficult to say.

"Do sit down," said Dorothea, rolling a chair forward. "Am I wanted for anything? I shall be so glad if I can do anything."

"I will not stay," said Miss Noble, putting her hand into her small basket, and holding some article inside it nervously; "I have left a friend in the churchyard." She lapsed into her inarticulate sounds, and unconsciously drew forth the article which she was fingering. It was the tortoise-shell lozenge-box, and Dorothea felt the color mounting to her cheeks.

"Mr. Ladislaw," continued the timid little woman. "He fears he has offended you, and has begged me to ask if you will see him for a few minutes."

Dorothea did not answer on the instant: it was crossing her mind that she could not receive him in this library, where her husband's prohibition seemed to dwell. She looked toward the window. Could she go out and meet him in the grounds? The sky was heavy, and the trees had begun to shiver as at a coming storm. Besides, she shrank from going out to him.

"Do see him, Mrs. Casaubon," said Miss Noble, pathetically; "else I must go back and say No, and that will hurt him."

"Yes, I will see him," said Dorothea. "Pray tell him to come."

What else was there to be done? There was nothing that she longed for at that moment except to see Will—the possibility of seeing him had thrust itself insistently between her and every other object; and yet she had a throbbing excitement like an alarm upon her—a sense that she was doing something daringly defiant for his sake.

When the little lady had trotted away on her mission, Dorothea stood in the middle of the library with her hands falling clasped before her, making no attempt to compose herself in an attitude of dignified unconscious-ness. What she was least conscious of just then was her own body. She was thinking of what was likely to be in Will's mind, and of the hard feelings that others had had about him. How could any duty bind her to hardness? Resistance to unjust dispraise had mingled with her feeling for him from the very first, and now in the rebound of her heart after her anguish the resistance was stronger than ever. "If I love him too much it is because he has been used so ill:"—there was a voice within her saying this to some imagined audience in the library, when the door was opened, and she saw Will before her.

She did not move, and he came toward her with more doubt and timidity in his face than she had ever seen before. He was in a state of uncertainty which made him afraid lest some look or word of his should condemn him to a new distance from her; and Dorothea was afraid of her own emotion. She looked as if there were a spell upon her, keeping her motionless and hindering her from unclasping her hands, while some intense, grave yearning was imprisoned within her eyes. Seeing that she did not put out her hand as usual, Will paused a yard from her and said with embarrassment, "I am so grateful to you for seeing me."

"I wanted to see you," said Dorothea, having no other words at command. It did not occur to her to sit down, and Will did not give a cheerful interpretation to this queenly way of receiving him; but he went on to say what he had made up his mind to say.

"I fear you think me foolish and perhaps wrong for coming back so soon. I have been punished for my impatience. You know—every one knows now—a painful story about my parentage. I knew of it before I went away, and I always meant to tell you of it if—if we ever met again."

There was a slight movement in Dorothea, and she unclasped her hands, but immediately folded them over each other.

"But the affair is matter of gossip now," Will continued. "I wished you to know that something connected with it—something which happened before I went away, helped to bring me down here again. At least I thought it excused my coming. It was the idea of getting Bulstrode to apply some money to a public purpose—some money which he had thought of giving me. Perhaps it is rather to Bulstrode's credit that he privately offered me compensation for an old injury: he offered to give me a good income to make amends; but I suppose you know the disagreeable story?"

Will looked doubtfully at Dorothea, but his manner was gathering some of the defiant courage with which he always thought of this fact in his destiny. He added, "You know that it must be altogether painful to me."

"Yes—yes—I know," said Dorothea, hastily.

"I did not choose to accept an income from such a source. I was sure that you would not think well of me if I did so," said Will. Why should he mind saying anything of that sort to her now? She knew that he had avowed his love for her. "I felt that"—he broke off, nevertheless.

"You acted as I should have expected you to act," said Dorothea, her face brightening and her head becoming a little more erect on its beautiful stem.

"I did not believe that you would let any circumstance of my birth create a prejudice in you against me, though it was sure to do so in others," said Will, shaking his head backward in his old way, and looking with a grave appeal into her eyes.

"If it were a new hardship it would be a new reason for me to cling to you," said Dorothea, fervidly. "Nothing could have changed me but—" her heart was swelling, and it was difficult to go on; she made a great effort over herself to say in a low tremulous voice, "but thinking that you were different—not so good as I had believed you to be."

"You are sure to believe me better than I am in everything but one," said Will, giving way to his own feeling in the evidence of hers. "I mean, in my truth to you. When I thought you doubted of that, I didn't care about anything that was left. I thought it was all over with me, and there was nothing to try for—only things to endure."

"I don't doubt you any longer," said Dorothea, putting out her hand; a vague fear for him impelling her unutterable affection.

He took her hand and raised it to his lips with something like a sob. But he stood with his hat and gloves in the other hand, and might have done for the portrait of a Royalist. Still it was difficult to loose the hand, and Dorothea, withdrawing it in a confusion that distressed her, looked and moved away.

"See how dark the clouds have become, and how the trees are tossed," she said, walking toward the window, yet speaking and moving with only a dim sense of what she was doing.

Will followed her at a little distance, and leaned against the tall back of a leather chair, on which he ventured now to lay his hat and gloves, and free himself from the intolerable durance of formality to which he had been for the first time condemned in Dorothea's presence. It must be confessed that he felt very happy at that moment leaning on the chair. He was not much afraid of anything that she might feel now.

They stood silent, not looking at each other, but looking at the evergreens which were being tossed, and were showing the pale underside of their leaves against the blackening sky. Will never enjoyed the prospect of a storm so much: it delivered him from the necessity of going away. Leaves and little branches were hurled about, and the thunder was getting nearer. The light was more and more somber, but there came a flash of lightning that made them start and look at each other, and then smile. Dorothea began to say what she had been thinking of.

"That was a wrong thing for you to say, that you would have had nothing to try for. If we had lost our own chief good, other people's good would remain, and that is worth trying for. Some can be happy. I seemed to see that more clearly than ever, when I was the most wretched. I can hardly think how I could have borne the trouble, if that feeling had not come to me to make strength."

"You have never felt the sort of misery I felt," said Will; "the misery of knowing that you must despise me."

"But I have felt worse—it was worse to think ill—" Dorothea had begun impetuously, but broke off.

Will colored. He had the sense that whatever she said was uttered in the vision of a fatality that kept them apart. He was silent a moment, and then said passionately—

"We may at least have the comfort of speaking to each other without disguise. Since I must go away—since we must always be divided—you may think of me as one on the brink of the grave."

While he was speaking there came a vivid flash of lightning which lit each of them up for the other—and the light seemed to be the terror of a hopeless love. Dorothea darted instantaneously from the window; Will followed her, seizing her hand with a spasmodic movement; and so they stood, with their hands clasped, like two children, looking out on the storm, while the thunder gave a tremendous crack and roll above them, and the rain began to pour down. Then they turned their faces toward each other, with the memory of his last words in them, and they did not loose each other's hands.

"There is no hope for me," said Will. "Even if you loved me as well as I love you—even if I were everything to you—I shall most likely always be very poor; on a sober calculation, one can count on nothing but a creeping lot. It is impossible for us ever to belong to each other. It is perhaps base of me to have asked for a word from you. I meant to go away into silence, but I have not been able to do what I meant."

"Don't be sorry," said Dorothea, in her clear tender tones. "I would rather share all the trouble of our parting."

Her lips trembled, and so did his. It was never known which lips were the first to move toward the other lips; but they kissed tremblingly, and then they moved apart.

The rain was dashing against the window-panes as if an angry spirit were within it, and behind it was the great swoop of the wind; it was one of those moments in which both the busy and the idle pause with a certain awe.

Dorothea sat down on the seat nearest her, a long low ottoman in the middle of the room, and with her hands folded over each other on her lap, looked at the drear outer world. Will stood still an instant looking at her, then seated himself beside her, and laid his hand on hers, which turned itself upward to be clasped. They sat in that way without looking at each other, until the rain abated and began to fall in stillness. Each had been full of thoughts, which neither of them could begin to utter.

But when the rain was quiet, Dorothea turned to look at Will. With passionate exclamation, as if some torture screw were threatening him, he started up and said, "It is impossible!"

He went and leaned on the back of the chair again, and seemed to be battling with his own anger, while she looked toward him sadly.

"It is as fatal as a murder or any other horror that divides people," he burst out again; "it is more intolerable—to have our life maimed by petty accidents."

"No—don't say that—your life need not be maimed," said Dorothea, gently.

"Yes, it must," said Will, angrily. "It is cruel of you to speak in that way— as if there were any comfort. You may see beyond the misery of it, but I don't. It is unkind—it is throwing back my love for you as if it were a trifle, to speak in that way in the face of the fact. We can never be married."

"Some time—we might," said Dorothea, in a trembling voice.

"When?" said Will, bitterly. "What is the use of counting on any success of mine? It is a mere toss up whether I shall ever do more than keep myself decently, unless I choose to sell myself as a mere pen and a mouthpiece. I can see that clearly enough. I could not offer myself to any woman, even if she had no luxuries to renounce."

There was silence. Dorothea's heart was full of something she wanted to say, and yet the words were too difficult. She was wholly possessed by them: at that moment debate was mute within her. And it was very hard that she could not say what she wanted to say. Will was looking out of the window angrily. If he would have looked at her and not gone away from her side, she thought everything would have been easier. At last he turned, still resting against the chair, and stretching his hand automatically toward his hat, said with a sort of exasperation, "Good-bye."

"Oh, I cannot bear it—my heart will break," said Dorothea, starting from her seat, the flood of her young passion bearing down all the obstructions that had kept her silent—the great tears rising and falling in an instant: "I don't mind about poverty—I hate my wealth."

In an instant Will was close to her and had his arms round her, but she drew her head back and held his away gently that she might go on speaking, her large tear-filled eyes looking at his very simply, while she said in a sobbing childlike way, "We could live quite well on my own fortune—it is too much—seven hundred a year—I want so little—no new clothes—and I will learn what everything costs."

***

Dorothea never repented that she had given up position and fortune to marry Will Ladislaw, and he would have held it the greatest shame as well as sorrow to him if she had repented. They were bound to each other by a love stronger than any impulses that could have marred it. No life would have been possible to Dorothea that was not filled with emotion, and she had now a life filled also with a beneficent activity which she had not the doubtful pains of discovering and marking out for herself. Will became an ardent public man, working well in those times when reforms were begun with a young hopefulness of mediate good that has been much checked in our days and getting at last returned to Parliament by a constituency who paid his expenses. Dorothea could have liked nothing better, since wrongs existed, than that her husband should be in the thick of a struggle against them, and that she should give him wifely help. Many who knew her, thought it a pity that so substantive and rare a creature should have been absorbed into the life of another, and be only known in a certain circle as a wife and mother. But no one stated exactly what else that was in her power she ought rather to have done.

***

Some never ceased to regard Dorothea's second marriage as a mistake; and indeed this remained the tradition concerning it in Middlemarch, where she was spoken of to a younger generation as a fine girl who married a sickly clergyman, old enough to be her father, and in little more than a year after his death gave up her estate to marry his cousin—young enough to be his son, with no property, and not well-born. Those who had not seen anything of Dorothea usually observed that she could not have been "a nice woman," else she would not have married either the one or the other.

Certainly those determining acts of her life were not ideally beautiful. They were the mixed result of young and noble impulse struggling amidst the conditions of an imperfect social state, in which great feelings will often take the aspect of error, and great faith the aspect of illusion. For there is no creature whose inward being is so strong that it is not greatly determined by what lies outside it. A new Theresa will hardly have the opportunity of reforming a conventional life, any more than a new Antigone will spend her heroic piety in daring all for the sake of a brother's burial: the medium in which their ardent deeds took shape is forever gone. But we insignificant people with our daily words and acts are preparing the lives of many Dorotheas, some of which may present a far sadder sacrifice than that of the Dorothea whose story we know.

Her finely-touched spirit had still its fine issues, though they were not widely visible. Her full nature, like that river in which Cyrus broke the strength, spent itself in channels which had no great name on the earth. But the effect of her being on those around her was incalculably diffuse: for the growing good of the world is partly dependent on unhistoric acts; and that things are not so ill with you and me as they might have been, is half owing to the number who lived faithfully a hidden life, and rest in unvisited tombs.

A MAN CALLED PETER

THE COURTSHIP OF PETER AND CATHERINE MARSHALL

CATHERINE MARSHALL

AN EXCERPT

I was twenty, and allergic to figures. Unfortunately, the required college algebra had figures, lots of them. Dr. Henry Robinson, a brilliant scholar in his own field, and the head of Agnes Scott's mathematics department, undertook personally to escort me through the wilderness. But mathematics was not Dr. Robinson's only talent. He had side lines, such as a romantic interest in match-making and a vital concern for the then much-discussed cause of prohibition. I came in for both, because it was he who arranged my first meeting with Peter Marshall. Along with an Emory University freshman, Dr. Robinson had scheduled the Reverend Peter Marshall and me to speak at a prohibition rally at a little town near Atlanta.

For two full years I had longed to know this young Scotsman whom I had frequently heard preach. Who could have heard such sermons as "Agnostics and Azaleas" or "Rosary of Remembrance" and failed to glimpse the poetry in this man's soul or the deep earnestness of his desire to take men and women by the hand and lead them to God? Both attributes appealed to me strongly; for at this stage (I might as well admit) I was in love with love, fancied myself a poet, and, more important, was groping to find my way out of an inherited Christianity into a spiritual experience of my own.

One of my youthful self-indulgences was a journal in which I poured out my hopes and dreams and let my poetic urge have full reign. In it I had written earlier: "I am neither right with myself nor with God. I can never enjoy life until I learn why I am here and where I am going—" And then a few pages on: "I have never met anyone whom I so want to know as Mr. Marshall."

My letters to my parents in the little town of Keyser, West Virginia,

where my father was pastor of the Presbyterian Church, had also been
including comments about Peter Marshall for some time. In January, 1934, I
had written to them:

*Carol (one of my New England friends) and I went to Westminster again
yesterday to hear Peter Marshall.*

*Westminster is a rather small church—but very quiet and worshipful. Mr.
Marshall conducts beautiful services, and I like him more each time I go. He's only
twenty-eight (I was mistaken, Peter was actually thirty-one at the time) and has
had just four years of experience, but believe me, he's something already.*

*I have never heard such prayers in my life. It's as if, when he opens his mouth,
there is a connected line between you and God. I know this sounds silly, but I've got
to meet this man!*

There was, however, no apparent way to meet him. To me, a college
girl, Peter Marshall, the clergyman, seemed almost as inaccessible as a man
from Mars. Since I was very young and quite transparent, it must have been
obvious to my parents that all of my idealism, as well as my natural girlish
romanticism, was rapidly centering upon this young Scottish minister.

You see [I explained in another letter], *as far as Mr. Marshall is concerned,
he doesn't even know I exist—I've never met such a young man with so much real
power. You feel it the minute you step inside his church. He's oh, so Scotch, and very
dignified, but he has a lovely sense of humor.* [Then I added self-consciously] *All
this is awfully silly, isn't it? Oh, shucks, I wish I'd stop thinking about the man!*

The night of the prohibition rally was, therefore, very important to me.
At long last I was going to meet Peter Marshall. My romantic soul said that
the event must have the proper setting. I had suggested to Dr. Robinson that
he pick me up in the Alumnae garden. In my imagination I could see Mr.
Marshall marching down between the rose arbors to get me, while I waited
for him, holding in one graceful hand a copy of *Sonnets from the Portuguese* and
dreamily trailing the other through the lily pond.

Dr. Robinson picked me up in the garden all right, but merely tooted his horn; so I climbed into the back seat by the boy from Emory. Mr. Marshall was sitting beside Dr. Robinson in front. I expected him to be thinking about his speech. Instead, he immediately turned around to ask, "What's this I hear about my being engaged? Dr. Robinson says that you said—"

I flushed and stammered, "I—I did hear some rumors to that effect."

"Don't believe everything you hear, my dear girl. I certainly am not even about to be married."

He pronounced the word "mar-r-ied" with a very broad "a" and a rolling of the "r's."

I remembered then another story I had heard about him. One night in prayer meeting, he had been talking about gossip and had remarked that everyone in the church seemed to know better than he when he was going to be "mar-r-ied" and whom he was going to "mar-r-y."

"I'd like this clearly understood," he went on, grinning like a small boy, "I'm not going to get mar-r-ied till I'm good and ready. I'm good enough now, but I'm not ready." This remark soon went the rounds.

The village to which we were going was some twenty miles away and seemed to have a general store, six houses, and a schoolhouse set in a grove of trees. A large group of farmers and their wives from the surrounding countryside came, bringing with them numerous assorted wriggling children and some babes in arms. They apparently had some curiosity to know why we thought the county should not go wet. Free schoolbooks had been cannily promised by the local politicians out of the tax from beer.

The night was blustery, with a wind from the south and frequent flashes of lightning. Soon the schoolroom was filled with people packed in around the old potbellied stove.

The choir was solicited from the audience by a gray-haired man who assured all bashful recruits that the choir was not going to sing an anthem. For this mercy we were grateful. He managed to get together an assortment of folks who looked as if they had stepped out of a Dickens novel. After they had self-consciously filed into the rows of cane chairs facing the audience, the meeting began, as it was to end, with the singing of revival hymns strange to us. The gray-haired man kept waving his arms and urging the choir on. The bass, a large red-faced man in the back row, tried harder, and, as a result, looked as if he might have a stroke any minute. The tremolo of the tall, thin woman in the front row became almost turbulent under his heckling.

Peter, standing beside me, managed to read the music, growing more and more enthused, finally entering into the spirit of the evening and enjoying himself immensely. Whenever I stumbled over the unfamiliar music, he would give me a nudge of encouragement to "car-r-y on."

One by one, we were then elaborately introduced, listened to patiently, and given more applause than we deserved. Frankly, I can't remember much about what we said. The county promptly went wet.

On the way home Peter said, "May I see you sometime this week? I've wanted to know you for a long time." And when I clearly showed my great astonishment, he added, "Not even ministers are blind, you know."

Six dates, four chaperones, and a dozen months later we were engaged.

How it came about I still regard as one of God's nicest miracles and the first big evidence of God's hand on my life.

All public speakers develop pet expressions and clichés. Peter had his, and was often teased about them. Usually, during these years, they were alliterative. For example, whenever the announcement of a recent marriage was made in Westminster Church's bulletin, almost invariably it would end with words bearing the Marshall touch: "May He who has admitted these young people into the halls of highest human happiness richly bless them in their new life."

Peter was an increasingly popular speaker in the city of Atlanta and throughout the South. Moreover, he was now in the full swing of all that is involved in a thriving city parish. Indeed, he was so busy baptizing infants, writing sermons, calling, bowling on the church team, teaching the Boudeleon class, holding meetings, and admitting people "into the halls of highest human happiness" that there was little time for personal dates. Mostly, we saw each other only as he drove me back to the college after some church service.

Even that took the help of Miss Ruby Coleman, his secretary. As I made my way slowly toward the church door through the crush of the crowds that came to hear him, Miss Coleman would appear, seemingly rising out of the floor like a one-woman orchestra.

"Mr. Marshall requested that I ask you please to wait until he is through speaking to people. He would like very much to drive you back to Decatur."

I waited.

On Mother's Day I had heard Peter preach "Keepers of the Springs," and had been profoundly stirred. Other sermons like "Dancing in Tears" and "Youth and the Stranger" made it clear that he was holding up fluttering white banners of premarital chastity for both men and women, and that as far as women were concerned, he was an idealist and a romanticist.

His own words give best his philosophy of marriage:

"Marriage is not a federation of two sovereign states. It is a union— domestic, social, spiritual, physical. It is a fusion of two hearts—the union of two lives—the coming together of two tributaries, which, after being joined in marriage, will flow in the same channel in the same direction . . . carrying the same burdens of responsibility and obligation.

"Modern girls argue that they have to earn an income, in order to establish a home, which would be impossible on their husband's income. That is sometimes the case, but it must always be viewed as a regrettable necessity, never as the normal or natural thing for a wife to have to do.

"The average woman, if she gives her full time to her home, her husband, her children . . . if she tries to understand her husband's work . . . to curb his egotism while, at the same time, building up his self-esteem, to kill his masculine conceit while encouraging all his hopes to establish around the family a circle of true friends. . . .

"If she provides in the home a proper atmosphere of culture, of love, of music, of beautiful furniture, and of a garden . . . If she can do all this, she will be engaged in a life work that will demand every ounce of her strength, every bit of her patience, every talent God has given her, the utmost sacrifice of her love.

"It will demand everything she has and more. And she will find that for which she was created. She will know that she is carrying out the plan of God. She will be a partner with the Sovereign Ruler of the universe.

"And so, today's daughters need to think twice before they seek to make a place for themselves, by themselves in our world today. . . ."

"He still places women on such a pedestal," I confided in my journal, "much as my father's generation did, and he seems quite old-fashioned in some ways—especially toward marriage and the home. Yet, I wonder if I shall ever meet anyone whom I admire so much—Peter, with an inheritance of the best of the European tradition, and an acquisition of the best of the American. Peter, who has such an acute appreciation for beauty, such a delightful sense of humor. I don't think he's really a scholar, but except for that, why must the embodiment of all my ideals be twelve years older than I, and still as remote as the South Pole?"

Like the rest of young America, I would never have taken the philosophy of marriage Peter advocated from any of the older generation, but we took it from him, liked it, and came back for more.

Was it possible, I wondered, under the stimulus of his thinking, that women in seeking careers of their own, were seeking emancipation from their own God-given natures, and so were merely reaping inner conflict? Could this be one of the basic reasons for the failures of so many marriages today? Could God have created us so that, ideally, we achieve greatest happiness and greatest character development as our husband's career becomes our own, and as we give ourselves unstintingly to it and to our homes? I was not sure, but it was worth pondering deeply.

"It suddenly occurred to me today," I wrote, "that with all my wondering about what I am supposed to do with my life when I graduate this year, I have scarcely consulted God about His plans for me. . . . " I didn't know it then, but His plans were incredibly wonderful.

Meanwhile it had become something of a distinction to have one's wedding ceremony performed by Peter Marshall. If possible, he wanted three conferences before the ceremony with each couple he married—one with the prospective bride, one with the groom, and a final joint conference. Books on marriage were also loaned to them, and the suggestion was made that they see their physicians and exchange health certificates. Health certificates were not required by the state of Georgia at that time.

"People are so funny," Peter would say to the young couple. "They demand certificates for their horses, their dogs, and their cattle, but their sons and daughters are married off with little or no attention to the hereditary strains of their partners. . . ." If folks resented thus being put in a category a little lower than the animals, they dared not show it. The young Scotsman was so obviously in earnest. Then too, he had a point.

The three premarital conferences were used to make sure that the couple had a spiritual foundation for marriage. "The perfect marriage must be a blend of the spiritual, the physical, the social, and the intellectual," he would say. "We are souls living in bodies. Therefore, when we really fall in love, it isn't just a physical attraction. God has opened our eyes and let us see into someone's soul. We have fallen in love with the inner person, the person who's going to live forever. That's why God is the greatest asset to romance. He thought it up in the first place. Include Him in every part of your marriage, and He will lift it above the level of the mundane to something rare and beautiful and lasting."

He liked to say to young people: "There are mysteries all around us. . . . Take, for example, this strange phenomenon of falling in love. Have you ever asked the question, 'How will I know when I fall in love?' I have. I've asked it many times. I've asked it of blondes and brunettes, of redheads and bald heads, and people here and there. The strange thing is that I have always received the same answer, namely, 'Don't worry, brother, *you'll know.*' Exactly, that's the point. You can't have any understanding ahead of personal experience. And as that is true of falling in love, so it is true of finding God."

Peter first knew on a Sunday night in May, 1936. I had been asked to review a book on prayer for Westminster's Fellowship Hour. After the talk, when Peter spoke to me, there was profound respect in his blue-gray eyes, and there was something else too—a certain glint I had not seen there before and didn't quite know how to interpret. He lost no time in making a dinner date with me for the following Saturday night. Then we went into the evening service, where I made the mistake of sitting within three pews of the front.

Love promptly went to my stomach. The stone pillars and the Good Shepherd window behind the pulpit began to swim alarmingly. I was too sick to be embarrassed when Peter mentioned my name from the pulpit in connection with the talk I had just given. By the time he began his sermon, I knew it would be disastrous to stay.

As I rose to begin the longest walk in history, the voice from the pulpit trailed off, and there was dead silence, broken only by the staccato clicking of my heels on the stone floor. I could feel Peter's eyes boring into my back every step of the way up the long aisle. Not until I was well out into the foyer and into the sympathetic hands of the deacons, did the voice resume.

The college infirmary received me that night and attempted to diagnose this strange stomach ailment. The head nurse, properly starched, and equipped with a strong nose for sniffing out lovesick maidens, had her suspicions.

The next day, Peter and Miss Coleman, his secretary, were eating lunch at Martha's Tea Room, next door to the church. As a rule, they used that time to talk about church business or sermons or plans for Ruby's approaching marriage to Willard Daughtry. On this particular day, however, Peter was unusually quiet. Ruby noticed that he seemed tense and introspective.

Suddenly, he said, "You know, every time I meet a nice girl, she leaves town."

Ruby knew what he meant. She had been watching the slow unfolding of our friendship. She knew that in less that a month I would be graduating and leaving Atlanta.

"Well, look," she asked in her quiet way, "can't you do something about it?"

For a long moment Peter did not reply. He appeared to be in deep thought. Carefully, he buttered a roll. Then "Maybe I can."

He did do something about it—within the next hour.

In the early afternoon, the infirmary telephone at Agnes Scott rang, and the solicitous voice on the other end had a familiar Scottish accent.

"I'm talking from Miss Hopkins' office," the voice said. "I have secured her permission to come over and see you. May I?"

I gasped. No mere man—unless armed with a medical diploma—had ever, in all the college's history, been allowed inside the infirmary. Male visitors were simply taboo. After all, the young ladies were not properly clothed! How Peter had prevailed on Miss Hopkins I couldn't even imagine.

"I—I really don't think you'd better," I said hastily. "I'm well enough to dress and come over. I'll meet you in the colonnade in ten minutes."

It was an awful mistake. Ever afterward Peter accused me of having thwarted his only chance for fame with future generations of Agnes Scotters. If I hadn't interfered, he might even have rated some day a bronze plaque on the infirmary wall in commemoration of the occasion.

The glint that had been in his eyes the night before was still there. Soon it became perfectly apparent what it was. It represented a Scotsman's clear-cut decision and a Scotsman's rock-ribbed determination. He knew what he wanted now, and he went after it with the same vigor and dispatch with which the "Ladies from Hell" had stormed Saint Quentin. All he lacked was the bagpipe accompaniment.

Yet he framed his proposal in gentle words, like the delicate embroidery surrounding the strong, simple words of an old sampler. I did not feel that I could give him an immediate answer. We agreed to pray about it separately. Years before, Peter's life had been solemnly dedicated to his Chief. Both of us felt that the important thing now was to find out what God wanted for us. Were our paths to separate at this point, or was it possible that we together would be a greater asset to the Kingdom of God than we could ever be separately? My heart dictated the answer, but I was fearful that my heart might obscure God's mind on the matter.

As unskilled and immature as I was in prayer, God chose this time to teach me a great lesson. I learned that just because God loves us so much, often He guides us by planting His own lovely dream in the barren soil of our human hearts. When the dream has matured, and the time for its fulfillment is ripe, to our astonishment and delight, we find that God's will has become our will, and our will, God's. Only God could have thought of a plan like that!

As I took my last college exams and wandered about the campus in something of a daze, it seemed to me that Someone's benediction was resting on my head. What seemed too good to be true was true. I was having my first object lesson in the fact that nothing is impossible within the providence of God, and that the more beautiful the dream, the more chance it has of fulfillment. There remained only the pleasant task of telling Peter.

I chose a moment when we were driving from Decatur to Atlanta.

"There's something I must tell you," I began.

In the semidarkness, I could see a strained look cross Peter's face.

"Good . . . or bad?" he asked tensely. Then, a moment later, simply, "Thank the Lord!"

For several moments he drove along without saying anything more. When finally he stopped the car beside the road, it was to bow his head and pray the most beautiful prayer of his life. God was in every part of that life, he was God's, and with God he wanted to share this supreme moment. Only then did he take me in his arms.

Graduation was only two days off. By then, "with some embarr-r-assment," Peter had met my family, had taken them to see Atlanta's famous Stone Mountain, with rare diplomacy had complimented my little sister, Em, on her new patent-leather shoes, and had agreed to exchange duplicate stamps with my brother Bob. Being a very practical son of the heather, he even discussed his finances with my father and described his insurance program in detail, "Because," he said, "you have a right to know that your daughter will be taken care of."

Justice Florence Allen, a woman of simplicity and charm, made the principal address for commencement. Peter was there, sitting with my family.

"I thought you seemed pale," he wrote afterward, "as you knelt before Miss Hopkins to receive your hood. I have never been so moved or impressed with any commencement. Of course, not before had my hopes and my whole life been wrapped up in a member of the class, not before had my heart been invested. I wonder if it was an omen that the girls sang 'Annie Laurie'? I hardly needed that to start the tears."

Late that night we came back to an almost-deserted campus. I was to leave the next day.

The ancient oaks cast heavy shadows on the driveway, and the moon shone on heavy white magnolia blossoms. Main Hall had seen thousands of girls come and go. The venerable red-brick, ivy-covered walls had stood sentinel over many a tender farewell.

"If anybody had told me three months ago," said Peter, "that I would be standing in front of Main Hall telling the girl I love good-bye and not caring whether all Decatur was at my back and all Atlanta at my front, I would have thought they were crazy."

The night watchman, standing somewhere in the shadows, discreetly looked the other way.

"Our life together will be a poem, a song, a monument to Love, and a memorial to the Holy Spirit who brought us together. I hope there will never be any real good-byes. God gave you to me, and I'll leave you in His hands. May He keep you always."

As Peter drove away, the night watchman stepped out of the shadows to see me safely into the dormitory. He walked along, his flashlight bobbing, his huge bunch of keys jangling, solemnly agreeing that leave-takings were sometimes hard.

I thought then that I was going to spend the next year teaching school in the mountains of West Virginia. I didn't know it, but already Peter had quite a different idea.

The halls of highest human happiness were closer than I knew.

***

Agnes Scott's commencement was on a Tuesday. By Wednesday I was on my way north to spend a few days with my Tennessee grandmother. That night Peter was busy speaking at other commencement exercises in Atlanta. It was his eighth such address that season.

Having shaken the last hand in sight, he beat a hasty retreat and climbed wearily into his car. The exertion of speaking had drenched his shirt with perspiration and completely wilted his collar. Even the back of his white coat was wet. Though it was now eleven at night, there was no sign of relief from the intense heat. The breeze made by the moving car might as well have been fanned from a furnace door.

Peter always reacted violently to the heat. Under its relentless, sinister influence, as he regarded it, he felt completely thwarted, and became sure that life wasn't worth living. In addition, on this particular night, he was lonely and somehow at a loss. Could the events of the last few days have been just a beautiful dream? They seemed so now. Under a sudden compulsion to communicate with me in any way that he could, he turned the car around and headed for the nearest telegraph office.

The girl in the Western Union office was hot too. Seated on her tall stool, she watched the businesslike hands of the wall clock creep toward a merciful midnight. At that moment Peter strode through the side door. He too looked up at the wall clock, frowned slightly, and reached for the nearest yellow pad and chained pencil.

Instantly the girl was wide awake. There was a decisiveness about this man that fascinated her. His face looked strained, she thought, and there were beads of perspiration on his upper lip. Repeatedly he wiped his face, and repeatedly a recalcitrant lock of damp curly hair kept falling back on his forehead. But as his big hand moved across the page, the tense look vanished, and a smile appeared at the corners of his mouth.

Carefully, he signed his name, putting beneath it a precise line with two dots. He hesitated a moment before handing it to the girl, then resolutely shoved it across the counter.

"Make it a night letter," he said.

The girl circled the NL and began reading what he had written. Her pencil ran along the first three sentences, then paused.

"M'm . . . oh, I see . . . unforgettable memories and thrilling hopes—" her voice trailed off.

Peter flushed violently and looked away, trying to hide his obvious embarrassment.

"This is to go to Johnson City, Tennessee, sir? It's exactly . . . exactly forty-five words. That will be forty-eight cents, sir."

As the girl handed Peter the change from a dollar bill, his eyes met hers. Suddenly, he grinned sheepishly, and in spite of herself, the girl almost laughed aloud.

In Johnson City I was awakened the next morning by some member of the family stuffing a yellow envelope into one relaxed, outstretched hand. It was the night letter. I read it and marveled at the goodness of God and the temerity of Peter.

It read:

HOPE YOU HAD A SAFE PLEASANT TRIP STOP TODAY

HAS BEEN SO EMPTY AM MISSING YOU TERRIBLY STOP
UNFORGETTABLE MEMORIES AND THRILLING HOPES WILL
HELP TIME PASS STOP AM THINKING OF YOU CONSTANTLY
AND WILL WRITE TOMORROW STOP LIFE IS WONDERFUL
REMEMBER I LOVE YOU DARLING GOD BLESS YOU
    PETER

Soon the promised letter arrived:

Dearest Catherine,

How last week dragged on leaden feet—while I was waiting to hear from you. I really did not expect to hear until Friday afternoon or Saturday morning, but when no letter or card had arrived on Saturday morning, I explored all the torments of the lovelorn. I thought all kinds of things! I suffered agonies of secret pain. You see, I was waiting for the first expression, the first reassurance.

You will never know with what transports of joy I received your precious letter sent special delivery. It came about 10:30 last night as I was working on my evening sermon. I read it with a bursting heart. I could have wept, and did—a little—and I thanked the Lord right then and there for giving me such happiness and such a wonderful sweetheart. Never in my life have I known such happiness and joy and peace. I cannot help thinking of the words of the hymn: "Peace, peace, the wonderful gift of God's love." Everything is turning out so much better than I could have planned it, because He is planning it. It was far better to get your wonderful letter at 10:30 last night than in the morning. It meant more to me then, for I had hoped all day and longed!

I had called—on Saturday to see if she had heard from you! And that was silly—and she said so! This morning at Sunday School I told her I had received a Special last night, and she smiled and asked if I was going to let her read it? Darling, I am so happy! I love you so much!

It was so hard leaving you on Tuesday night. I stood gazing after you a long time. I can never be the same again. I am a different person now, praise the Lord, and you have made all the difference. My heart is in your keeping for ever and ever. I live from now on to serve Him and to make you happy. Life can hold nothing more satisfying or more glorious than this—the joy of building with you, a home that will be a temple of God, a haven and a sanctuary, a place of peace and love, of trust and joy.

Thus began a correspondence rare in the annals of love-making. Certainly, there have been plenty of passionate love letters before. Literature has also preserved a few in which there runs a deeply spiritual note. There have been lovers sufficiently detached to write in a humorous vein. But I doubt if many series of letters, before or since, have more uniquely combined all three attributes.

Peter had the happy capacity of sometimes laughing at himself; so his letters were spiced with drawings of small faces wearing over-eloquent expressions. He said that I was responsible for his current cardiac condition, and that I ought to be ashamed of myself; and at the end of the sentence there was a drawing of an imp with his hair over his eyes looking pleased with himself. He complained that he had had no letter from me today, and none the day before, and the imp wore an expression of infinite sadness. Would the men in our wedding party really have to wear spats? He hoped not! That face wore the corners of its mouth turned down almost to its boot tops.

The letters never failed to include a weather report. This was characteristic of Peter, since the weather was of utmost importance to him. From May till October he suffered with America's heat, and he saw no reason why he should suffer in martyred silence.

Rain, rain, rain, sultry weather, close, stuffy, depressing. I can't even think, I'm so hot, much less write sermons.

Or he would say:

It is still hot here—terribly humid—and I am almost reduced to homicide. If this keeps up—well—it just can't do that! Something will have to burst, the weather or myself.

Sometimes a note on the weather even crept into his frequent telegrams:

LET THIS BE FORGETMENOTS AND SWEETHEART ROSES FOR SUNDAY STOP LAST TWO WEEKS WITHOUT YOU HAVE BEEN MONTHS STOP WEATHER NOT TOO HOT STOP I LOVE YOU DARLING

In his eyes there was nothing incongruous about the juxtaposition of the most lyrical expression of his love alongside a detailed analysis of the weather. He simply assumed that I, like him, would be just as much interested in the one as the other.

He was then thirty-four years old. For years he had dreamed of the day when he might have a home of his own. His wistfulness for it had crept into many a sermon, and perhaps all unknown to him, had colored many a public prayer. In one of his early sermons, he had sketched a vivid word picture of a home he knew whose characteristics were now interwoven with this home of his dreams:

"I was privileged, in the spring, to visit in a home that was to me—and I am sure to the occupants—a little bit of Heaven.

"There was beauty there. There was a keen appreciation of the finer things of life, and an atmosphere in which it was impossible to keep from thinking of God.

"The room was bright and white and clean, as well as cozy. There were many windows. Flowers were blooming in pots and vases, adding their fragrance and beauty.

"Hyacinths and lilies of the valley had been placed gracefully and lovingly before a little shrine where the family could worship.

"Books lined one wall—good books—inspiring and instructive—good books—good friends. Three bird cages hung in the brightness and color of this beautiful sanctuary, and the songsters voiced their appreciation by singing as if their little throats would burst.

"Nature's music, nature's beauty—nature's peace. It seemed to me a kind of Paradise that had wandered down, an enchanted oasis—home.

And now that this home of his dreams was about to materialize, he could not bear the thought of waiting another year. I had been planning to teach school. Why did I want to do that? He delicately pursued this point through several letters, then followed up with a quick trip to Johnson City so that he might personally plead his case.

He did not have to twist my arm to persuade me. I had found my heart's home, and I knew it. So the decision was made. We would be married in early November, in my home church, the First Presbyterian Church of Keyser, West Virginia. Peter went back to Atlanta in the mood of a knight returning victorious from battle. The only catch was that, for a time, he had to be a somewhat restrained knight. There always remained the danger of gossip.

Since getting back [he admitted], *I have been in Atlanta, but not of it. I never knew I'd be so thrilled over anything. My grin becomes more sheepish every day, my preoccupation more pronounced. In short, every indication points to the imminent incarceration of the writer as a dangerous lunatic! I know I must look stupid as I go around, and I want to tell everybody why I feel like this, and all about it.*

It seemed wise to tell the session of the church of our engagement before the news of it leaked out grapevine fashion or was formally announced. From Covington days onward, Peter had always made his elders his confidants. The result was an extraordinary depth of mutual respect, unity, and affection man to man.

At his request, the men gathered in his study immediately following the morning service. It was a gracious room to which they came, clearly reflecting their young minister's taste. There was a fireplace with the inevitable seascape above it, and low bookshelves around two sides of the room filled with the theological books he was collecting. The walls were palest blue, and the carpeting deep-blue broadloom. Soft June air poured in through the open windows.

As the men came in, Peter stood leaning against the mahogany desk. He knew, at that moment, how much he loved all these men, with that depth of affection known only to those who have shared many things. A procession of pictures flitted across his mind—an all-night vigil in the bare hospital corridor with Mrs. Zoll and her daughters; the awful inadequacy of his comfort for a big man shaken with sobs; the quiet pride in a father's eyes as his only daughter, a vision of loveliness in white lace and tulle, came slowly down the long candlelit aisle; the look of surprise and joy on Dr. Hope's face (the dean of Westminster's session) the night the session meeting turned into a celebration for his fifty-third wedding anniversary.

Something of the emotion of the moment was written on Peter's face, so that the men sensed that this would be an unusual meeting.

"Gentlemen," he began, and his Scottish burr seemed softer than usual, "I have asked you to come here, to share with you something that I feel you should know first, even before your wives. This will be just once you can scoop them on the latest gossip!" he grinned, then quickly grew serious again.

"Most of you are much older than I. During the three years of this present ministry, you have come to be to me, individually and collectively, what a father would be. I want to tell you this morning, just as I would tell my own father, were he here on earth, of the happiness that has come to me. I hope to be mar-r-ied in the fall, perhaps around the first of November. The girl is Miss Catherine Wood. Some of you have met her." He broke off suddenly, his face crimson.

Mr. Pomeroy leaped to his feet and gripped Peter's hand. "That's the best news I've heard in this church. You've waited a long time, boy. I wish you all the happiness in the world."

Soon all of the men were clustered around him, laughing, shaking hands, slapping him on the back, and offering him their congratulations.

They were genuinely glad, Catherine [he wrote me afterward]. *You ought to have seen their faces. I dared not look myself, for I was quite embarrassed—but some of them must have been studies. When you know these men as I do, you will love them too. They're the salt of the earth.*

About the same time Peter broke the news to his mother in Scotland. Immediately she wrote him:

> *Coatbridge, Scotland*
>
> *July 3, 1936*
>
> *My dear Peter,*
>
> *I received your letter of June 17th. We were in Troon for June month.*
>
> *Well, my boy, I did not know you were interested in any special girl. But this I do know. I have kept asking the Lord to guide you in all your actions and in all your plans, whether in your work or in your choice of a life partner. Peter, this is no surprise, and I feel it is the best of all things to come to you.*
>
> *I remember how fond you were of that verse, "Seek ye first the Kingdom of God and His righteousness, and all these things shall be added unto you." Then when I think of you and Miss Wood praying about each other at the same time, I am sure it is an answer to prayer.*
>
> *I have the happiest thoughts about it all. She is a daughter of the manse, and her training and education will make her just what you need in a life partner.*
>
> *I wish you every success in all you undertake, and hope that Miss Wood will find in you her heart's desire, and that you will find in her all your happiness. So may the Lord's blessing rest on you both.*
>
> *The years are flying fast, and we are getting older. I had my 66th birthday. Thank you for your remembrances.*
>
> *My love and best wishes and congratulations to you both. Perhaps*

someday I will meet her and you in your new home. Thanks for telling me
about your plans. I am happy.

    All my love,

    Mother

And to me she wrote, with a gentle reserve, typical of her:

    Coatbridge

    August 8, 1936

    My dear Catherine,

    This is the letter of a mother who dearly loves her son, to one whom
she is soon to welcome as her son's wife.

    It is a difficult letter to write, especially since we are so far apart
and have not met. Yet why should it be difficult, when all I want to say is
how happy I am because my boy is happy—and to ensure you a mother's
welcome into her own heart.

    Peter has told me some of the things he carries in his heart about you,
of which a mother loves to learn. I am sure this happy event is in answer to
our prayers, and that is enough to put our minds at rest. God only gives to
His own dear ones the best—and that is how I feel about you and my Peter
coming together.

    With much love to you from Peter's mother.

    Janet Findlay

Always in Peter there was a practical businessman as well as poet—a
curious combination that Scotland loves to nurture in her sons. So he wrote
an ecstatic half-page description of the engagement ring he had bought, and
then added that he had been fortunate enough to secure it at the wholesale
price. Another day he was sorely tempted by a sale on flat silver at one of
Atlanta's department stores. Then he found a salesman friend who offered
him furniture at half price.

Of course, people laugh at this trait in Scotsmen, while Scotsmen condescendingly endure the crude jokes, knowing them to be the best, most continuous free advertising in the world.

Dreams carried around in one's heart for years, if they are dreams that have God's approval, have a way suddenly of materializing. One September afternoon Peter found his dream house standing on the crest of a hill—and, best of all, it was for rent at only sixty dollars a month. Tall pines stood sentinel over a rambling cottage with casement windows. Peeping in, Peter saw that the living room had an open fireplace, in which he could imagine logs crackling. At the bottom of the hill on which the house stood, there was a little ravine through which a clear stream sang its way. One approached the house by a rustic footbridge and many stone steps.

Peter sent me snapshots, a detailed floor plan, and pages of description. In his mind's eye, he could already see rock gardens, azaleas, clumps of daffodils and iris beside the brook, a vegetable garden in back, hammocks under the trees, and the top of the garage a plaza where we could entertain our friends on summer evenings. He even saw himself raising chickens. In his enthusiasm it never occurred to him that innumerable preaching engagements, wedding conferences and ceremonies, calls, church meetings, and sermon writing would inevitably crowd out the gardening and chicken raising, and that there would never be time for lying in hammocks under the pines. It was always to be that way.

Even then, we were forever bumping into already scheduled ecclesiastical duties and trying to detour personal plans around them. *I find I have a wedding scheduled for Friday afternoon. If I could just persuade the bride to move it up one hour.* Or, *A funeral on Sunday afternoon delayed my departure. I'm sorry, darling.*

In between the epidemic of Atlanta weddings and eight series of preaching engagements all the way from Athens, Georgia, to Eagle River, Wisconsin, we managed to see each other six times that summer. Peter drove seven thousand miles to achieve it.

There was even trouble finding a date for our wedding that wouldn't interfere with something or other. A two weeks' meeting in Chattanooga, scheduled to end four days after our wedding, was moved up so that it concluded four days before the wedding. That gave Peter time to write a Sunday sermon, preach it, pick up his going-away suit, pack his bag, and drive 750 miles. The meeting, he said, would be "his pre-matrimonial workout." So it proved to be.

In July he had supplied the then-vacant pulpit of the New York Avenue Presbyterian Church in the nation's capital. Dr. Joseph Sizoo had resigned some months previously to go to the Collegiate Church of St. Nicholas in New York. What had seemed routine pulpit supply quickly turned into something more significant. The people of New York Avenue were immediately impressed with the young Scotsman.

The personalities of another group of men who subsequently proved themselves "to be the salt of the earth" now obtruded themselves into our lives. There was Mr. Frank Edington, New York Avenue's session clerk—tall, slim, Chesterfieldian in manner, his neat gray goatee making him look as if he had stepped out of the mid-nineteenth century. There were Mr. Edward Martin, the manager of the Lee House Hotel, Judge Claude Porter, and Mr. Adam Weir—all fine men.

The negotiations, then begun, were not to be concluded for another fourteen months. Meanwhile, already there was the agony of indecision, the inner conflict, the prayer and quiet waiting that were always to attend the search of God's will in this matter of calls to other churches.

Our periods of separation during that time were marked with long letters in which we tried to appraise the decision before us. Peter cheerfully admitted how he pined for these letters and laughed at his own eagerness. He preached at Cedartown, Georgia, each night during a week when the temperatures stayed at 95 degrees night and day.

It has been four days since I have heard from you [he chafed], but I

*know I'll get a letter in the morning, because I called up Ruby in Atlanta,
and she told me she had forwarded a letter from you.*

Said the next letter:

*You were very kind to write me twice this week. In fact, you saved
my life, that's all. Harry Petersen—the minister here—was sorry for me
and would go to the post office twice a day to indulge me. In desperation, I believe he was almost at the point of making up a letter for me—so
that the services might proceed—only he could never have imitated your
writing. No human being could do that!*

Couples whom he counseled had often wondered how this young
preacher would act when he finally fell in love. Peter knew he could not escape
being watched. Above all else, he despised hypocrisy. Hence, he insisted that
he and I had to do everything he had advised others to do. His idealism not
only "soared through mother-of-pearl skies on frigates of romance" but also
stooped to embrace health examinations, insurance policies, and budgets.
I had to read the same books he had lent to others. Dutifully, we each went
to our doctors and exchanged health certificates. We discussed relatives and
made a budget. He made it clear to me in words that admitted of no duplicity
that he had practiced the continence for the unmarried that he had preached.

This idealism of Peter's was no mere sentimentality, for it was rooted
and grounded in the love of Christ. Indeed, every sermon Peter preached
was a word drama, whose gigantic backdrop was a picture etched in bold
strokes of God's age-long courtship of the human race. To the preacher, all
human history was but the tale of God's tender wooing of the self-willed,
stubborn hearts of men and women—a drama that culminated in the Cross.
No romance could ever equal the romance of Calvary. But when, perchance,
a little of the love of God spilled over into the hearts of a man and woman—
and when that love was blessed and sanctified by Christ—there was true
romance, a "marriage made in heaven."

We found time for less serious things in the summer, such as long hours spent playing games like Monopoly, Parcheesi, and Yacht. Peter came honestly by his honorary title of G.G.P.—abbreviation for Great Game Player, bestowed on him by my young brother and sister. My family thought it would look impressive on his church bulletin—thus, "Peter Marshall, D.D., G.G.P."

The day of our wedding saw a cold rain falling, "an ideal day for staying home and playing games," Peter said. It was indeed. During the morning, I put the finishing touches to my veil, and wrestled with a new influx of wedding gifts swathed in tons of tissue paper and excelsior. I gathered the impression that Peter was rollicking through successive games of Yacht, Parcheesi, and Rummy with anyone who had sufficient leisure to indulge him. That was all right, but I thought he was carrying it a bit too far when, thirty minutes before the ceremony, he was so busy pushing his initial advantage in a game of Chinese Checkers with my little sister Em, that he still had not dressed.

Shortly before we left for the church, a card and a telegram arrived. The card was addressed to the bridegroom-elect. It was from three of Peter's seminary friends and read:

> *The great event will probably put scores of girls back into circulation.*
> *Our sympathy to Catherine.*
> *Cecil Thompson*
> *Bill Stewart*
> *Sam Cartledge*

The telegram was from Westminsterites, who could not resist this golden opportunity to rib their preacher with one of his own favorite expressions. It said:

> CONGRATULATIONS ON YOUR ADMISSION TO THE HALLS
> OF HIGHEST HUMAN HAPPINESS
> THE DEACONS, WESTMINSTER CHURCH

The morning after we were married, I opened my eyes to find Peter lying propped up on one elbow, staring at me intently from the vantage point of the other bed. Apparently he had been staring for some time. His inscrutable expression didn't make it quite clear whether he had been thinking, "Oh, you gorgeous creature!" or "How did this happen to me?"

Upstairs, in the Lee House, seven men and a lone woman, Mrs. C. S. Goodpasture, were waiting for us. They constituted the Pastoral Committee of New York Avenue Church, whose duty it was to find a new minister. There wasn't time to eat breakfast; so Peter left the room hurriedly, calling over his shoulder, "Take your time dressing, Catherine. I'll start the ball rolling, and when the men want to see you, I'll telephone you to come on up."

Considering the effect his words had on me, he might as well have said, "I'll call you when we're ready to throw you to the wolves."

The room was fragrant with flowers sent by Mr. Martin, the manager of the Lee House and the chairman of the Committee on Pastor. I dressed carefully, with unsteady hands, trying to ignore the butterflies in the pit of my stomach.

I was just twenty-two, knew the city of Washington only as a schoolgirl tourist, and had not met any of the members of New York Avenue Church. When the telephone rang, I steeled myself, and said meekly, "Yes, darling, I'll be right up."

Of course, the committee was graciousness itself, and quickly put me at my ease. They were not unmindful of the fact that we had been married only the afternoon before, but they were sure, they said, "that we wouldn't mind combining a little church business with our honeymoon. Wasn't it convenient that we had come through Washington on our way to New York?" To them—these men of the world, skilled in the affairs of government and finance—we must have seemed terribly young and inexperienced. Looking back, I know that it was altogether typical that our married life began with a church committee meeting.

THE GREATEST OF THESE:
The Love Story of God and Man

ADAPTED FROM THE BIBLE

RETOLD BY VICKI J. KUYPER

The noonday sun beats down relentlessly on the rocky incline dotted with people. They mingle in and out of groups, looking from afar like a flock of sheep aimlessly wandering about in an unfamiliar field. The young, the old and everything in between. Friends, family and strangers. The hopeful. The hopeless. The curious. The confused. They sit, stand, shuffle, slouch, shift their weight from one sandaled foot to another. They fidget with stones from the ground or the hems of their garments.

They feel like intruders without quite knowing why. Something about this moment feels eerily private, like something they should not be witness to. Yet the people in the crowd can't turn away. Their eyes keep returning to the figure on the crest of the hill. As storm clouds begin to gather overhead, the afternoon sky turns an ashen gray. The murmur of the crowd fades to hushed whispers. They know something catastrophic is happening, but what? It seems like a strange setting for the most unique proposal of all time.

There have been hints of what's to come, of the depth of love about to be revealed. But only the One Who Loves the Souls of Men knows how the proposal to His beloved will play out over the next few days. No detail has been overlooked. There will be wine and music. Wine turned to vinegar, soured and stale. The rhythm of nails being driven through wood, through flesh. The Bridegroom-To-Be has spared no expense. Today He offers the gift of Himself.

As He looks out over the crowd, the pain in His heart feels more raw and relentless than that in His hands and feet. Tears of love and longing fill His eyes as He envisions His future bride. He knows her inside and out. Her likes and dislikes. What makes her smile or laugh or cry. Her hopes, dreams, fears and failures.

He knows her beauty is timeless, running deeper and truer than a poet's words—though His beloved rarely recognizes that beauty in herself. She's like a princess from a fairy tale, royalty toiling in the ashes while clothed in rags. Though He cherishes His beloved's beauty, He's not unaware that His chosen bride can be fickle, selfish, moody and coarse. He's not the first love she's turned to in her life. But He knows His beloved has no other real prospects other than Him. If He turned His back, she'd be lost—she would surely die.

The sky has turned from ash to slate. A wild wind whips across the hillside. A ripple of movement waves through the crowd as people pull their outer robes more tightly around them and shield their eyes against the blowing dust. Then as suddenly as it began, the wind is still. It's as if the world itself has paused to hear the words the man on the cross is about to say: "It is finished." Then He's gone.

A flash of lightening cuts through the black sky like a knife through flesh. Thunder echoes off the rocky slope, scattering the crowd. It all seems so wrong, so backward. How could it be "finished" before the proposal's complete?

The night is filled with questions and tears. The next day passes much the same way. What promised to be the greatest love story of all time now looks like nothing more than romantic make-believe. Just another fairy tale. Just another empty promise. Just another man. Until the dawn of the third day—

Rumors rise with the sun. From mouth to mouth, from home to home, word of Bridegroom-To-Be's bold return from the dead spreads like the light of the coming day. Yet one encounter, then another, and another prove the rumors to be reality. The Bridegroom lives! His proposal is now complete.

The Bridegroom-To-Be extends an engagement ring to His beloved. It's a family heirloom, untarnished by time. Its smooth gold band speaks of eternal faithfulness and promises kept. The band holds a single multi-faceted stone, a polished jewel that seems to sparkle with unequaled brilliance—the symbol of a love that's proven stronger than death and will endure longer than time.

"Will you choose Me?" the Bridegroom-To-Be asks softly, with hope in His eyes. "I will love you with an everlasting love. I'll forgive the past and give you real hope for the future. Through My eyes, you'll come to see the beautiful bride you were meant to be."

The proposal hangs in the air, love expectantly poised, waiting for a reply.

You are the one He seeks, the one He conquered death to win. Will you accept His proposal? Will this love story have a happy ending?

AN OLD SWEETHEART OF MINE

JAMES WHITCOMB RILEY

An old sweetheart of mine!—Is this
Her presence here with me,
Or but a vain creation of
A lover's memory?

A fair, illusive vision
That would vanish into air
Dared I even touch the silence
With the whisper of a prayer?

Nay, let me then believe in all
The blended false and true—
The semblance of the old love
And the substance of the new,—

The then of changeless sunny days—
The now of shower and shine—
But Love forever smiling,—
As that old sweetheart of mine.

This ever-restful sense of home,
Though shouts ring in the hall.—
The easy-chair—the old bookshelves
And prints along the wall;

The rare Habanas in their box,
Or gaunt churchwarden-stem
That often wags, above the jar,
Derisively at them.

As one who cons at evening
O'er an album, all alone,
And muses on the faces
Of the friends that he has known,

So I turn the leaves of Fancy,
Till, in shadowy design,
I find the smiling features of
An old sweetheart of mine.

The lamplight seems to glimmer
With a flicker of surprise,
As I turn it low—to rest me
Of the dazzle in my eyes,

And light my pipe in silence,
Save a sigh that seems to yoke
Its fate with my tobacco
And to vanish with the smoke.

'Tis a fragrant retrospection—
For the loving thoughts that start
Into being are like perfume
From the blossom of the heart;

And to dream the old dreams over
Is a luxury divine—
When my truant fancies wander
With that old sweetheart of mine.

Though I hear beneath my study,
Like a fluttering of wings,
The voices of my children
And the mother as she sings—

I feel no twinge of conscience
To deny me any theme
When Care has cast her anchor
In the harbor of a dream—

In fact, to speak in earnest,
I believe it adds a charm
To spice the good a trifle
With a little dust of harm,—

For I find an extra flavor
In Memory's mellow wine
That makes me drink the deeper
To that old sweetheart of mine.

O childhood-days enchanted!
O the magic of the Spring!—
With all green boughs to blossom white,
And all bluebirds to sing!

When all the air, to toss and quaff,
Made life a jubilee
And changed the children's shout and
Laugh to shrieks of ecstasy.

With eyes half closed in clouds that ooze
From lips that taste, as well,
The peppermint and cinnamon
I hear the old School-bell,

And from "Recess" romp in again
From "Blackman's" broken line

To—smile, behind my reader,
At that old sweetheart of mine.

O face of lily-beauty,
With a form of airy grace,
Floats out of my tabacco
As the "Genii" from the vase;

And I thrill beneath the glances
Of a pair of azure eyes
As glowing as the summer
And as tender as the skies.

I can see the pink sunbonnet
And the little, checkered dress
She wore when first I kissed her
And she answered the caress

With the written declaration that,
"As surely as the vine
Grew 'round the stump," she loved me—
That old sweetheart of mine.

Again I made her presents,
In a really helpless way,—
The big "Rhode Island Greening"—
I was hungry too, that day!—

But I follow her from Spelling,
With her hand behind her—so—
And I slip the apple in it—
And the Teacher doesn't know!

I give my treasures to her—all,—
My pencil—blue and red,—
And, if little girls played marbles,
Mine should all be hers instead—

But she gave me her photograph,
And printed "Ever Thine"
Across the back—in blue-and-red—
That old sweetheart of mine!

And again I feel the pressure
Of her slender little hand,
As we used to talk together
Of the future we had planned—

When I should be a poet,
And with nothing else to do
But write tender verses
That she set the music to. . . .

When we could live together
In a cozy little cot
Hid in a nest of roses,
With a fairy garden-spot,

Where the vines were ever fruited,
And the weather ever fine,
And the birds were ever singing
For that old sweetheart of mine.

When I should be her lover
Forever and a day,
And she my faithful sweetheart

Till the golden hair was gray;

And we should be so happy
That when either's lips were dumb
They would not smile in Heaven
Till the other's kiss had come.

But, ah! my dream is broken
By a step upon the stair,
And the door is softly opened,
And—my wife is standing there:

Yet with eagerness and rapture
All my visions I resign
To greet the living presence
Of that old sweetheart of mine.

MY DEAR AND LOVING HUSBAND

ANNE BRADSTREET

If ever two were one, then surely we.

If ever man were lov'd by wife, then thee.

If ever wife was happy in a man,

Compare with me, ye women, if you can.

I prize thy love more than whole Mines of gold

Or all the riches that the East doth hold.

My love is such that Rivers cannot quench,

Nor ought but love from thee give recompetence.

Thy love is such I can no way repay.

The heavens reward thee manifold, I pray.

Then while we live, in love let's so persever

That when we live no more, we may live ever.

SMALL IS THE TRUST
WHEN LOVE IS GREEN

ROBERT LOUIS STEVENSON

Small is the trust when love is green
In sap of early years;
A little thing steps in between
And kisses turn to tears.

Awhile - and see how love be grown
In loveliness and power!
Awhile, it loves the sweets alone,
But next it loves the sour.

A little love is none at all
That wanders or that fears;
A hearty love dwells still at call
To kisses or to tears.

Such then be mine, my love to give,
And such be yours to take:-
A faith to hold, a life to live,
For lovingkindness' sake:

Should you be sad, should you be gay,
Or should you prove unkind,
A love to hold the growing way
And keep the helping mind:-

A love to turn the laugh on care
When wrinkled care appears,
And, with an equal will, to share
Your losses and your tears.

LET LOVE GO, IF GO SHE WILL

ROBERT LOUIS STEVENSON

Let love go, if go she will.
Seek not, O fool, her wanton flight to stay.
Of all she gives and takes away
The best remains behind her still.

The best remains behind; in vain
Joy she may give and take again,
Joy she may take and leave us pain,
If yet she leave behind
The constant mind
To meet all fortunes nobly, to endure
All things with a good heart, and still be pure,
Still to be foremost in the foremost cause,
And still be worthy of the love that was.
Love coming is omnipotent indeed,
But not Love going. Let her go. The seed
Springs in the favouring Summer air, and grows,
And waxes strong; and when the Summer goes,
Remains, a perfect tree.

Joy she may give and take again,
Joy she may take and leave us pain.
O Love, and what care we?
For one thing thou hast given, O Love, one thing
Is ours that nothing can remove;
And as the King discrowned is still a King,
The unhappy lover still preserves his love.

BY NIGHT WHEN OTHERS SOUNDLY SLEPT

ANNE BRADSTREET

By night when others soundly slept
And hath at once both ease and Rest,
My waking eyes were open kept
And so to lie I found it best.

I sought him whom my Soul did Love,
With tears I sought him earnestly.
He bow'd his ear down from Above.
In vain I did not seek or cry.

My hungry Soul he fill'd with Good;
He in his Bottle put my tears,
My smarting wounds washt in his blood,
And banisht thence my Doubts and fears.

What to my Saviour shall I give
Who freely hath done this for me?
I'll serve him here whilst I shall live
And Love him to Eternity.

THE LOVE SONG OF SOLOMON

BOOK OF SONG OF SOLOMON,

KING JAMES VERSION

The Song of songs, which is Solomon's.

Let him kiss me with the kisses of his mouth:
for thy love is better than wine.
Because of the savour of thy good ointments
thy name is as ointment poured forth,
therefore do the virgins love thee.
Draw me, we will run after thee:
the King hath brought me into his chambers:
we will be glad and rejoice in thee,
we will remember thy love
more than wine: the upright love thee.

I am black, but comely,
O ye daughters of Jerusalem,
as the tents of Kedar,
as the curtains of Solomon.
Look not upon me, because I am black,
because the sun hath looked upon me:
my mother's children were angry with me;
they made me the keeper of the vineyards;
but mine own vineyard have I not kept.
Tell me, O thou whom my soul loveth,

where thou feedest,
where thou makest thy flock to rest at noon:
for why should I be as one that turneth aside
by the flocks of thy companions?

If thou know not, O thou fairest among women,
go thy way forth by the footsteps of the flock,
and feed thy kids beside the shepherds' tents.

I have compared thee, O my love,
to a company of horses in Pharaoh's chariots.
Thy cheeks are comely with rows of jewels,
thy neck with chains of gold.
We will make thee borders of gold with studs of silver.

While the king sitteth at his table,
my spikenard sendeth forth the smell thereof.
A bundle of myrrh is my well-beloved unto me;
he shall lie all night betwixt my breasts.
My beloved is unto me as a cluster of camphire
in the vineyard of Engedi.

Behold, thou art fair, my love; behold,
thou art fair; thou hast doves' eyes.
Behold, thou art fair, my beloved, yea, pleasant:
also our bed is green.
The beams of our house are cedar,
and our rafters of fir.

I am the rose of Sharon, and the lily of the valleys.

As the lily among thorns, so is my love among the daughters.

As the apple tree among the trees of the wood,
so is my beloved among the sons.
I sat down under his shadow with great delight,
and his fruit was sweet to my taste.
He brought me to the banqueting house,
and his banner over me was love.
Stay me with flagons, comfort me with apples:
for I am sick of love.
His left hand is under my head,
and his right hand doth embrace me.
I charge you, O ye daughters of Jerusalem,
by the roes, and by the hinds of the field, that ye stir not up,
nor awake my love, till he please.

The voice of my beloved!
behold, he cometh leaping upon the mountains,
skipping upon the hills.
My beloved is like a roe or a young hart:
behold, he standeth behind our wall,
he looketh forth at the windows,
shewing himself through the lattice.
My beloved spake, and said unto me,
Rise up, my love, my fair one, and come away.
For, lo, the winter is past, the rain is over and gone;
The flowers appear on the earth;
the time of the singing of birds is come,
and the voice of the turtle is heard in our land;
The fig tree putteth forth her green figs,

and the vines with the tender grape give a good smell.

Arise, my love, my fair one, and come away.

O my dove, that art in the clefts of the rock,

in the secret places of the stairs,

let me see thy countenance,

let me hear thy voice; for sweet is thy voice,

and thy countenance is comely.

Take us the foxes, the little foxes, that spoil the vines:

for our vines have tender grapes.

My beloved is mine, and I am his:

he feedeth among the lilies.

Until the day break, and the shadows flee away,

turn, my beloved, and be thou like a roe or a young hart

upon the mountains of Bether.

By night on my bed I sought him whom my soul loveth:

I sought him, but I found him not.

I will rise now, and go about the city in the streets,

and in the broad ways I will seek him whom my soul loveth:

I sought him, but I found him not.

The watchmen that go about the city found me:

to whom I said, Saw ye him whom my soul loveth?

It was but a little that I passed from them,

but I found him whom my soul loveth:

I held him, and would not let him go,

until I had brought him into my mother's house,

and into the chamber of her that conceived me.

I charge you, O ye daughters of Jerusalem,

by the roes, and by the hinds of the field,

that ye stir not up, nor awake my love, till he please.

Who is this that cometh out of
the wilderness like pillars of smoke,
perfumed with myrrh and frankincense,
with all powders of the merchant?
Behold his bed, which is Solomon's;
threescore valiant men are about it,
of the valiant of Israel.
They all hold swords, being expert in war:
every man hath his sword upon his thigh
because of fear in the night.
King Solomon made himself a chariot
of the wood of Lebanon.
He made the pillars thereof of silver,
the bottom thereof of gold,
the covering of it of purple,
the midst thereof being paved with love,
for the daughters of Jerusalem.
Go forth, O ye daughters of Zion,
and behold king Solomon with the crown
wherewith his mother crowned him in the day of his espousals,
and in the day of the gladness of his heart.

Behold, thou art fair, my love; behold, thou art fair;
thou hast doves' eyes within thy locks:
thy hair is as a flock of goats, that appear from mount Gilead.
Thy teeth are like a flock of sheep that are even shorn,
which came up from the washing;
whereof every one bear twins,

and none is barren among them.
Thy lips are like a thread of scarlet,
and thy speech is comely:
thy temples are like a piece of a pomegranate within thy locks.
Thy neck is like the tower of David builded for an armoury,
whereon there hang a thousand bucklers,
all shields of mighty men.
Thy two breasts are like two young roes that are twins,
which feed among the lilies.
Until the day break, and the shadows flee away,
I will get me to the mountain of myrrh,
and to the hill of frankincense.
Thou art all fair, my love; there is no spot in thee.
Come with me from Lebanon, my spouse,
with me from Lebanon: look from the top of Amana,
from the top of Shenir and Hermon,
from the lions' dens,
from the mountains of the leopards.

Thou hast ravished my heart, my sister,
my spouse; thou hast ravished my heart
with one of thine eyes,
with one chain of thy neck.
How fair is thy love, my sister, my spouse!
how much better is thy love than wine!
and the smell of thine ointments than all spices!
Thy lips, O my spouse, drop as the honeycomb:
honey and milk are under thy tongue;
and the smell of thy garments is like the smell of Lebanon.
A garden inclosed is my sister, my spouse;

a spring shut up, a fountain sealed.
Thy plants are an orchard of pomegranates,
with pleasant fruits; camphire, with spikenard,
Spikenard and saffron; calamus and cinnamon,
with all trees of frankincense; myrrh and aloes,
with all the chief spices:
A fountain of gardens, a well of living waters,
and streams from Lebanon.

Awake, O north wind; and come, thou south;
blow upon my garden,
that the spices thereof may flow out.
Let my beloved come into his garden,
and eat his pleasant fruits.

I am come into my garden, my sister, my spouse:
I have gathered my myrrh with my spice;
I have eaten my honeycomb with my honey;
I have drunk my wine with my milk.

Eat, O friends; drink, yea, drink abundantly,
O beloved.

I sleep, but my heart waketh:
it is the voice of my beloved that knocketh, saying,
Open to me, my sister, my love, my dove,
my undefiled: for my head is filled with dew,
and my locks with the drops of the night.
I have put off my coat; how shall I put it on?
I have washed my feet; how shall I defile them?
My beloved put in his hand by the hole of the door,

and my bowels were moved for him.
I rose up to open to my beloved;
and my hands dropped with myrrh,
and my fingers with sweet smelling myrrh,
upon the handles of the lock. I opened to my beloved;
but my beloved had withdrawn himself,
and was gone: my soul failed when he spake:
I sought him, but I could not find him;
I called him, but he gave me no answer.
The watchmen that went about the city found me,
they smote me, they wounded me;
the keepers of the walls took away my veil from me.
I charge you, O daughters of Jerusalem,
if ye find my beloved, that ye tell him,
that I am sick of love.

What is thy beloved more than another beloved,
O thou fairest among women?
what is thy beloved more than another beloved,
that thou dost so charge us?

My beloved is white and ruddy,
the chiefest among ten thousand.
His head is as the most fine gold,
his locks are bushy, and black as a raven.
His eyes are as the eyes of doves by the rivers of waters,
washed with milk, and fitly set.
His cheeks are as a bed of spices, as sweet flowers:
his lips like lilies, dropping sweet smelling myrrh.
His hands are as gold rings set with the beryl:

his belly is as bright ivory overlaid with sapphires.

His legs are as pillars of marble,

set upon sockets of fine gold:

his countenance is as Lebanon,

excellent as the cedars.

His mouth is most sweet:

yea, he is altogether lovely.

This is my beloved, and this is my friend,

O daughters of Jerusalem.

Whither is thy beloved gone,

O thou fairest among women?

whither is thy beloved turned aside?

that we may seek him with thee.

My beloved is gone down into his garden,

to the beds of spices, to feed in the gardens,

and to gather lilies.

I am my beloved's, and my beloved is mine:

he feedeth among the lilies.

Thou art beautiful, O my love, as Tirzah,

comely as Jerusalem, terrible as an army with banners.

Turn away thine eyes from me,

for they have overcome me:

thy hair is as a flock of goats that appear from Gilead.

Thy teeth are as a flock of sheep which go up

from the washing, whereof every one beareth twins,

and there is not one barren among them.

As a piece of a pomegranate are thy temples

within thy locks.

There are threescore queens, and fourscore concubines,
and virgins without number.
My dove, my undefiled is but one;
she is the only one of her mother,
she is the choice one of her that bare her.
The daughters saw her, and blessed her;
yea, the queens and the concubines, and they praised her.
Who is she that looketh forth as the morning,
fair as the moon, clear as the sun,
and terrible as an army with banners?

I went down into the garden of nuts to see the fruits of the valley,
and to see whether the vine flourished,
and the pomegranates budded.
Or ever I was aware, my soul made me like
the chariots of Amminadib.

Return, return, O Shulamite;
return, return, that we may look upon thee.
What will ye see in the Shulamite?
As it were the company of two armies

How beautiful are thy feet with shoes,
O prince's daughter! the joints of thy thighs are like jewels,
the work of the hands of a cunning workman.
Thy navel is like a round goblet,
which wanteth not liquor:
thy belly is like an heap of wheat set about with lilies.
Thy two breasts are like two young roes that are twins.
Thy neck is as a tower of ivory;

thine eyes like the fishpools in Heshbon,
by the gate of Bathrabbim:
thy nose is as the tower of Lebanon
which looketh toward Damascus.
Thine head upon thee is like Carmel,
and the hair of thine head like purple;
the king is held in the galleries.

How fair and how pleasant art thou,
O love, for delights!
This thy stature is like to a palm tree,
and thy breasts to clusters of grapes.
I said, I will go up to the palm tree,
I will take hold of the boughs thereof:
now also thy breasts shall be as clusters of the vine,
and the smell of thy nose like apples;
And the roof of thy mouth like the best wine
for my beloved, that goeth down sweetly,
causing the lips of those that are asleep to speak.

I am my beloved's, and his desire is toward me.
Come, my beloved, let us go forth into the field;
let us lodge in the villages.
Let us get up early to the vineyards;
let us see if the vine flourish,
whether the tender grape appear,
and the pomegranates bud forth:
there will I give thee my loves.
The mandrakes give a smell,
and at our gates are all manner of pleasant fruits,

new and old, which I have laid up for thee,
O my beloved.
O that thou wert as my brother,
that sucked the breasts of my mother!
when I should find thee without,
I would kiss thee; yea, I should not be despised.
I would lead thee, and bring thee into my mother's house,
who would instruct me: I would cause thee to
drink of spiced wine
of the juice of my pomegranate.
His left hand should be under my head,
and his right hand should embrace me.
I charge you, O daughters of Jerusalem,
that ye stir not up, nor awake my love, until he please.

Who is this that cometh up from the wilderness,
leaning upon her beloved?

I raised thee up under the apple tree:
there thy mother brought thee forth:
there she brought thee forth that bare thee.

Set me as a seal upon thine heart,
as a seal upon thine arm:
for love is strong as death;
jealousy is cruel as the grave:
the coals thereof are coals of fire,
which hath a most vehement flame.
Many waters cannot quench love,
neither can the floods drown it:

if a man would give all the substance of his house for love,
it would utterly be contemned.

We have a little sister, and she hath no breasts:
what shall we do for our sister in the day
when she shall be spoken for?
If she be a wall, we will build upon her a palace of silver:
and if she be a door, we will inclose her
with boards of cedar.
I am a wall, and my breasts like towers:
then was I in his eyes as one that found favour.

Solomon had a vineyard at Baalhamon;
he let out the vineyard unto keepers;
every one for the fruit thereof was to bring
a thousand pieces of silver.
My vineyard, which is mine, is before me:
thou, O Solomon, must have a thousand,
and those that keep the fruit thereof two hundred.

Thou that dwellest in the gardens,
the companions hearken to thy voice:
cause me to hear it.

Make haste, my beloved,
and be thou like to a roe or to a young hart
upon the mountains of spices.